CW00704969

IRONY THROUGH PSYCHOANALYSIS

Giorgio Sacerdoti

IRONY THROUGH PSYCHOANALYSIS

Giorgio Sacerdoti

translated by
Geraldine Ludbrook

forewords by
Joseph Sandler
and
Cesare Musatti

Karnac Books
London 1992 New York

English edition first published in 1992 by
H. Karnac (Books) Ltd.
58 Gloucester Road
London SW7 4QY

Distributed in the United States of America by
Brunner/Mazel, Inc.
19 Union Square West
New York, NY 10003

Italian edition, *L'ironia attraverso la psicoanalisi*,

British Library Cataloguing in Publication Data.

Sacerdoti, Giorgio
Irony Through Psychoanalysis
I. Title II. Ludbrook, Geraldine
150.19

ISBN 1 85575 010 4

Printed in Great Britain by BPCC Wheatons Ltd, Exeter

CONTENTS

FOREWORD TO THE ENGLISH EDITION

Joseph Sandler

The Oxford English Dictionary defines irony as a figure of speech in which the intended meaning is the opposite of that expressed by the words used. In his outstanding book Professor Sacerdoti applies a psychoanalytic point of view to irony and examines the dynamics of this form of expression in its conscious, preconscious, and unconscious aspects. The author poses the question of why irony has been relatively ignored by psychoanalysts, and he responds by showing that Freud had used a limited and rather obsolete definition of irony. He adds, more significantly, that psychoanalysts have paid little attention to the history of ideas, which have also influenced psychoanalysis. He asks why, if irony as a rhetorical device can be considered as one form of expression of thought that can achieve particular concreteness and liveliness, it has acquired a predominantly negative connotation, and why psychoanalysts have not made greater use of it. One need only think of the rhetorical value of Antony's saying, "For Brutus is an honourable man". Over the years, there has been a progressive undervaluation of the communicative potential of irony, with psychoanalysts laying greater stress on its narcissistic and pregenital aspects. This, as Sacerdoti suggests, may be a reflection of defensive activity aiming at the rejection of anything that might act as a bridge between what is conscious and what is unconscious. One must add, of course, that the fear of one's own sadism must play a significant role in prompting such defence. In this connection we can understand Charles Lamb's warning, "Clap an extinguisher on your irony, if you are unhappily blessed with a vein of it". Clearly, analysts need to exercise enormous caution in their use of irony as a vehicle for communication, and they need to be sure that the patient's narcissism can contain the ironic comment and will not be threatened. Yet with some patients such comments can be most effective, provided that the analyst is never sardonic, mocking, or scornful.

The book is divided into four substantial chapters, each a profound contribution in its own right. The first examines recent developments in regard to the concept of irony and the attempts at its classification arising from studies of rhetoric and of literary criticism. This is followed by an account of the psychoanalytic literature on the topic.

In chapter two Sacerdoti points out that the question of how we recognize or fail to recognize irony applies to ourselves as well as to the communications of others. The question of whether it is possible and useful to recognize unconscious irony is considered in some detail, and the notion of *latent irony* is introduced through a number of impressive clinical examples. Irony, and its position in regard to consciousness–unconsciousness, is related to the antitheses of playful–serious and play–work. Consideration of such issues appears to be fundamental to a study of irony in the bipersonal analytic field, particularly if we regard irony as being characterized by the contrast between appearance and reality and by the possibility of perceiving both at the same time.

The notion of latent irony, in its preconscious and unconscious aspects, is examined in relation to psychoanalytic theory in chapter three. The author considers that the analytic situation, as it develops and is resolved, can be considered "ironic" in two senses. On the one hand, it may be seen in terms of the development of common interpersonal relationships, in the form of representation through the opposite, insofar as what is initially placed in the foreground is the analyst's "appearance" in the analysand's world, while the analyst's "being" emerges with the progression of the analysis and the resolution of the transference, ultimately marking the end of the analytic relationship. On the other hand, the development of this relationship from appearance to reality draws it closer to the mechanism of irony, defined as the conflict between two different aspects of what is signified by a dramatic structure.

The final chapter is particularly interesting. Starting from the question of why Freud's work on jokes (1905c) seems to have been detached from the rest of his work [with the exception of his later paper on humour (1927d)], an explanation is sought through an examination of some of the elements involved in the conception of "Freud as ironist". Sacerdoti also looks at the characteristics and dynamics of the Jewish joke, in which self-directed irony is particularly noticeable.

There is no doubt that this book makes a significant step forward in both the understanding and the application of the ironic view, something that has a particular connection with the development and expression of insight.

FOREWORD TO THE ITALIAN EDITION

Cesare Musatti

During the Fascist period in Italy, psychoanalysis could only be practiced clandestinely, and even writing about it was forbidden. In 1945, when the war ended and freedom for psychoanalysis had also been won back, Joachim Flescher, a Galician Jewish psychoanalyst who had lived secretly in Italy during the war, contacted the few psychoanalysts left in the country (Perrotti, myself, and one or two others) and founded a journal entitled *Psicoanalisi*.

He wrote, asking me to contribute an article for the first issue, which was about to be published. I sent him one entitled "L'impressione di finzione nella situazione analitica". I no longer have any copies of the journal in which the article appeared, nor indeed of the article itself.

My intention in the article was to point out the considerable differences between the manner of speaking used by the analyst and patient during the session and that used in real conversation once the session is over. Naturally this concerns more the patient's manner of speaking than that of the analyst, who naturally provokes this kind of dialogue but then lets the patient speak, merely intervening whilst following the patient's exposition at the same level. The patient, on the other hand, has to express what comes to him from a more profound level, that is, from the unconscious.

In fact, a skilful analyst does not use the second manner of speaking at all, or he keeps it to a minimum (for example to settle the times of the next sessions, holidays, questions of fees, etc.).

I therefore claimed that the relationship between the two during the analytic session is different from the ordinary relationship between people discussing real things and actual events, and from personal relationships following a logical, rational principle.

This difference produces the impression that the analytic session is a "simulation", a kind of performance.

When I later became interested in the various experiments in psychodrama and also took part in the use of this kind of psychotherapy with patients, it seemed to me a more explicit expression of what takes place in every analysis. Thus, each analysis is a play, a simulation, a performance.

Obviously, I had discovered nothing new.

The fact that Freud had dealt with what we call "jokes"—*Witz* in German—is important here. Freud (1905c) entitled his work on *Witz*: "Jokes and their Relation to the Unconscious".

The way in which the unconscious speaks—undoubtedly connected with the most archaic forms of human language—differs from the way we reason. Jokes are told neither during a meeting between statesmen dealing with problems of international relations, nor during a business lunch—unless, of course, they are used to break the ice of pure reason, to create a new atmosphere, and to alter the approach to problems when certain difficulties arise between two opposing positions.

In his work, Freud not only discusses jokes, but he also deals with other forms of expression such as humour or, simply, the comic. He attempts to order all this material, which is characterized by the fact that it departs from the field of serious discourse (as is usually imposed on children by adults) and separates our irrationalities from our consciousness as far as possible. They are thus related to the unconscious zone of our personality.

In the analytic relationship, the barrier between the rational and the irrational must come down. This is why the dialogue that takes place during analysis is "outside the accepted limits". We reason as we do in serious matters for things that cannot seem serious in terms of ordinary thought. "Let's play games", says one of Sacerdoti's patients.

Freud was not happy with his own work on *Witz*. It is the only book of his that was never reprinted after the first edition, except naturally for its inclusion in the complete works published during Freud's lifetime: *Gesammelte Schriften*.

In my opinion, Freud's reasons for dissatisfaction were three-fold.

The first concerns the fact that any analysis of jokes immediately destroys the mechanism that produces the humorous effect. The effect is expressed through laughter, which, by means of a complex dynamic process, concludes the listener's reception of the joke, discharging the emotional charge accumulated from the beginning of the telling into laughter. However, if analysis of the *Witz* mechanism means that the humorous effect is lost, then the whole point of the exercise vanishes, leaving us with nothing. Thus Freud's book becomes boring and only interests professional psychoanalysts, in the same way that jokes repeated too often to a group of people who have already heard them become boring.

The second reason for Freud's dissatisfaction comes from another fact. The jokes he deals with derive mainly from the *Witz* of the Oriental Jews and are linked to their particular ways of life. Alternatively, they come from Heinrich Heine, who, despite his apostasy, was also a typical Jew who knew how to personify his people's spirit.

It is, therefore, very specific material. I may also personally add that, during the Fascist period, when I was writing the *Trattato di psicoanalisi* (published in 1957) as a text-book for the psychology course I was teaching at Padua University, I wanted to expound on the treatment of the joke following Freud's method, but without using Jewish stories, for a certain caution was necessary given the climate of the time. I was, however, unable to find any other material in other cultures or languages, either modern or ancient, that could be adapted to the model used by Freud.

English humour is quite another thing, as are the epigrams of antiquity. Only Jewish stories fit the scheme put forward by Freud. Psychoanalysis is itself so permeated with its Jewish origins that it irritated Freud to point out this aspect as well, while persisting with the book on Jewish *Witz*.

There is, however, a third reason for Freud's dissatisfaction. As well as dealing with jokes, he also examined humour and the comic. But comedy, wit, and humour do not constitute the only material that can stimulate laughter and possess the characteristic of the double meaning—that is, material that can be interpreted literally and, at the same time, reveal something lying underneath. Many expressions with a double meaning exist, and they are avoided by serious people, people who prefer reason and are reluctant to give in to the seduction of unconscious thought.

In this book, Giorgio Sacerdoti considers irony. Irony, too, is prohibited material—at least beyond certain limits—and it has its own specific characteristics. In the joke, the Jewish *Witz*, certain masochistic mechanisms can be perceived, along with an element of self-defence. This is the case of the poor Polish Jew who reveals his own faults to a listener, who is ready to allow his aggressiveness to explode. The Jew has found a way of protecting himself from this aggressiveness. It is a way of demonstrating that one's own awareness of one's defects is greater than that of those who criticize (or who could be potential critics). In the same way, irony releases a certain aggressiveness, veiled by a slight and apparently innocuous disguise. It must be carefully measured, for, if the aggressiveness is hidden too well, it disappears completely and no trace of irony remains—at least for the object of it. If, on the other hand, it is not hidden well enough, it becomes diluted offensiveness, which is nothing like irony.

Irony can serve as an aggressive weapon by people who fear that by exposing themselves excessively they will provoke a violent reaction in others at a level of reality. It must therefore be used with care—unless, of course, all this takes place within the theatre of the analytic session. The analysts quoted here by Sacerdoti examine this kind of irony.

In the various different kinds of plays that make up the analytic theatre, where the scene enacted always has a subplot, the play of irony also has a role in the ambivalent relationship of transference and countertransference.

The patient's and the analyst's unconscious systems often use ironic cues with each other in the kind of fencing match that takes place in the analytic session. The material is certainly complex, and, having studied the observations mentioned in the previous works of modern psychoanalysts, Sacerdoti provides us here with a synthesis that, despite its complexity, throws some light onto the network of dynamic elements subject to the play of irony.

This was no easy task to undertake, because, in addition to the difficulties encountered by Freud in his work on jokes, which are met with in part here as well, there are also the problems that arise from a certain elusiveness of irony. There are situations that may appear ironic to some and yet not to others. It is thus necessary to investigate the sum total of the processes—partly conscious and partly unconscious—that convey the impression. Furthermore, it is necessary to consider the personal relationship between the person expressing the irony and the person who is the object of it.

This book is by no means easy reading. But for those interested in the study of the psychic mechanisms that form the basis of human communication in the analytic situation in particular, but also in ordinary relationships between people, there is much to be learned from the numerous ideas put forward here for consideration.

INTRODUCTION

In his clinical work, as also in his theorization—which in the best Freudian tradition is a function of praxis—the analyst constantly questions himself in order to grasp the psychic reality of the analysand and its development through himself and through his relationship with the analysand, working on what *seems to be*. And the answer to his self-questioning (in fact the term "irony" derives from εἴρων—"he who questions") is always a temporary and incomplete one. The tension for completeness is maintained up to and beyond the end of the analysis at a clinical level, up to and beyond any formulation at a theoretical level. There is no illusion of finding a universally valid fixed formula that applies like a symbolic passe-partout or a boring cliché.

Psychoanalysis, "countervision in perpetuity" (Erikson, 1977), just as the double vision of appearance and reality that is characteristic of irony, never ceases to surprise. And it may, in fact, come as a surprise that irony—which, extending the concept to the preconscious and unconscious levels, inevitably permeates every psychoanalytic exploration, even if only because of its fictional aspects (*eironeia*)—has remained a marginal object in psychoanalytic studies. This surprising fact is the subject of this book. Naturally, the aim is not to eliminate the surprise, but merely to re-locate it.

The relative lack of interest psychoanalysts have shown in irony can only be attributed in part to Freud's statement that to understand irony the unconscious is not required to be brought in. His theoretical consideration of irony on the basis of a restricted and slightly obsolete definition parallels his practically never having dealt with it. It is in contradiction, however, to his capacity for ironic vision and his recognition of ambiguity as a constituent element of irony. In fact, in his own ironic expressions he reinforces what he explicitly states: that irony easily risks being misunderstood. His statement about the clarity of the signs of irony—although according to Kerbrat-Orecchioni (1976) it is perhaps contradictory, and unduly generalized given his own receptive capacity—could have influenced his having considered ironology irrelevant for a scholar of the unconscious.

In order to extend the study of ironic dynamics to the preconscious and unconscious levels, it would seem opportune to begin with the verification of the legitimacy of such a broadening within the analytic situation. It is, in fact, above all on the basis of clinical material that the acceptability of a latent irony, of "ironic work", and the like, may be evaluated. On the other hand, the search for ironic aspects in psychoanalytic theorization seems to fall essentially within the province of the spirit of the founder of psychoanalysis. This perspective may shed some light both on the conceptualization of the analytic situation and process, and also on the *querelle* concerning the beginning, the evolution, and the role of metapsychology.

In the light of the gaps existing in the psychoanalytic literature, it would be opportune to give some attention to both the recent evolution of the concept of irony and the attempts to classify it in the sphere of literary criticism, as well as to the psychological dynamics working in irony in not only élite but also popular contexts. Taking this into consideration, the *jüdische Witz* must also be re-evaluated on those terms. At best, the *Witz* can be employed as a paradigm of how irony persists, even under conditions of external reality that would seem to obliterate it. The conditions of the Eastern European Jews were certainly of this kind, at least up until last century. Today they exist in part once again, *mutatis mutandis*, albeit in a more generalized and universal manner.

Adorno (1951), for example, claims that today the medium for irony has disappeared, insofar as ideology merely duplicates reality, and "there is no fissure in the rock of what is, including truth". The claim may be at least re-assessed by bearing in mind what corresponds to "truth" at an unconscious level that clinical psychoanalysis makes it possible for us to understand. From a consideration of the correspondences, a closer examination of the theme of se-duction becomes necessary in a comparison with social reality. I use the term "se-duction" here (and, elsewhere, "ana-logically", "in-difference", "con-vince" etc.) to refer to the original etymology of the compound word that has today been lost in common use.

Although as a general rule seduction can be considered included in rather than "foreclosed" (*entworfen*) by psychoanalysis (Baudrillard, 1979) with regard to other primal phantasies, it can perhaps be admitted that Freud excluded to a certain degree or attempted to avoid se-duction (on the path to truth) in his work on *Witz* (1905c), which also explains why it is not very amusing.

In addition to this work, there are many other examples of how Freud allowed himself to be se-duced by ironic and self-directed ironic dynamics (extended to include also latent aspects) and then returned to the path to truth, to inner reality. Before the collapse of his theory on seduction and the aspirations to fame and fortune associated with it, Freud depicted himself as the abandoned bride in his letter to William Fliess of 21 September 1897 (1887–1904). He noticed, however, that he felt no shame; on the contrary, he experienced a sense of triumph rather than of defeat. Here, as elsewhere (see chapter four, the section on "Freud as ironist"), it would be misleading—just as in many *jüdische Witze*—to emphasise the narcissistic, masochistic, nihilistic, or destructive aspects, to the detriment of the constructive and communicative elements, both on an intra- and an interpersonal level.

There is perhaps the need at a universal level—and to the same degree as was necessary until last century in the ghettos of Galicia—for a kind of irony and self-directed irony that takes place in the sphere in which genitality prevails. In any case, at a clinical, theoretical, and doctrinal level, psychoanalysis today can undoubtedly benefit from a certain capacity for irony and self-directed irony.

On the other hand, if irony as a rhetorical device is to be included amongst the attitudes that the expression of thought assumes for the purpose of making itself more concrete and more vivid, we may ask ourselves as psychoanalysts why irony in common use has come to take on a significance in which its negative aspects prevail. It may be thought that such a deterioration could be ascribed to a kind of defence mechanism in which anything that might connect the unconscious and the conscious, the "primary process" and the "secondary process", is removed. This would support the observation that other useful defence mechanisms might meet a similar fate. We need only mention the decline of the metaphor and the deterioration of other concepts close to irony such as parody, the destructive aspects of which are emphasized. By a kind of nemesis (itself included in this group, as its significance has deteriorated in common use from its original meaning of giving someone what they deserve), which is perhaps linked to the frequent use of contrast to move from appearance to reality, irony risks deterioration through exaggeration, not knowing where to stop, a grotesque absence of limits in both its use and its reception. There is also the risk of its effect being lost through being over-explained.

I trust that readers will kindly bear in mind my mentioning these dangers, whilst accepting them as inherent to the subject, each time they feel that a gratuitous effort is required of them because of what has sometimes been left implicit.

IRONY THROUGH PSYCHOANALYSIS

CHAPTER ONE

Irony through a psychoanalytic lens

Notes on the recent evolution of the concept of irony and on attempts at classification

In recent studies on rhetoric and literary criticism, irony and parody have been revalued in terms of their communicative, relational (especially in the case of irony), and innovative value. Their constructive aspects have been highlighted, whilst the destructive aspects—those that are traditionally emphasized—have been reappraised as being subordinate and functional to the positive elements insofar as they are a healthy and necessary *mise en crise* of the anachronistic, stereotyped, inauthentic elements reduced to clichés.

Irony is based on the contrast between the appearance initially presented by the ironist and the reality that is subsequently revealed. Parody, in the definition of literary criticism, is based on the contrast between a sub-text—that is, a pre-existing, previous text—and the new text, which has a critical, ironic detachment from the original text. And the irony is "more elating than disparaging, or more analytically critical than destructive. . . . The author—and consequently the reader—makes a kind of structural superimposition of texts, setting the old in the new" (Hutcheon, 1978, pp. 468–469), according to Goethe's rule quoted by Freud (1912–13): "What thou hast inherited from thy fathers/Acquire it to make it thine" p. 158). [Freud stresses rather the degradation of what is exalted, obtained "by destroying the unity that exists between people's characters as we know them and their speeches and actions, by replacing either the exalted figures or their utterances by inferior ones" (1905c, p. 201).]

The reasons for which irony has become the mechanism that the novelist of metafiction uses to highlight parodic contrast must, according to Hutcheon, include parallelisms of structure, as well as similarities of strategy. Irony and parody both work at two levels—what is visible and what is implicit—and the implicit level derives its meaning from the context.

Hutcheon notes that parody itself is structurally an act of incorporation. As such, it does not try to humiliate or ridicule the underlying material but, rather, seeks a reconciliation with it through the use of irony. The artist cannot ignore what has preceded him. But if the parodic act is an act of synthesis, its function and strategy are, paradoxically, those of separation and contrast.

Also in the light of the fact that a valid attempt to classify types of irony is missing from the psychoanalytic literature, it is worthwhile to examine briefly what literary criticism can offer in this regard. It is particularly useful because, if we review the literature on irony—or, rather, different kinds of irony—to see what, according to different authors, defines and characterizes them, thus permitting their classification, we rediscover certain elements that are usually taken into consideration when an attempt is made to focus on the psychoanalytic process and the conditions necessary for it to take place, and what distinguishes it from other forms of psychotherapy.

Knox (1972), for example, when considering the classification of kinds of irony, points to the significance of four variable factors: the field of observation, the degree of conflict between appearance and reality, an inherent dramatic structure, and, finally, the philosophical–emotional aspect.

Muecke (1969, 1970) attempts a broad classification according to the degree to which the real meaning is hidden. He pays particular attention to the structural elements ("verbal" irony and "situational" irony) on which the ironic conflict rests. He then makes a distinction between "corrective" irony on which the ironic conflict rests in which "one term of ironic duality is seen . . . as effectively contradicting, invalidating . . . or . . . modifying the other" (1969, p. 23), and irony that is primarily non-corrective, although it may be "heuristic" and thus correspond to Knox's paradoxical irony. In the former, "psychic tension is generated but rapidly released" (pp. 25–26), whereas in the latter no element releases the psychic tension generated by the ironic contradiction.

Muecke also moves on to a correlation, on the one hand between corrective and specific irony—which involves "single victims and victimizations, single exposures or aberrancy in a world otherwise moving on the right track . . ." (pp. 119–120)—and on the other, between non-corrective and general irony—in which life itself, or every general aspect of life, is fundamentally and inevitably seen as an ironic state of things. The distinction between two fields of observation or two different concepts of irony is of historical importance, as Muecke shows, because the extension of the concept of irony from specific to general was one of the principal inventions of the German Romanticists, and a sense of general irony greatly characterizes modern thought. Knox (1973) notes that when Schlegel and his contemporaries began to invent new kinds of irony, they matched general and paradoxical irony exactly. However, as time passed, general irony began to be seen as capable of assuming all the other aspects as well. And most of our "modern" conceptions of irony stem from the German Romanticists, although the concept of romantic irony has been widely misunderstood and misrepresented.

In Muecke (1978) it can be seen that the perception of situations of "general irony" is probably as old as philosophical thought. From a historical point of view, it is to be found in

Classical antiquity, and examples of "dramatic irony" can be found in the Bible (see also Vossius, 1643; Good, 1965). "Dramatic" irony, like "general" irony, is part of "situational" irony and can be distinguished from "verbal" irony. Verbal irony allows a meaning that "literally" is not there—and a meaning, moreover, that contradicts the meaning that *is* there—to be read into a set of words. In situational irony, on the other hand, it is possible to observe a person serenely unaware that he is in an awkward situation, especially when he believes he is in the contrary situation to the one in which he actually finds himself.

Ironic situations can be invented or presented with a satirical purpose by those who wish to expose hypocrisy, wilful ignorance, pride, confident folly, rationalizing, or vanity. According to Muecke (1970), the victim to be exposed is identified in these corrective or normative uses of irony. In "metaphysical" or general irony, however, the ironist sees the whole human race as the victim of an irony inherent in the human condition.

In Muecke's view, with Christian theology's denial of any radical conflict between Man and Nature—Man is the Lord of Creation—or between Man and God—Man is the son of a loving God—it is hardly surprising that general irony did not appear in modern Europe until Christian ideology lost its power to convince. Considering these observations and simplifying to some degree, it might be supposed that a kind of historical oscillation existed between two visions, one inevitably and irrevocably conflictual and the other substantially aconflictual. However, even earlier than Freud we can find ironic representations that do not fit into such a schematic categorization. The very story of Job, which Muecke quotes as an example of dramatic irony, may be interpreted not as Job's ignorance—his not knowing he is the subject of a wager between God and Satan—but, rather, in terms of the dramatization of intrapsychic appeals with the consequent possibilities of modifying them.

The artist is in an ironic position for various different reasons. In order to write well, he must be both critical and creative, both subjective and objective, both enthusiastic and realistic, both emotive and rational, both a conscious and also an unconsciously inspired artist. His work concerns the real world, even though it is fiction. Thus what he creates is considered something that is "ambivalently both art and life" (Muecke, 1970, p. 20):

> Romantic Irony is the irony of a writer conscious that literature can no longer be simply naive and unreflective but must present itself as conscious of its contradictory, ambivalent nature. The author's "presence of mind" must now be a principal element in his work, alongside the equally necessary but "blind" driving force of enthusiasm or inspiration. [p. 78]

In this sense, ironic literature is literature in which there is a constant interplay of objectivity and subjectivity, of freedom and necessity, of the appearance of life and the reality of art. The author is immanent in every part of his work as its creative vivifying principle, and at the same time he transcends his work as its objective "presenter".

Introduction to the concept of latent irony

It is hardly necessary to note that the ease with which the ironist moves or "plays" between two registers—which could be considered dialectic pairs—is basically the ease required of the analyst and also of the "good analysand" (see Greenson, 1967) in order to carry out the analytic work fruitfully. Trying to summarize the similarities and differences in a few brief words, we can recall that although a series of contradictions, antinomies, and ambivalences tends to make itself conscious, all this is not an end in itself, but in successful analysis—with the exclusion of directive positions—it leads to the possibility of an adequate synthesis. This does not, however, derive from specific work in this sense, but from a greater capacity of the ego in the presence of a mutated intrapsychic situation, concerning which we need only mention the aspect comprising the overcoming of the (instinctual) drive ambivalence as a means of access to the postambivalent or genital position. The individual can thus neither deny nor scotomize the contradiction's of external reality, nor can he link the drive ambivalence to the incongruities or contradictions of reality in order to set up a perverse game. He must resolve them, in the sense of being able to choose—which, in the case of the analytic situation, coincides with the end of the analysis.

It is the drive dimension that introduces into the discussion on analysis an element that is generally missing from the discussion on irony, or at least leads it to an impasse right at the point where the discussion comes close to the above-mentioned possibilities regarding analysis. Kierkegaard (1841), for example, claims that "true" irony (unlike rhetorical irony) does not generally wish to be understood. This naturally brings us back to the question of how we recognize—or fail to recognize—irony, even when we are the ones to use it. Returning to the discussion regarding the drive dimension, in light of the fact that it may be translated into terms of the unconscious, the question arises—and it is a basic one for us—as to whether it is operatively useful to consider the possibility of unconscious or latent irony.

Certainly different answers lead to different approaches regarding the question of how to recognize irony, especially our own. For example, if a certain contrast between appearance and reality is a basic characteristic of irony, an awareness of the contrast is a necessary condition for the recognition of the irony (Muecke, 1970). However, this simple statement obviously has different levels of significance, depending on whether or not the unconscious dimension is introduced

The generalizations that analysts know so well in analysis, and which can be traced back to defence mechanisms (such as intellectualization in a general manner) regarding insight and which concern something more concrete and emotionally important—the body, in short, and therefore tangible contact in the relationship with the analyst—are closely linked to the general themes known as the "fundamental contradictions" of general irony, as has already been seen. On the other hand, a few ironologists (not many, to tell the truth) in a general way have observed the existence of similarities between certain descriptions by analysts and those by ironologists. Thus Muecke (1970), for example, who is perhaps the ironologist who has dwelt most closely and with greatest depth on this point, observes that

> The operations of the unconscious are described in terms similar to those we use when talking of irony: a man intends to say one thing but by a "Freudian slip" he says something quite different and so reveals his real preoccupations, as in the Irony of Self-betrayal; artists through their unconscious "choice" of subjects, motifs, or images, reveal meanings they did not intend; the concept of "compensating" enables us to reverse the ostensible meaning of everything men say or do. In our conscious life we have all the "innocent awareness" of the typical victim of irony who assumes that things are what they appear to be. This makes us all unconscious hypocrites living a "life of continuous and uninterrupted self-deception", as the Satanic angel in Mark Twain's *Mysterious Stranger* puts it. The things which we say happen to us against our will may really be the things which we secretly will to happen; the unconscious may have its reasons, which reason knows nothing of, for falling sick or into debt, for crashing the car or losing the job, or failing the examination. [p. 74]

There is in fact a marked resemblance between ironic speeches, which are essentially those of general irony, and psychoanalytic speeches, which are divulgatory in nature. As I have observed elsewhere (Sacerdoti, 1977a), the divulgation of psychoanalysis is an operation that is often and at the best of times ambivalent, both for those to whom it is clearly directed, who are more likely to emerge hurt than helped, and also for psychoanalysis itself, which is more likely to be distorted. The most common reaction will be an increase in resistance, if divulgation is not in fact already an expression of this. Speeches aimed at eliciting a sincere interest or desire for non-intellectual knowledge—the only one that can be fruitful also in an inter-disciplinary field (and I believe this to be true for all disciplines)—are different. I believe that Booth's (1974) study follows the latter line and is perhaps one the analyst can most usefully support, although—or, more precisely, because—

it does not discuss the unconscious. We will therefore deal with it after having briefly discussed the principal contributions psychoanalysts have made to ironology, attempting to trace a few guidelines along which a reciprocal and non-superficial collaboration could take place.

The psychoanalytic viewpoint

Historical outline

The relative lack of interest analysts have shown for irony can partly be traced back to Freud's (1905c) statement that irony, although very close to wit, can be understood without having to "bring in" the unconscious. Within certain limits this may suit the kind of irony Freud, then Reik (1929) and Winterstein (1932), schematically refer to—that is, representation by the opposite (sparing contradiction).

However, if it is true that antiphrasis is the basic ironic transformation, simple verbal inversion is nothing more than one of many possibilities: Morier (1975) lists four inversions and nine other forms of ironic "écarts". Furthermore, as Muecke (1978) notes, it is not in fact these inversions and discardings that mark the presence of irony, but, rather, the incompatibility between the literal meaning of the text and its context. Freud (1905c) observed that irony is exposed to the danger of being badly understood or not understood at all, and there is unanimous consensus regarding this "danger". It would, however, seem to contradict what he himself says about the signs of irony, as Kerbrat-Orecchioni (1976) points out: "It is not easy to see how irony 'easily risks remaining misunderstood' if these indices really 'clearly indicate that one thinks the opposite of what one says'" (p. 15).

It seems to me that Freud's contradiction could be explained by his having kept to the classic and slightly obsolete definition of irony, without developing what he probably sensed (and what made him say that irony easily risks being misunderstood)—that is, that the ambiguity that is part of irony specifically requires the unconscious (or the preconscious) both of the person delivering the message and that of the person receiving it to be brought in.

Furthermore, the dynamics of the relational point of view is complex and mobile. In fact, it would be possible to expect a relationship in which the listener may perceive an ironic aspect which was, in actual fact (or perhaps not), limited to an unconscious (or preconscious) level in what the other person was saying. In analysis, the distinction would be between the analyst's countertransferential intuition and his transferential experience. A good example of both these possibilities (and here the choice is left to those who may benefit from it) is the following Jewish anecdote told by Landmann (1960, p. 42) in which the shift of emphasis and the recognition of the literal aspects are played upon . To the quartermaster's question: "Why must a soldier die *gladly* for his emperor?" a recruit replies: "You're right, why must he *die*?" (my italics). In the answer, the position of masochistic submission and indoctrination breaks down; free association allows the emergence of the free thinker in whom the super-ego is no longer archaic and sadistic, but an ally of the ego. The anecdote (which can also be read as a dramatization of the intrapsychic dynamics) does not tell us how the officer reacts—that is, whether the joke manages to win him over. If this were so, the officer might no longer feel himself to be the object of the irony but might, rather, discover himself to be an ironist and thus an ally of the recruit, whilst the object of the irony would be the Kaiser and the military institution. It would seem to point out both the social nature of irony (as Freud had already noted regarding the comparison between the *Witz* and the—asocial—dream) and also its "antisocial" potential regarding a certain type of society. According to Alexander (1969), on the other hand, the first emotional state that leads to this kind of mental representation we call irony is anger against injustice, against persistent offensive reality. Bitterness transforms anger into hate, which involves an imperative action in an attempt to obtain justice and revenge. It is not, however, a bloody revenge—irony is used to ridicule and discredit the person who has offended.

Irony and ambiguity

Let us return now to the problematic aspect of the deciphering of irony. As has already been mentioned, it is connected with the ambiguity of irony itself (see also Kerbrat-Orecchioni, 1976). The psychoanalytic literature on ambiguity, which deals with the unconscious and preconscious aspects, could thus be useful to us for a study of the same aspects in irony. At the same time, it will be necessary to define better the relationship between irony and ambiguity.

Like other terms that refer to characteristics of the primary process and, above all, to the connections between it and the secondary process, 'ambiguity' is a term easily used with negative and often moralistic connotations in ordinary language. Isay (1977), who defines "ambiguity in language" as verbal obscurity that allows a phrase or a group of phrases more than one interpretation, reviews the psychoanalytic literature. He recalls how Freud often refers to ambiguities in connection with their use in the manifest context of dreams as "verbal bridges" between the manifest and the latent.

With reference to Dora's case, Freud (1905e [1901]) observes that

> Ambiguous words (or, as we may call them, "switch-words") act like points at a junction. If the points are switched across from the position in which they lie in the dream, then we find ourselves on another set of rails; and along this second track run the thoughts which we are in search of but which still lie concealed behind the dream. [p. 65n.]

He had already expressed similar concepts in "*The Psychopathology of Everyday Life*" (1901b).

In "Delusions and Dreams in Jensen's 'Gradiva'", Freud (1907a) gives the following definition of verbal ambiguity:

> But whence comes this striking preference for ambiguous speeches in *Gradiva*? It is no chance event, so it seems to us, but a necessary consequence of the premises of the story. It is nothing other than a counter-part of the two-fold determination of symptoms in so far as speeches are them-

> selves symptoms and, like them, arise from compromises between the conscious and the unconscious. It is simply that this double origin is more easily noted in speeches than, for instance, in actions. And when, as is often made possible by the malleable nature of the material of speech, each of the two intentions lying behind the speech can be successfully expressed in the same turn of words, we have before us what we call an "ambiguity". [p. 85]

And in "Psychoanalysis and the Establishment of the Facts in Legal Proceedings", Freud (1906c) not only stresses the importance in analysis of the search for the signs that suggest ambiguity, but he also observes how a similar search can "for a while" become the object of irony, both for the analysand and also for "medical colleagues":

> We quite generally regard even slight deviations in our patients from the ordinary form of expression as a sign of some hidden meaning and we are quite willing to expose ourselves for a while to the patient's ridicule by making interpretations in that sense. Indeed we are on the lookout for remarks in which the hidden meaning glimmers through an innocent expression. Not only patients but medical colleagues who are ignorant of the technique of psychoanalysis and its special features are incredulous about this and accuse us of being too clever and playing with words; but we are nearly always in the right. After all, it is not difficult to understand that the only way in which a carefully guarded secret betrays itself is by subtle, or at most ambiguous, allusions. [p. 110]

This passage from Freud is important, for it establishes a connection between ambiguity and irony. This involves an overcoming of the previously-mentioned "contradiction" that Kerbrat-Orecchioni points out in Freud when she discusses irony, saying, on the one hand, that the signals are clear and, on the other, that irony easily risks being misunderstood. It is in fact in terms of the latter statement that in the passage we are examining Freud tips the scales. What Freud explicitly points out is the link between the patient's ambiguity and his (conscious) ironization regarding the analyst who, searching for clues, believes he is perceiving (mistakenly according to the patient) "remarks which suggest any ambiguity and in which the hidden *meaning glimmers through an innocent expression*" (1906c, p. 110, my italics).

We know (Muecke, 1970), however, that an expression of a certain innocent type and at the same time a certain transparency of the opposite (guilty) type are precisely the essence of irony. [The example Freud gives stems from that of the criminal: "In the case of the criminal it is a secret which he knows and hides from you, whereas in the case of the hysteric it is a secret that he himself does not know either, which is hidden even from himself" (p. 108).] Thus the patient actually (consciously) ironizes on the fact that the analyst is proceeding with an ironic reading of the (unconsciously ambiguous) text he has been presented by the patient himself. It is this ironic reading that is perceived by certain medical colleagues who "accuse us of being too clever and playing with words". Perhaps they, too, behave just like the patients.

The position of the criminal is in this regard characterized by Freud for its similarities and differences with respect to the patient. This matter is discussed again in chapter two with regard to the psychopathological/delinquent alternative.

Kris and Kaplan (1948), after having distinguished between certain types of verbal ambiguity, which they call disjunctive, additive, conjunctive, integrative, and projective, note that words, images, and fantasies spring to mind because of their emotional charge, and that the primary process clearly shows the tendency to concentrate numerous meanings into a single symbol, thus satisfying several emotional needs.

For Rogers (1978), "the trouble with the word 'ambiguity' is that it is not ambiguous enough. Standard usage tends to limit its denotational range to multiplicity of meaning within the realm of conscious thought or ideation, though nothing in its root meaning of 'lead, drive, wander about' would appear to impose such a limitation" (p. 68). In his opinion, a comprehensive term is required to express two broad kinds of meaning: ideative and emotive. He uses the term "ambiguity" to characterize a language that generally speaking can be said to refer to conscious or unconscious thoughts or emotions. Having established this distinction, Rogers defines "modal ambiguity" as a characteristic of every ambiguous structure—be it a word, a phrase, or a poem—that reflects or calls upon either or both of the two modes of psychic functioning, the primary and the secondary process. He proposes that this concept be subdivided into intermodal and intramodal ambiguity. "A metaphor, image, word, or phrase having coordinates in both primary- and secondary-process mentation can be said to possess intermodal ambiguity" (p. 69). For Rogers, metaphor is a natural vehicle for modal ambiguity. It provides an effective method for "tracing" the principal elements of a repressed idea, because it carries out the double function of "being instrumental to the conscious intention, but of providing *at the same time* a switch off opportunity for a peripheral or repressed train of thought which is in a state of activation" (Klein, 1967, p. 119-120; my italics).

All this seems extraordinarily close to the modern definition of irony given by scholars of rhetoric and literary criticism. It must at once be pointed out that the relationships between formal aspects and those that emphasize content may also be inverted—the former corresponding to the "deep" level and the latter to the superficial level as we often (although not always) happen to verify in analysis. According to Muecke (1970) some kinds of non-ironic art and literature can be characterized as being in fact the object of a single vision that is immediately perceptible, since the formal properties either constitute an opaque surface, so to speak, which retains all our attention, or disappear in favour of the equally absorbing content they transparently reveal.

> Art and literature should, therefore, if we may go by contraries, have both surface and depth (cf. perspective!), both opacity and transparency, should hold our attention at the formal level while directing it to the level of content. Irony would combine McLeish's Imagist or post-Imagist slogan:
>
> A poem should not mean
> But be

with Browning's "messagism" (if we can apply the following lines to the little "world" of a poem):

> This world's no blot for us,
> Nor blank; it means intensely . . .

and rewrite them as:

> An ironic poem should both mean
> And be

with the rider that the elements of "meaning' and "being" should oppose one another. [p. 5]

Preconscious and unconscious levels in the emission and reception of ironic messages

If we now bear in mind the fact that, according to Muecke, the above-mentioned opposites in irony should be simultaneously perceptible, although the latter (the "deep") should not make the former (the "superficial") disappear, we must take note of the similarities and differences between the basic situation of the irony and the situation that corresponds to one of the fundamental vicissitudes of the (instinctual) drives: the transformation into the opposite (see also chapter two).

It could be said that the differences begin when the transformation into the opposite is used as a defence mechanism and, removing one of the terms of the pair of opposites, does not allow it to "glimmer" (at the level of the conscious ego) through the opacity of the other (see chapter three). Every ambiguity is thus eliminated, with the risk of displacement (cf. "reaction formation") and, in short, the risk that not only is a resolution, a choice, eluded but so is a perception of the problem.

Ironic play brings with it, instead, other risks. Briefly and schematically, what interests us here is the risk that it may remain play indefinitely. However, ironic play can well use ambiguity as a temporary means of arriving at an active and serious choice with greater strength. And this may be the basis on which a fundamental distinction between ironies could be founded.

Booth (1974) understands this well, and he proposes calling "unstable ironies" those in which the truth asserted or implied is that no stable reconstruction can be built from the ruins revealed through the irony.

> The author—insofar as we can discover him, and he is often very remote indeed—refuses to declare himself, however subtly, for any stable proposition, even the opposite of whatever proposition his irony vigorously denies. The only sure affirmation is the negation that begins all ironic play: "this affirmation must be rejected", leaving the possibility, and in infinite ironies the clear implication that since the universe (or at least the universe of discourse) is inherently absurd, all statements are subject to ironic undermining. [p. 240]

On the other hand, when ironic play at a certain point reveals the underlying reality, Booth calls this "stable irony". In this case, irony takes on communicative importance; the ironic author is perceived as being "my kind of man because he enjoys playing with irony, because he assumes my capacity for dealing with it, and—most important—because he grants me a kind of wisdom; he assumes that he does not have to spell out the shared and secret truths on which my reconstruction is to be built" (p. 28).

Booth constantly notes that anyone dealing seriously with irony sooner or later seems to face the transition of "stable" irony/"unstable" irony, no matter what name is given to it. Muecke (1970), for example, calls it the transition between "specific" or "rhetorical" irony (corrective or normative) and "general" irony etc.

This is not all, however. In terms of interpersonal relations, keeping in mind all the possible combinations between the two pairs of conscious/unconscious and playful/serious that can occur, it is possible to reassess what Freud (1905c) states about how it is not necessary to bring in the unconscious to understand irony:

> Representation by the opposite . . . forms the core of another pleasurable way of expressing a thought, which can be understood without any need for bringing in the unconscious. I am thinking of *irony*, which comes very close to joking and is counted amongst the sub-species of the comic. . . . Its essence lies in saying the opposite of what one intends to convey to the other person, but in sparing him contradiction by making him understand—by one's tone of voice, by some accompanying gesture, or (where writing is concerned) by some small stylistic indications—that one means the opposite of what one says. Irony can only be employed when the other person is prepared to hear the opposite, so that he cannot fail to feel an inclination to contradict. As a result of this condition, irony is exposed particularly easily to the danger of being misunderstood. It brings the person who uses it the advantage of enabling him readily to evade the difficulties of direct expression, for instance in invectives. It produces comic pleasure in the hearer, probably because it stirs him into a contradictory expenditure of energy which is at once recognized as being unnecessary. [p. 174]

Immediately before this passage, Freud speaks of the technique of joke and, after giving some examples of representation by the opposite, adds another two. One is taken from Shakespeare's *Julius Caesar*, but Freud limits it to the final moment: "When Mark Antony, after he has made a long speech in the Forum and has reversed the emotional attitude of his audience round Caesar's corpse, finally claims once more: 'For Brutus is an honourable man . . .', he knows that the people will now shout back to him the true sense of his words: 'They were traitors: honourable men!'". The other example is that of *Simplizissimus*, a humoristic weekly which "describes a collection of incredible pieces of brutality and cynicism as the expression of 'men of feeling'". And Freud adds: "But we call this irony and no longer a joke. The only technique that characterizes irony is representation by the opposite" (p. 73). Two things can be observed in these examples: Freud's limitation of irony to the narrow field of representation by the opposite, and, furthermore, in this field the non-consideration of ambiguity. In the first example, his non-consideration is linked to his concentration on the moment in which the signals of irony become clearly indicative, not so much through an explicit revelation but, rather, through an increase in the capacity for comprehension the ironist allows the receiver. The example, therefore, belongs to the kind of irony in which at a certain point the ambiguity dissolves. It is for this reason that Booth calls it "stable", insofar as it reaches a point at which it stops, clearly indicating where reality lies.

According to Booth (1974, pp. 41–42), the famous scene from *Julius Caesar* is particularly demonstrative of two of the four types of judgement required when reading stable irony. When Mark Antony first says that "Brutus is an honourable man", the invitation is merely to agree or disagree. However, irony dramatizes the choice and renders it more actively ours. [Booth himself notes that in this case "the reader will find himself choosing, perhaps unconsciously" (p. 41); the message works along paths which go beyond the conscious sphere, even where ambiguity is overcome.] As the scene proceeds, the audience begins to perceive that Mark Antony is being ironic, and it is forced to make the ironic leap. The irony asserts itself and thus also asserts recognition of the author's skill in its use. If "both irony and ambiguity are 'pluralistic' ways of speaking, evasions of committed speech", the irony that disorients by resisting univocal interpretation, irony that evades committed speech, is "only a branch of a great and ancient art; even those modern works which are rightly celebrated for their rich ambiguity reveal, on close inspection, large tracts of stable irony—what Muecke calls "rhetorical" irony—about which no careful reader experiences any ambiguity whatever" (p. 48).

The last categorical statement seems to be linked to two interconnected elements: the fact that Booth, although he mentions it, deals neither with the unconscious level nor, in principle, with the preconscious level, and also the fact that in the case of stable irony, he tends to leap straight to the final stage (that of stability) and stress its characteristics, almost forgetting those of the preceding stages, although he has shown them too (see the discussion of the classic passage from Shakespeare above). In stable irony there is a whole procedure which, like the process used by psychoanalysts capable of adopting irony, is also activated by the desire to seek uncertainty, by the ability to tolerate it, and by the need to resolve it (Isay, 1977). Booth (1974) himself clarifies his thought more precisely when, examining the fact that poets often create deliberate ambiguities, he observes that there are great rewards in double vision. He adds that many literary works "not only can be but should be read in several different and even contradictory ways. But am I entitled to use that word should? If so even these works rule out some readings—namely, the unambiguous!" (p. 127).

A certain critical argument that hails the discovery of ambiguities as a major achievement could induce readers to live "with blurred senses and dulled attention" (p. 172) and to deprive themselves of the delights of precise and subtle communication that skilful ironists provide. Booth quotes Kierkegaard with reference to the boredom that results, not only in literature, but in the whole of life, when everything is ironized. Inflation is undoubtedly a form of psychological defence. In this case the defence seems to concern not only the above-mentioned pleasures but also the possibilities of insight offered by irony and ambiguity. According to Isay (1977, p. 449), during analysis ambiguity always communicates an unconscious desire or intention and the defence against this desire or intention. And we know (Wangh, 1979) that a situation of this kind is at the root of boredom.

Using this as a basis, we might now better see Booth's "unstable" irony (which, unlike stable irony, unceasingly and constantly referring to something else, leads to nihilism) as the expression of a mainly defensive action and, more precisely, of an inflation of irony, which thus loses its positive importance.

Sperling (1963), dealing with "exaggeration as a defence", mentions romantic irony and Heine in particular as exemplifying expression of the passion that precedes the sober counter theme. Through the close examination of clinical psychoanalysis, he proposes to verify the hypothesis that such a sequence illustrates a conflict in which the ego gains control over a derivative of the id. "To use Freud's simile in explaining romantic irony, after the rider has been taken by his horse for some distance, he regains his strength and directs the horse where he wants it to go" (p. 543). Rather than in these terms, I believe the sequence could be put forward in terms of its aspects or traits, which are playful or serious, respectively. What interests us is, in fact, not so much that the ego (re)gains control of the id, but, rather, *how* this might take place. It could happen, for example, by treating appearance first seriously and then going on to show that it was only a game, a way of playing (with) the appearance and of revealing the contrasting reality with greater effectiveness. In humour, seriousness is hidden beneath the apparent joke and there is generally not that contrast between the two registers—often inverted with respect to irony—which is a rule in irony.

Naturally, if the target of the irony is systematically established by the opinions of others rather than by appearance (according to a procedure incorrectly defined as Socratic), in ironic play, attacks directed against self or others will easily predominate over the achievement of the vision of reality.

As we have already mentioned, Booth (1974) observes that a great deal has been made of the aggressive–destructive aspect and too little of the communicative and even community aspects. There is no need to add to the list of ironic examples—unless we are choosing the examples in order to dramatize particularly the use of victims—to discover that the creation of amiable communities is often much more important than the exclusion of naive victims (who, I might add, may be persecutors in reality and/or fantasy). "Often the predominant emotion when reading stable ironies is that of joining, of finding and communing with kindred spirits" (p. 28).

When reviewing *A Rhetoric of Irony*, Muecke (1978, pp. 483ff) notes that Booth seems uninterested in the ironies that communicate nothing, that deny or seem to deny everything. That is, however, basically also the position of the analyst regarding material with no communicative importance. One must merely add that this very denial and absence are still elements that at that moment characterize the analytic relationship and as such should be noted and analysed.

It has been seen that, at its extreme, this kind of unstable irony merges with relativism, scepticism, nihilism, and pluralism, "a world of quicksand and miasmas where the reader loses all contact and all sense of his solidarity with the ironist"

(Muecke, 1978, p. 483). Obviously this sensation of loss can be used in the sphere of countertransference in analysis. However, the classification Booth makes from a rhetorical point of view of the deliberate procedures of irony can usefully be kept in mind by the analyst. The reader's reconstructions of covert or overt irony are certainly more limited from this point of view than the reconstructions the analyst aims at insofar as he is not content with reconstructing the field of intentionality and is not satisfied with understanding a passage of overt irony and reconstructing a covert irony. The reconstruction or unfolding must obviously also concern the patient's unconscious, and the analyst's insight is naturally dependent on the patient's acquisition of insight. When the analyst communicates, therefore, he will take into account those elements (essentially their location in the patient's preconscious) which lead him to judge the communication as timely. The communicative and constructive potential of (stable) irony structures the relationship rather than being structured by it.

The relational aspect has been considered little in psychoanalytic writings or has been considered in a pregenital or narcissistic key. According to Alexander (1969, p. 450), from a teleological point of view, one of the functions of irony in the total psychic economy is revenge. Another function is that of altering the surroundings and correcting its errors; yet another is that of preventing defeat and the narcissistic wound, depression, and the loss of self-esteem.

On the whole, it seems that in psychoanalysis a concept of irony in which regressive, defensive, or destructive elements prevail is highlighted. This would account, for example, for its association with sarcasm rather than with parody, to which irony—although different—is closer.

According to Reik (1929), the roots of irony, like those of sarcasm, are to be found in the oral sadistic stage, whilst humour (Winterstein, 1932) derives from the initial oral stage. What Reik misses is that a fundamental condition of irony is that the force both of the apparent meaning and of the real one is felt, whilst with sarcasm the apparent meaning is practically absent.

Irony will, however, be differently characterized according to the type of relationship—that is, according to whether it is pseudo-objectal or narcissistic or objectal with a predominance of pregenital or genital levels. This is valid both for its emission and for its reception. Regarding this last point, it must be noted that it is certainly the most neglected in the psychoanalytic literature and not only in Freud's writings but strangely even more so in the wealth of writings on countertransference that has since followed. Irony, on the other hand, poses special temptations for our weaknesses, especially our pride, and those who under-read and those who over-read see themselves on a conscious level as good readers. Our pride is more engaged in being "right" about irony, says Booth (1974), than about other things that could seem more important. "If I am wrong about irony, I am wrong at deeper levels than I like to have exposed" (p. 44). Different receptivities will in turn influence the emission of ironic messages. Irony can happily be used when praying to Jehovah, himself a great ironist, but not when writing to the governor to ask his pardon for a murderer. Here the words of Heine on his deathbed come to mind: "*Dieu me pardonnera. C'est son metier*" [God will pardon me. That is his job].

Summary of main points and some expectations

I should like to conclude this chapter with a summary of the principal points made so far.

It was probably on the basis of an inadequate consideration of the ambiguity of the signals of irony that Freud, although he observed that irony easily risks being misunderstood, considered that its understanding did not require the involvement of the unconscious. It is suggested that this contributed to the relative lack of interest psychoanalysts have shown for irony. Moreover, analysts have underestimated its communicative potential, highlighting instead its narcissistic and pregenital aspects, almost as if to confirm the "deterioration" the concept of irony has suffered, especially since the German Romanticists. A brief analysis of this follows, with the inclusion of a comparison with parody, which is closer to irony than is sarcasm.

With the Romanticists, the concept of irony broadened from the specific to the general (Muecke, 1969). General irony was identified with paradoxical irony (Knox, 1972) and was also seen as being able to take on all the other aspects of irony (the field of observation, the degree of conflict between appearance and reality, the inherently dramatic structure, and the philosophical and emotional aspects).

According to this interpretation, we may observe a similarity between ironic and psychoanalytic speeches; it is, however, at a divulgatory level. More promising in terms of finding a possible interdisciplinary meeting point is the concept of the ironist as a person who moves between two registers that are considered dialectic pairs. He is someone who is able to do this by following two fundamental modalities: what Booth calls "unstable" irony (analogous to "general" irony), in which the only truth affirmed and implied is that no stable reconstruction can be made from the ruins revealed through irony, and "stable" irony (analogous to "specific" irony), in which not only is the reconstruction rendered possible, but communication is also favoured. The communication stems from the understanding that the secret, shared truths on which the reconstruction must be based are not to be revealed.

In the psychoanalytic relationship, both the patient and the psychoanalyst emit and receive messages that can be considered as ironic. Their study can obviously assume greater importance if the qualification is extended from the conscious to the preconscious and unconscious levels. The extension seems justified, in other words worth investigating, at least within the analytic situation.

To conclude, I should like once more to recall and compare some of the points that have been developed or even merely touched on and which seem particularly pertinent when dealing with the topics in the following chapters. They are:

1. the definition of irony that Freud (1905c) seems to adopt;

2. the relationship Freud notes—albeit *en passant*—which exists between irony and ambiguity;
3. the possibilities of insight and communication that Freud recognizes in ambiguity;
4. the deductions that can be made in the light of Freud's statement that irony easily risks being misunderstood; he probably refers to a concept of irony that is different from the restricted concept mentioned in point 1, for which only Freud's affirmation that the unconscious need not be brought in can be held valid;
5. Booth's distinctive characteristics of "stable" and "unstable" irony, respectively;
6. the distinction between ambiguity as a means and ambiguity as an end in both meanings of the term, highlighting the temporal dimension; in the first sense, ambiguity can be reintroduced into the concept of stable irony from which only the second sense is excluded; the second meaning represents the characteristics of unstable irony and, markedly, that of "infinite, unstable" irony;
7. the possibility of a convergence in certain aspects between infinite, unstable irony and pregenitality, and between stable irony and genitality;
8. the analogies between the double vision of irony (Muecke, 1970) and those of "countervision in perpetuity" of psychoanalysis (Erikson, 1977).

From all this emerges a certain convergence in terms of the following affirmations:

1. We can legitimately speak of latent ironies–that is, those not consciously experienced as such.
2. Although in the field of literary criticism (or of psychoanalysis applied to literature) there are works that highlight ironies moulded by the author's unconscious, and although we may admit that a complete rhetoric of irony should, in theory, take into account the deeper communings authors invite us to, what literary critics and analysts do in terms of

this must be treated with great caution (Booth, 1974, p. 241).

3. On the other hand, the few psychoanalytic works on irony do not take into consideration the unconscious dimension of irony and thus do not contain the attempts mentioned above based on clinical material, which, in my opinion, would be more useful than those of applied psychoanalysis. This is a brief indication of what this study wishes to examine, beginning with the documentation that follows in chapter two. Exceptions to this are Rosen (1977), who deals with it in terms of the comic, and perhaps Schafer (1976) who of the various "psychoanalytic visions of reality" gives importance generically above all to the ironic vision, together with the tragic vision.

CHAPTER TWO

Ironic aspects in clinical psychoanalysis

Some examples and a discussion of latent ironies

In this chapter I intend to illustrate the concept of latent irony using mainly personal clinical material.

A first case (Case A) allows us to observe how the patient's expression of both libidinal and aggressive instincts towards the analyst may take:

1. the form of play at a conscious (or preconscious) level and a serious form at an unconscious level;
2. a serious form at a conscious level and the form of play at an unconscious level.

This was the case of a patient (see Sacerdoti, 1979) married to a man who virtually dominated her but who, it seems, was not without an ironic side to him (which the patient seemed for a long time to lack), even though it was somewhat rough and served his aggressive narcissism, which colluded with the patient's conspicuous masochistic elements. She justified her capitulations by saying that she was afraid her husband would kill her. Her conviction [the fact that she was *con-vinced* of this by her husband expressed the sadomasochistic collusion in which the husband's role was that of *con-vincer*] was not objectively justified (despite the fact that her husband was indeed a violent man): the fact that it could not be attacked by criticism seemed to be linked, amongst other things, to the patient's inability to see the situation ironically.

The analytic fragment that follows provides an example of the situation noted above at point 1.

The patient, who was obsessively fixated with the problem of reaching orgasm, had decided to terminate the analysis at a time that coincided with an important job opportunity in a distant city. Hence, she speeded up an extra-marital relationship that had begun recently, with counterproductive effects. She thus came to the final session dramatizing the event as something irreparable, for full sexual satisfaction should have been reached, or so she hoped, while the analysis was still under way ("now or never"). She thus tended to blame me for this development, digging up the more negative moments of the analysis in a crescendo that brought her to sever our relationship on a sour note. I insisted that she was staging a dramatic epilogue, whilst, all things considered, the last act seemed more like a farce. That very day she rang, asking to have one more session.

In this session, amongst other things, she brought up old fantasies she had never mentioned before in which I was present as a victim of the Nazi extermination. She had already earlier and repeatedly mentioned physically destructive fantasies, more or less clearly concerning me, which were, however, couched in totally improbable terms. This could no longer be said—at least at an atemporal level—of the fantasies she was now describing, which made explicit reference to my Jewishness. [On the basis of this material, the question of the total bracketing-off of (outer) reality and the exclusivity of the interpretation of transference (see, for example, Greenson, 1967) could be rediscussed by examining, to remain in the same theme, its grotesque aspects.] Moreover, it was virtually impossible for her to be ironic about them, unlike her previous fantasies. But this was in fact able to be overturned, insofar as it indicated the presence and activity in the analytic relationship of quite a different—libidinal—part of herself which, right at the point at which it was taken seriously, could also, rather than being denied, be distanced and invested elsewhere, without its being degraded or misunderstood. The patient recounted, for example, that she had read books by Singer with great interest and that she associated him with the analyst. Since then she has continued—albeit at less frequent intervals due to the geographic distance—good analytic work: the relationship now contains a stable and obvious positive transference that was previously absent or very sporadic. At the same time the patient has developed her first important, satisfying sentimental and sexual relationship.

It therefore seems that the reappropriation in the sphere of transference of her more "serious" impulses, both aggressive and libidinal, has become possible for the patient by moving through play (preconsciously experienced as such) with her lover, when the planned end of the analysis (or rather of the analyst, given her tendencies for concrete thought) was coming near. The "serious" resentment then manifested towards the analyst was just that, but it was farcically assimilated with that experienced in the game played with her lover, with the aim of excluding other much more serious associations—both in the aggressive and in the libidinal sphere—as well as the possibility of making its co-existence conscious (with all the problems but also the prospect of the fusion of instincts). My highlighting the playful aspect, now obviously preconscious, probably allowed her to accept *in extremis* the demolition of her own *mise-en-scène* aimed at convincing herself of the legitimacy of the *j'accuse* towards a frustrating and antilibidinal analyst, recognizing it as a game that had reached its end and about which she could, and indeed had to, ironize. She was thus offered the possibility of recognizing how, within the analytic relationship, the existence of a playful space (or register) previously palmed off as serious (cf. "pseudo work"), had allowed her to discover another authentically serious space that had until then remained, at least at the relational level, inconceivable.

This same patient also showed the situation described above in point 2: the expression of instinctual drive that manifests itself through a serious form at a conscious level and a playful form at an unconscious level.

The patient used to make reductive remarks concerning the analyst's comments, mainly by taking them out of context. Thus, for example, when, with regard to her extreme masochism on a general level in the relationship with her husband, I stated that in some way she must have gone along with it, she perceived the comment, as I realized much later, as a judgement, or even, as an order. This could also be, at an unconscious level, a kind of caricature of the "reductionist" aspect of the analyst's approach. In any case, at a conscious level, it was by attaching herself to the literal aspect of the analyst's comment, isolating it from its context, that the patient was able to give it superegoic significance, feeling herself to be the victim and the analyst to be a judge who, by condemning, might in turn be condemned by her. The ironic intention remained, however, totally unconscious for her (and for a long time impossible for the analyst to grasp).

Rosen (1977, pp. 320–321) emphasizes how in analysis obsessive subjects often react by reducing what the analyst states to trivialities through a distortion of the form and content. This is often carried out by ignoring the invitation implicit in the interpretation to a collaborative exploration that could resolve some ambiguities of the interpretation itself and thus extend its significance. [The patient's reduction of what the analyst says is in some aspects similar to that carried out by certain critics of psychoanalysis and which, with the addition of projection mechanisms, results in psychoanalysis being accused of reductionism.] (It could be said that the patient's reaction was the opposite of the recruit's in the story told by Landmann.) Rosen compares this to what happens in many literary parodies, in which the comic effect is derived from a similar artifice consisting of the reduction of the many complications of the author's theme to a single banal statement.

The recovery of the unconscious playful aspect in my patient's transferential movements (see Meltzer, 1973) not only failed in the here and now, but it was kept away (as I later discovered) by my slightly ironic comment. (Probably the indices of my irony were not clear enough in relation to a countertransferential ambiguity.) The above-mentioned recovery was made easier for me, by analogy, by the possibility of grasping the patient's attachment to the literal, concrete meaning not only of what I but also of what she said. Thus, when, in referring to these themes, at a certain point she said that I was on her husband's side, I realized that this represented for her a kind of plastic representation of the transference from the husband to the analyst.

Briefly anticipating what is discussed in chapter three, I would like to observe here that, by analogy with oneiric work, "ironic work" (like that of *Witz*) may also be considered something that, based on the consideration of verbalizability—instead of, as in dreams, on the consideration of the representability (Freud, 1900a)—serves to give an acceptable verbal (rather than a mainly figurative) form. This is naturally only the "appearance". The irony, or, rather, some of its forms, could thus be the finished product analogous to the manifest aspect of dreams. Through this work (of irony), inner censorship is "played". Moreover, as irony is social, like *Witz* (Freud), unlike dreams, which are asocial (Freud), also the other (or another) can be "played".

I shall try to simplify this by using a fragment taken from an analysis—Case B—in which, unlike the previous example, the development of a space in which to play together (see Winnicott, 1971) was not possible during analysis and therefore neither was there another space in which to work seriously, for both were obliterated by the patient's pre-occupation with the alternative: playing the analyst/being played by the analyst.

The patient (a student who had been at university for years without completing his degree) wrote me a letter that began: "Some time ago my father wrote to you to ask whether I might enter psychoanalysis. . . ." (In Italian, the patient made the mistake of writing "*intra*prendere" [to undertake] as "*intrapp*rendere, which alluded to the verb "*intrapp*olare" [to trap].) The thing he feared most was the "concatenation" of the doubts and scruples that paralysed him: just when he decided to get down to studying seriously, they even affected his breathing, which was held back: this brought him to a state of "absence", which was diagnosed and treated as a case of petit mal epilepsy. The patient broke off the analysis, giving the excuse that he no longer wished to cost his father even more money, shortly after having felt himself "*entrapped*" in a session when it emerged that his favourite hobby, floriculture, might be an alibi, and that there existed the possibility of it becoming a serious thing.

In this case (and the mere idea of it anguished him) not only would he no longer have a condition (that of not earning) that was always available as a valid reason for rationalizing his flight from the analysis, but the different meaning floriculture would have taken on would have altered a certain equilibrium of the patient's psychical economy to which, as a hobby, it contributed. It seems to me that this case is a good example of how complex the links between "partial pleasure" and "reproductive pleasure" are and how remaining in the sphere of the former may act as a defence against the latter, even at a level of "sublimation", thus avoiding a "return of what is substituted into what substitutes" (Freud 1916–17):

> This displaceability [of the component instincts of sexuality] must operate powerfully against the pathogenic effect of a frustration. Among these protective processes against falling ill owing to deprivation, there is one which has gained special cultural significance. It consists in the sexual trend abandoning its aim of obtaining a component or a reproductive pleasure and taking on another which is related genetically to the abandoned one, but is itself no longer sexual and must be described as social. [p. 345]

Turning his hobby into a job—that is, into a productive activity—would have meant for the patient associating pleasure with productivity; it would no longer be gratuitous, but something serious inserted in reality; he would have had to recognize himself and therefore also show he possessed a work tool. Whilst floriculture remained a hobby, the pleasure of planting [*Pflanzungslust*] could remain a substitutive object; if it were to become a job, a productive activity [*Fortpflanzungslust*], reproductive pleasure, it could no longer be considered as a substitutive object; there would be a return (or an appearance) of what is substituted into what substitutes.

Faced with this possibility, his fear was so great that the patient preferred to give up, to remain in the preventive self-castrating position—a flight from adult sexual identity—and castrate the therapist, rather than expose himself to similar risks (the irony of the fate certain analyses are unable to avoid, perhaps partly because the analyst is unable to grasp an unconscious irony in the patient).

As Kubie (1951) states, it is never the symbol that becomes unconscious, but the link with what it may represent. In this way, the "symbolic process" may lead to masking and misleading rather than really representing the trend of the inner psychological experiences. These distorted, masked experiences may become sources of disturbance, since, as long as they remain inaccessible to every conscious approach, they will remain inaccessible also to corrective experiences, to developments that may create suitable conditions to satisfy needs. This is fundamentally the path by which discontinuity enters our psyche and creates an inner dictatorship in human lives. This inner dictatorship tends to keep the status quo (and therefore to oppose the analysis which could break the repetition, taking the Ego where the Id dominates), mainly precisely through the interruption of the paths of communication between the "symbol" and what it represents. Hence the defence, avoidance, sabotage before something that could re-establish communications or links, as in the case mentioned above. For the moment I shall stop here as far as the problem of the dynamics of the relationships between the playful and serious aspects is concerned. [The fear of being able to move from "doing for fun" to "doing for real"—and the isolation of the two registers—is in my opinion particularly frequent in obsessive patients in relation to the aggressive component of ambivalence.] I shall limit myself here to noting, *à propos* of the "regard (*Rücksicht*) for verbalizability" mentioned above, two expressions of unconscious irony that I did not recognize as such immediately: "Enter analysis", in the light of feeling oneself "*entrap*ped", shortly followed by flight, was more concretely "*entrap*" a psychoanalyst as the patient had already done with the neuropsychiatrists by using "absence"—that is, such a massive presence that it obliterated any diagnostic space they might have had. Here it must be remembered with Freud (1916–17) that:

> Jokes, too, often make use of allusion. They drop the precondition of there being an association in subject-matter, and replace it by unusual external associations such as similarity of sound, verbal ambiguity, and so on. But they retain the precondition of intelligibility: a joke would lose all of its efficiency if the path back from the allusion to the genuine thing could not be followed easily. The allusions employed for displacement in dreams have set themselves free from both of these restrictions. They are connected with the element they replace by the most external and remote relations and are therefore unintelligible. [p. 174]

The analogies with dreams are therefore much greater if we may consider ironic those products that show themselves to be such only through a hermeneutic work, which in some way runs back over another work. The other work—even given the differences due to the material utilized and also to the fact that the product is "finished" and presented to the consciousness, and necessarily also to the other, awake not asleep—is the work that has rendered the ironic intention unrecognizable, also allowing the subject to continue to "sleep", even in the analytic relationship.

It now seems pertinent to give a brief example of the integration, from this point of view, between behaviour and dream, which may be connected in another obsessive patient (Case C). In a phase in which the character defences were giving way, especially regarding aggressiveness, a patient related the gaffes he frequently committed with friends; his motility had altered, he himself felt and seemed more "awake". He occasionally persisted in taking some of my comments out of context, especially when he could link them to notions of psychoanalytic theory or technique. This procedure was in all likelihood operating when he shortly before decided to abstain from masturbation, after he had spoken of it as something that might have a defensive role. Abstinence, however, seemed for the patient, apart from having an aspect of caricature within the psychoanalytic relationship, also as having a serious (working) aspect. Whilst he was slowly emerging, amongst other things, from an inhibition towards reading, the patient came to one session with a biography of Jung, hastening to add that he had never much liked him. He later dreamed that he was undergoing Jungian analysis. The individual sessions were represented by images contained in separate frames: they formed a strip, which was, in turn, clearly outlined. In the dream, he knew that by concentrating on this thing he saw in front of him, he would be able to go on sleeping.

For what interests us here, we need only observe that, following the manifest aspect, this dream—insofar as it is a means of communication in the analytic relationship—(re)constitutes the procedure of irony more typically than in the patient's behaviour. In it the patient (the author, but also the potential reader), turns to the analyst (reader, but also "muse", a term that is preferable here to "container", no matter how elastic), ironizing about a third person (no matter whether it represents a "split" part of the analyst).

I shall now describe Case D: the parodic remark a patient addressed to me, my interpretation of it, and some considerations, what interests us here being the possibilities of communication and insight (beyond conscious aspects) linked to this kind of relational procedure. Other observations regarding this case, both psychological and metapsychological, may be found in a previous work (Sacerdoti, 1977a). The remark was the reaction to a comment of mine that was felt to be too neutral and to which the patient responded with an ironic "Tickets, please". It was a humorous way of saying a serious thing, emphasizing the formal aspects of the statement and leaving the target (the analyst) implicit, recognizable through the link of caricatural resemblance with the analyst's tone and emotional stance (neutrality—indifference). My interpretation was dictated by the perception that—apart from the liberating aspect of the patient's parodic comment, made up of the possibility of attacking the analyst thanks to the synthesis operated in the caricature (cf. irony) and realized through the form (verbal and extraverbal) of the patient's expression—an aspect of repression (or perhaps, more precisely, one that tended to keep the other elements in the preconscious) existed in the remark, which could be highlighted through an analysis of the content —that is, emphasizing (shifting the emphasis to) what seemed banal (in this case the content).

The possibility of perceiving the (benevolent) "neutrality" as indifference is linked here to the eroticization of the transference and to the frustration connected therefore to abstinence. What emerges is that, from this point of view, what is serious (the analytic work) is experienced as a game, whereas what is a game—or, rather, the effect of a "game", its rules (eroticization of the transference and more generally the sexual developments of the relationship at the level of interior reality)—is experienced (imagined) as "doing seriously". We may here recall also Meltzer's (1973) considerations about the possibility of distinguishing play and work from pseudo-play and pseudo-work, respectively, merely on the basis of the analysis of the transference.

Therefore the patient's irony (in this case) should have been taken seriously; on the other hand, it was closer to sarcasm than to the expression of what Schafer (1976) calls the ironic vision of reality. It did not, therefore, help bear better the frustration, relativizing it and above all inserting it in the context and the real aim of the analysis agreed upon by mutual consent. There was therefore no point in the analyst placing himself at the same level, counterparodying for example the patient (see Rosen, 1977). This would in all likelihood have encouraged a kind of "split" that the patient seemed to tend to operate. Taking for granted my ability to conduct a kind of game, she turned to one image of me, whilst at the same time the target of the aggressive aspect of her irony was another image of me. I recognized both these aspects as classifiable at a partly conscious, partly preconscious level, but what seemed to be more characterizing was the separation between the two aspects, a separation that could have been reduced through an insight that pivoted around the aspects of the content, even favouring them with respect to the formal aspects the patient had highlighted. In the condensation operated by the remark quoted above, what remained overshadowed was the patient's tendency to feel masochistically in an impasse insofar as she was rejected by the analyst precisely because of the taboos connected to the setting imposed on her by the analyst (this latter element was expressed by the content). This I tried to summarize as follows: "You seemed annoyed at having noticed my lack of interest connected to your taking for granted that you had a ticket—that is, you were not breaking the rule." My interpretation tended to recover the serious aspect within the playful one to which the communication was at that moment linked. In fact, in the communicative aspect of the patient's irony, there was probably an invitation to play with the irony, which takes us back to what Booth (1974) says about the author of "stable" irony.

On the other hand, it may be seen that it is precisely the seriousness in the play and the play in the seriousness that may give the grandiose access to the feeling of self, without involving shame, feelings of inadequacy, and tortuous self-destruction; and yet in the forms of the relationship of the psychoanalysis an ever greater cleft is opened up between playfulness and seriousness, just as in the society in which we live (Morgenthaler, 1977, pp. 3-4).

This may limit the possibility of experiencing the play of the transference neurosis with the greatest seriousness and of finding, through the exploration this allows, better solutions than those adopted in the past. In the transference impact, "the psychoanalytical setting tends to reproduce, from the outset, the repetitive phases of the state of relative separation from early objects" (Stone, 1961, pp. 86–87). Thus both the struggle against separation and the progressive impulse directed against the attachment to an early object are expressed in the neurosis of transference. The tensions that emerge between the protagonists of this situation of "intimate separation" may be better managed in all their seriousness and dramatic force if a space for play remains.

This is, in my opinion, well represented in the following dream of another patient (Case E) during the first year of analysis:

> I was in the flat of an oculist friend of mine [the patient wears contact lenses that often make her eyes water during our sessions]; she is a brave and very sweet woman, who is now pregnant by her companion; they can't get married because although they are both separated, neither is divorced. My husband was sitting behind me; in came a thin, somewhat crazy man, who, holding a pin in his mouth, came so close that he pricked my face [the patient has often seen me as being ironic, like her father]. He is also holding a copper wire, and I think he is going to strangle me or tie me up. I ask my husband for help, and he replies that he'll find a way to help me all in good time. So I stretch out my hands and they lock with those of the man, as if in a game".

Interconnections between playful and serious aspects

In the examples mentioned thus far, we have emphasized the relational potential of irony (and parody) and interconnections between the playful and serious aspects, and between the conscious and unconscious level—interconnections that, by introducing these variables, require a broadening of the study of the basic contrast (between appearance and reality) of irony. This contrast may express itself or reveal itself not so much in the classical counterposition of opposites as in the contrasting of (or rather in the dialectic between) playful or joking aspects and serious or working ones, in that the former are placed in front as the appearance covering the reality of the latter or vice versa. Moreover, the apparent/real pair may be variously combined, in a *longitudinal section*, with the playful/serious pair, insofar as, for example, what initially appeared serious, but was in fact playful, may turn into something really serious, whether it appears serious or, vice versa, playful. The contrast between appearance and reality may fall or persist with inverted contents (all the possible combinations are basically imaginable). This dialectic pair (playful/serious or playful working) seems to be basic both for a psychoanalytic study of irony and for a study of irony in the psychoanalytic field, partly because it may stand at the meeting-point between a series of dialectic themes, themes of polarity or of pairs of opposites [*Gegensatzpaare*], which may be summarized, on the one hand, in the contrast between appearance and reality—characteristic of irony—and, on the other, in the great polarities that, according to Freud (1915c), dominate psychic life.

Freud (1908e [1907]) emphasizes how the opposite of play is not what is serious but what is real, and how "[the child] likes to link his imagined objects and situations to the tangible and visible things of the real world. This linking is all that differentiates the child's "play" from "phantasying" (p. 144).

Elsewhere (Sacerdoti, 1974) I have tried to show how, in the setting, the psychoanalyst, allowing himself to be experienced alternatively or even simultaneously as an imaginary object and as a real object, may favour not only "fantasizing" but also "playing" and moreover, on the one hand the distinction and, on the other, the undoing or the overcoming of the opposition between play and reality as well as (given the similarity of real and serious) between playful and serious aspects, between playfulness and seriousness. Freud (1908e [1907]) expresses something similar when he describes the so-called possibilities of recovery of the adult: "When the child has grown up and has ceased to play, and after he has been labouring for decades to envisage the realities of life with proper seriousness, he may one day find himself in a mental situation which once more undoes the contrast between play and reality" (p. 144). He continues by noting that the adult may be aware of the absolute seriousness that as a child he gave to his game and repeat, inverted, an analogous operation regarding his serious present occupations: freeing himself from their unbearable oppression, he thus wins "the high yield of pleasure afforded by humour" (p. 145). In Freud's later study on humour (1927d), which is centred on structural aspects, the emphasis is placed on the relationship between the ego and the superego and on the latter's quality of benevolence; what is therefore emphasized, in addition to the liberation, is the possibility of integration. I should like here to recall that liberation and the new synthesis (with inclusion of the old in the new) are today considered characteristic of parody, which is so close to irony. "From the novel of chivalry [the old *alibi et tunc* we might say, making a comparison with the analytic procedure] and from the new preoccupations about everyday reality [the *hic et nunc*] we have Don Quixote and the novel as we know it today" (Hutcheon, 1978, p. 474). For Freud (1905c) Don Quixote is originally a purely comic figure—an overgrown child—who ceases to be such when he takes his duties, promises, and idealism seriously.

But the analysis of playful situations and the contribution ethology provides also reminds us (see Sacerdoti, 1974) that the roots of clinical psychoanalysis stem from the biological substratum, which in turn, sets certain limits for it.

The fact that "infantile playfulness employed by the adolescent and the adult" is "an area of activity, of thought, of significance and of affection which psychoanalysts—even Melanie Klein —have not considered sufficiently" (Gillibert, 1973, p. 72) would therefore seem even less justified, albeit more understandable.

For Benassy (1973, p. 521) the serious/play (playfulness) pair of opposites cannot be expressed precisely in the usual metapsychological terms, not even from a genetic point of view. In his opinion, the serious/play pair exists before any other (conscious/unconscious, subject/object) distinction, before any formation of the ego, before the ego distinguishes itself from the id. He wonders if it is not the serious/play pair that provides the basis for an aspect of the ego/id distinction.

For Benassy, the serious/play opposition is therefore close to (but more primitive than) the reason/unreason, reality/fantasy, ego (representing reality)/id (representing the beginning of pleasure expressed by fantasy) bipolarity. In short, for Benassy the counterposition of the serious/play represents "above all the (regressive) opposition between the activities imposed by the reality the Ego will become responsible for and the activities (pure pleasures) that belong to the subject himself (before Narcissus knows he is Narcissus) as it is the Id" (p. 522).

I believe that this view strengthens the thesis set out above in which conditions of seriousness may co-exist at a conscious level and conditions of play at an unconscious level just as, vice versa, conditions of play at a conscious level and of seriousness at an unconscious level.

To ignore these possibilities in life means mainly running enormous risks in the former case and missing great opportunities in the latter; in psychoanalysis it basically means not being able to tune in to the patient's unconscious.

"Playing" and "being played"

Undoubtedly the fact that the analyst is aware of these themes increases both his capacity for insight and the ability of provoking insight in the patient by working and playing with him. On the other hand, it diminishes the possibility of his being played by the patient and (*absit iniuria verbis*) of playing the patient himself (see Favez, 1971) and in any case of playing the possibilities of the analysis (which may happen right from the first contact with the patient).

The playful/serious pair, together with the apparent/real pair, basically pose the problem of deception, and this, too, may be explored in analysis in its unconscious equivalents and at the limit of its biological roots. This is what I propose to do, following the thread of irony, with the clinical examples quoted in the section that follows.

In today's pathology, increasing importance is accorded to so-called character pathology, containing, however, egodystonic elements, which are those that bring the "patients" to analysis. Now, naturally at a conscious level, the motivation is almost always made up of "problems" (sometimes of dilemmas), which are presented as psycho-social in nature, but which concern the image of self as well as objects and relationships with them. The introduction of the unconscious dimension reveals other underlying problems or dilemmas that concern the image of the body, its functions and its relationships. Often the patient formulates the problem implicitly, and sometimes explicitly, in terms of appearance/reality, making options and opting himself for a greater closeness of his own image of himself (of the object and the relationship) to reality or to appearance [see later, in the section "Pairs of opposites and terminability of analysis", the example given by a patient of the equivalence of the pairs of truth–falsehood/emotional involvement–lack of emotional involvement opposites etc.]—in other words, opting for a greater appropriation or expropriation of the real (true, emotionally felt) aspects and, respectively, apparent (false, that is emotionally indifferent) aspects of the image of self; i.e. for a sincere or a fictitious image of self. The same dilemma, too, could be considered regarding the image of self (as well as that of the object and the relationship) as perceived in the messages of the other. It is basically the problem of self-deception and being deceived, to which must be added that of deceiving, in the transitive, active form, which generally appears later in the analytic relationship and which may offer special opportunities for interpretation.

Lacan (1964) states that on the path of deception the subject follows, the analyst is in a position to say, *"You tell the truth"*, and interpretation has no sense except in this dimension. The patient's "*I am deceiving you*" comes from the point at which the analyst waits for the subject and sends him, following the formula, his same message in its true meaning, that is in an inverted form. He tells him: *"In this* I am deceiving you, *what you send as a message is what I express to you, and doing this you are telling the truth."* Unmasking in analysis, therefore, takes place in the opposite direction to that of common language, in so far as, in emphasizing the truthful aspects (reality) that were concealed under the untruthful ones (appearance), it favours (or focuses on) the characteristics of communication of the patient's message, which emerge from the context, especially and above all the transference. In analysis, unmasking is not a way of ridiculing or degrading or joking (see Freud, 1905c) but, rather, a way of taking things seriously and re–qualifying them. [It may thus be comparable to parody, not in the traditional sense in which Freud understood it, but, rather, in the modern sense mentioned above. Here it is worth recalling that the word irony derives from the Greek *eirōnía*, which means 'fiction', for the ironist is he who—according to a certain image of Socratic irony—interrogates feigning ignorance and/or feigning to take seriously the opinions of others, which are necessarily the opposite of his. This confirms the negative evolution the concept of irony has undergone (like other concepts that have in common the characteristic of referring to something that can bridge the primary and secondary processes). Contrary to this cliché, the analyst could not do his work unless he felt really ignorant and unless he took the opinions of others really seriously. This obviously does not exclude the need both for a basic analytic "knowledge" and for room to play.]

This argument is illustrated in the clinical material that follows, which I believe is extremely representative of the vicissitudes—and in particular the equivalents and oppositions—of some of the aspects of the image of self, of objects, and of the relationship.

Examples broadened to the problem of pairs of opposites, with particular attention to self-image

In the cases that follow, the problem of procreation/inability to procreate/destruction of the child occupied in various ways a central position in the psychopathological picture and in the analytic relationship. The death of a new-born baby in one case and a miscarriage in the other were remembered as the killing of the child and of the foetus, respectively. The patient's dramatic alternative between believing her own memory (truthful) or not (deceiving herself) corresponded to her self-image either as a criminal or a madwoman and permitted a glimpse, despite the drama, of the superimposition of playful and serious aspects variously distributed between the horns of the dilemma at different levels of the conscious/unconscious polarity. The superimposition was particularly evident, in the sphere of the analytic relationship, in another patient—mentioned already for other aspects (Case A)—in which the theme of deception interconnected with those of frigidity and sterility.

These questions paradigmatically lent themselves to the study of the degree of primarity—and, respectively, to secondarity—of the fantasies and images, the different evaluation of which is the basis of different theoretical conceptions in psychoanalysis.

Given the centrality of the above-mentioned themes, the preconscious and unconscious equivalents that can be extracted from the analytic material quoted here quite extensively are particularly important.

Case F involves a 32-year-old patient who had undertaken analysis out of the fear of "relapsing" and out of the desire to "know the truth" about the death of her daughter. She had recently left a nursing home where she had spent some time after a nine-month stay in a psychiatric hospital, to which she had been admitted after a suicide attempt and an episode of acute psychosis (which passed in about a month) just after the sudden death during the night of her third child who was three months old. The patient, who was sleeping alone with the child (whose fingernails she had clipped, cutting a finger, just before going to bed), after swallowing a bottle of sleeping pills, had gone to the police, declaring that she had suffocated her daughter by sitting on her cot. The autopsy showed that death had been caused by suffocation from the regurgitation of milk in the child's windpipe.

Case G concerns a woman of 29 who asked to undertake analysis because of her painful and insistent obsessions with filicide (she had an only child of five) and of her fear of going mad, as well as a subdepressive state she connected to a miscarriage she had experienced six months previously, which she considered self-provoked. The patient's past revealed other interesting elements. At 12 or 13 she had had seizures that were considered epileptic (morpheic) and episodes of "sleepwalking". When her paternal grandmother, to whom she had been rude a few days earlier, died (when the patient was 16 or 17), she had the precise sensation of having killed her, and she suffered from amenorrhoea for the next nine months. After meeting her husband-to-be (whom she had first met as a child), she suffered from depression to the point that when she was 22 she was admitted to hospital and received electroshock treatment. She also had the obsessive idea that she could not tell her husband that when she was a child, his father had picked her up in his arms and had "interfered" with her. Later she had again suffered anxious depression and anorexia a few months after the birth of her son.

In both these cases, the problems at a conscious level essentially concerned the old healthy/(mentally) ill and innocent/guilty pair of alternatives, connected in such a way that neither choice was satisfying insofar as the "positive" solution of one automatically led to the "negative" one of the other. The alternatives thus were between madness or delinquency.

These conscious problems hid many other unconscious problems concerning other choices, which could also be seen as pairs of opposites.

The fantastic elements will be examined under the double register of desire and defence, leading to examples of how the active/passive antithesis, especially at the phallic and anal level, but also at the oral, and the related images of physical self lay at the basis of the image of mental self and, in particular, of the oscillations of this image between the poles of delinquency and madness. [According to Schafer (1968, pp. 189–190), whilst psychoanalysis has not reached a substantially psychoanalytic conceptualization of active/passive, a satisfying conceptualization is necessary in the context of subjective experience: we should thus speak in terms of active and passive. And naturally specific desires to love and be loved, to hit and be hit, to eat and be eaten etc. should play a prominent role in psychoanalytic formulations. In this regard, see also the important, if little-known, study by Rapaport (1953) published after his death. Rapaport did not publish this article, even though it was carefully finished, because his dual models of activity and passivity in relation to instincts still had to be completed by analogous models in relation to the outside world.]

The evolution of this problem in the sphere of transference was parallel to the progression or regression of the treatment (and, in one case, its being stopped and taken up again).

The possibility of grasping the dynamics, the interchanges between inner and outer reality, seems to have been assisted by the occurrence of "privileged" events: respectively, the sudden death of a daughter a few months old "remembered" by the patient as infanticide by suffocation, and a miscarriage for which the patient felt criminally responsible. [According to Winnicott (1935, p. 157), the changeover from the use of the term "fantasy" to that of "inner" reality implies a sufficient respect for the conscious and unconscious fantasy (and may aid a complementary rather than an antinomic vision of the fantasy/reality pair).]

Closely connected with what has been mentioned above, both patients had had psychotic experiences and had been admitted to psychiatric hospitals, which allowed them to glimpse, besides the unconscious significance underlying the conscious representation of "mental illness" and its alternative "delinquency", also those concerning "internment".

Moreover, especially in the case of G, in which the analysis was broken off by the patient before time and then taken up again two years later and finally concluded after the analyst had set a deadline, it was possible to trace back both what the so-called flight into healing and the healing according to analytical criteria, as well as its opposite, i.e. the installation of the illness, corresponded to at the level of inner conscious and unconscious reality.

All this has brought up once again the theme of the terminable and interminable analysis, linked to that of the initiability of the analysis.

To conclude, these cases illustrate how, also for the patient, the search for and the finding of the truth at a conscious level may make up the main aim of the analysis, and how, on the other hand, this may all serve to cover a "deception". The problem formulated initially in terms of the true/false antithesis helps to reveal the unconscious equivalents of this pair once brought into the relationship between the patient and analyst.

The active/passive antithesis

The oscillation of the image of self between the poles of delinquency and of madness often seems to correspond (see the material that follows) to oscillations between the male and female polarity. If this bipolarity may be seen with Freud (1915c, 1917c) as the expression at the phallic level of the more general active/passive antithesis (biological polarity), it also appears in the anal and oral aspects.

Patient F has read an article on sudden infant death and has previously read another on the characteristics of chromosomes in murderers. She shows resentment about the fact that the psychiatrists in the hospital had done nothing in the nine months she had spent there to investigate whether or not she had an extra chromosome. She does not appear to have any other notions concerning chromosomes, but concludes by remembering that differences exist between the chromosomes of the two sexes. In the next session she recounts the following dream: She is with a nurse who, using an instrument halfway between a pipette and a tweezer, is counting out the drops [chromosomes] of a liquid contained in a recipient halfway between a goblet and a test tube. She states there are eight, and that this is fine [i.e. there is no extra one]. The liquid is whitish [the patient associates the search for the chromosomes of the murderer with blood and the determination of sex with seminal liquid]. It is now up to her to make the determination, and therefore, following the nurse's instructions, she has to urinate a little [she has a catheter inserted]. She is worried both by the determination and by the difficulty of urinating a little [either all or nothing]. She recalls that she had had a catheter inserted when she gave birth for the second time, and she was very nervous about it as her husband had had a painful and complicated catheterization after the serious fracture of both bones of one leg.

In a previous dream, a man breaks into the house of a professor, which is rather dark and full of books [which reminded her of the analyst's study, and of that of a maternal uncle who had been paretic in his last years], intending to kill both the professor and his maid by shutting their heads in a box. Caught, he feigns the expression of an idiot, stupidly dribbling, and claims he has killed his daughter. After the dream of the chromosomes, *à propos* the dream about the professor, she remembers—amazed that she had not made the connection earlier—having read a thriller in which a couple was strangled. At first it seemed that the murderer was a woman, since the crime required little strength, but later it was discovered that it was really a man with only one arm. Immediately prior to the dream about the professor, the patient had cancelled several sessions and had repeatedly stated she wished to break off analysis.

The equivalent of being a murderer/having an extra chromosome/having a penis (as the catheter is partly inserted, partly protruding) is obvious. But being a murderer seems to be the alternative to being mad; in fact, her memories tell her that she has committed a murder. If they are right, she is not mad but has murdered; vice versa, if they are wrong, she has not murdered but is mad, she has lost her head (penis). In either case, her daughter is dead. This child, unlike the other two, was born after a pregnancy during which there had been arguments with her husband and between their respective families, and from the day she was born the child had been looked after like a daughter by her maternal grandmother, who had given her back to her mother only a few days before the child's death. It must be noted that the patient's mother, who was otherwise a good woman, had always had the bad habit of telling lies and had always been hostile towards her daughter's boyfriends (including her present husband), except for two, who later turned out to be homosexuals.

The patient's "breakdown" had begun with the birth, the experience of which was probably conditioned by the alternatives she had given herself: to keep the child as a penis (to be therefore a murderer—or thief—as far as her husband was concerned) or to lose her head–child–penis. The choice had probably been deferred by giving the child to her mother. The child's death poses a new situation in which the patient once again avoids a real choice by choosing both possibilities: murderer and madwoman (even a suicide, i.e. narcissistically omnipotent: being a murderer, i.e. with a penis–head, and mad, i.e. without it, in suicide the "autonomous" dramatization of the two sexual roles becomes possible for her).

The dream about the chromosomes probably contains a maternal transference. The difficult necessity for her to make the determination and limit her ambitions (urinating only a little) by herself can also be seen

In the dream about the professor there is a prevalently paternal transference. The terms of the alternative are, in any case, analogous. Self representation is, however, different: while the patient is represented in the dream by a man, the lying behaviour points to her identification with her mother (who had the "bad habit of telling lies", and the preferred choice is to be the murderer. Only when he is caught does the man retreat and pretend to be an idiot who has killed his daughter. Here, too, we are dealing with a non-choice insofar as both solutions (failed displacement and the return—breakthrough—of the repressed) are chosen. It must be noted that the patient considers herself to be, and is considered by others to be, far the least intelligent in the family.

The patient expresses doubts regarding the analysis, considering herself not to be up to it, and then not to be up to keeping the child. She thinks that if she lives with her husband (from whom she is at present separated), she has complexes, and therefore the analyst will have something to bring out; otherwise he won't. She is afraid of being sent back to the psychiatric hospital. Having heard that the analyst believes she wishes to be a man (*à propos* the dream about the chromosomes and another one in which she had a third nipple lower down and in the middle of her body) makes her very optimistic; she has the impression that this will resolve everything. She repeats that her complexes come when she is with her husband; if she does not go back to him, the analyst will have nothing to bring out.

She pays in advance, fearing she will be unable to come because of the bad weather. It is impossible for her to feel indebted; she prefers to be in credit. She has the idea she is not "rendering" in analysis (rendering is obviously giving back to the analyst what she has taken from him in inner unconscious reality).

She recounts a dream in which she is having sexual relations with her husband. She is lying on her back and cannot therefore understand how, even though she can feel her husband's penis (both inside and out), she cannot see him. The only position in which this would have been possible was a "sitting" one. She thinks this is a joke and it makes her laugh (as in the session prior to this dream). [The patient used the Italian word "*seduta*", which refers both to an analytic session and to the "sitting" position.]

In the same session she also tells of her dream about the professor. In the following session she recounts the following dream: "A brown horse [association: the analyst's bookcase] with large haunches mounted by a young boy was chasing me; I was running around a tree; I was scared it would crush me with its posterior". Association: 'fat-arse', said of annoying people—for example, in the past, of the analyst ("I've got to go and see that old fat-arse"). As a girl it was a name by which her mother in particular called her when she made mistakes: "Shut up you with your fat arse and big nose." In a dream she had had when married, a black horse with a black rider was chasing her, and she was running around a column like one at her school, thinking that if the horse caught up with her, she would be killed. Unlike in the later dream, her fear was of being trampled by the horse's hooves.

The problem of activeness as a defence from passiveness also appears in the comparison between the "murderer" of the child and the dream of the brown horse (being mother/heavy-on-top, instead of having the mother/heavy-on-top). With the analysis of the horse dreams emerges in particular that aspect of the active/passive polarity, at a mainly anal level, which corresponds to the controlling and destructive activity as defence from a passiveness signifying being controlled and destroyed.

After missing several sessions, she brings the following dream: "My mother-in-law was telling my daughter to eat up, be quiet and obedient, otherwise she would go to prison or to court. I, later, when the children had left, turned on my mother-in-law, particularly for the use of those two words". The alternatives are putting-in-the-mouth or going-into-prison.

Oral questions are therefore confused with phallic or anal ones.

After a deadline has been set for the analysis, Patient G begins again to have obsessions about killing her only child, following a conversation in which a woman commented (with regard to a newspaper article telling of a mother who had thrown her child out of the window): "They [mad people] should all be locked up [in the mental hospital]." At the time the patient had replied with spirit: "No, because there's no difference [between mad and sane people]", but later she had been assailed by doubts. During the night, half asleep, she had fantasized about using her husband's pyjamas to hurt her son. This fantasy was accompanied by the sensation–certainty that, while she was pregnant, she would never be committed to a mental hospital. She also recalled something her husband had said about the "inalienability" of the wife's property if husband and wife separate, and the deadline for the analysis set by the analyst.

It would also seem that as far as her desire/fear of "being inside" (a mental hospital, her mother), the fantasies of killing her child (connected also to an earlier miscarriage that had been followed by a depressive state and admission to the psychiatric hospital), of castrating her husband (who is lame), and of castrating the analyst (for whom, it is obvious from other elements, she has a paternal transference), corresponding to the "having inside" (like her mother), all signified defence (the defensive mechanism may be seen at other times to turn in the opposite direction). This defence had been activated at the moment in which the woman she was speaking to about the need to lock up all mad people reawoke in her the desire to be inside again. It could be classified—just as most of the cases in which the dialectic of being and having is at stake—as a defence of the kind that negates through fantasies. In the "solution" (non-solution) the patient was looking for when faced with the deadline fixed for the end of the analysis, we can see fantasies of omnipotence that basically concern the control and destruction of her father, at least initially (castration fantasies in the sense of active castration).

Thus in the following dream (after the assassination of John Kennedy): "The ceiling was falling down and I foresaw and followed its fall, saying one–two–three (tapping her foot)." The day before this dream, the patient has overheard a conversation in which, commenting on the assassination, a man was speaking about the possibility of killing God, and another man replied: "Let the ceiling fall in, then." The patricide–suicide here corresponds to the infanticide–suicide of the previous case (with highlighting of anal elements).

The true/false antithesis and the problem of deception in analysis

Parallel to the illustration of the active/passive polarity in its various unconscious equivalences, the cases we are examining also allow us to illustrate the equivalences, at the preconscious and unconscious levels, of the true/false polarity. These equivalences are closely connected, on the one hand with the metapolarity in which one pole is made up of a pair of opposites and the other of a pair of equals and, on the other, with the images of self oscillating between the (mentally) ill/healthy poles with the dynamics concerning falling ill and getting better. The latter theme, insofar as it is connected to the analysis, leads to the problem of deception also within the sphere of the analysis itself.

The true/false antithesis, together with the active/passive one, concerns the origin and the evolution of the "false Self" in that it is an operation that tends initially to hide for defence purposes the "true Self" (Winnicott, 1960) otherwise what is risked is death, madness, and castration; thus not falsifying, not lying, being truthful, may be mad or make mad. This obviously does not exclude the psychopathogenic potential of the lie, stressed amongst others by Bion (1970).

In Patient F—who had undertaken analysis above all "to know the truth" about the death of her daughter—the theme of cheating, of deception, had been experienced in transference at first only on an active plane; deceiving, in the sphere of paternal transference (the dream about the professor). In other words, I am an idiot (castrated), I do not have homicidal (castrating) intentions: it is what on a fantasizing plane is experienced as deception (inner reality, coinciding with desire). Deceiving the analyst is, on the other hand, a necessary presupposition for undertaking and continuing the analysis. She had, indeed, undertaken it out of the fear of relapsing (into madness)—that is, of losing her head–penis, therefore in order to avoid losing what she has not got.

The continuation of the analysis may be endangered if the patient (as in the dream about the professor) is not certain that the analyst can be deceived about her castrating intentions and, naturally, if she can no longer deceive herself on that matter.

Two different and opposite ways of breaking off analysis are: (1) on the grounds of health: "I'm fine, it's not worth my coming"—a realization of the fantasy of acquiring a penis ("flight into healing"); or (2) when coming to the analyst is experienced as a confirmation or even an attribution of the patient's illness: "So it means I'm not well, I can't keep my children, etc." Here there might be a disavowing mechanism, which is much more frequently seen in hospitalized cases (and not only amongst the patients). That is, not: "I'm in analysis because my head/penis is not alright", but: "My head/penis is not alright because I'm in analysis" (the term "flight from the iatrogenous illness" might be used to describe breaking off treatment on this basis).

In the same patient, concerning her desire to know the truth (about what happened—i.e. whether her daughter died or whether she killed her), there also appears the desire to experience actively the loss of her child–penis–faeces. To be a murderer means also (overdetermination!): "I have castrated myself, I have defecated, when I wanted to."

The passive aspect of the deception (being deceived) was later experienced on the transference plane, but it first appeared insistently in her relationship with her lying mother. It is closely connected to the reflexive aspect, i.e. to self-deception, which in turn plays a decisive role in the subjective evaluation—and perhaps in the determination—of the psychotic episode (and therefore also the fear of relapsing). [From a genetic point of view, this corresponds to emphasizing the importance of the lying mother in the formation of a weak ego (and superego).] In fact, if the patient deceives herself in her memories (having suffocated the child), it means she cannot trust her ability to perceive, or at least memorize, reality, to distinguish (in her memory) between fantastic and real elements: that is, she is (has been) mad. This is the same problem that her mother creates for her with her numerous comments and opinions about things that concern her—so much so that at times she feels she is going mad. Later, in analysis, her reaction towards her mother's lies alters, so that she doubts less and less her own ability to perceive things—in other words, her mother's well-denied aggressiveness towards her—and she reacts more and more with the exteriorization of her aggressiveness and her desire for independence from her mother.

Probably her mother's central latent negation (lie) (see Deutsch, 1933), as perceived by the patient, was: "It is not true that I don't have a penis—I have you" and her mother's anguish in seeing her give birth (anguish the patient herself fears experiencing when she will become a grandmother) sounds like: "You are no longer my penis—you have your own" (see her mother's hostility towards her daughter's boy-friends, except towards the two homosexuals).

One of Patient G's dreams, towards the end of the analysis, in addition to developing the theme of deception, also introduces the question of the terminability of the analysis.

I shall extract the following elements from the dream: "I was taking my husband and son to the station and I was sad because they were leaving [see, instead, above the inalienability of the wife's property if husband and wife separate, reassurance against the fear of losing what she does not have]. Then there were some false priests: one of them aimed a pistol at my husband and demanded three thousand lire. I said: 'You've been swindled, because I've been swindled too. My cousin told me that my father's funeral had taken place, and I said that I hadn't been able to go'." (The patient had been swindled of her father's inheritance by her brothers, and her husband always reproached her for having put up with this injustice virtually without protesting.)

In the dream it seems that the transference takes place to the analyst from the father, whom the daughter is able to mourn without needing to go to his funeral, therefore denying having killed him, and without claiming her inheritance (the penis). As the patient accepted having been "swindled"—that is, not having received the penis from her father because her brothers had received it—when the analyst who, as the object from whom separation was imminent, receives the paternal transference but who, as he aims the pistol, seems mainly to represent a fraternal transference, tries to swindle her by repeating the operation of taking away the penis from the husband–father, he is no longer able to do so, because in the meantime the patient has been "swindled". In other words, accepting the castration (see the departure of the husband–analyst with the child–penis), her brothers cannot this time swindle (castrate) her, because one cannot be cheated out of what one does not even fantasize possessing.

If they take the three thousand lire from her husband, they are not swindling her because the child is the husband's. If anything, there might be a small triumph in considering that the priest is swindled by his own desire to swindle (which is basically a reversal of the result of the analysis: that the patient abstained from castrating the analyst).

Unlike the dream in which the ceiling was falling, which, before the analyst's fixing a deadline for the analysis, represented a destructive solution, in this later dream another type of solution is represented: acceptance of the swindle–castration, non-attainment of the analyst–father's penis, acceptance of femininity, "healing", which allows her to no longer be swindled by the analyst.

It is obviously a projection of the swindle or deception, experienced by the patient at the moment of the insight concerning the desire that had led her to the analysis perceived as a promise by the analyst. The fantasy of healing is therefore here initially a fantasy of active castration, whilst at the end it is a fantasy of acceptance (working through) of her mourning for the death of her father and, in particular, of his inheritance, or penis.

When the patient gave up her desire to have the father–analyst's penis for herself—i.e. accepting the reality of the difference between the sexes—she also lost the fear of losing it. The child stays with her husband, and she will no longer be swindled—that is, swindle herself, deceive herself. Recovery and undeception coincide.

In the dream of the cheating priest, we may see deception (by the analyst) if we are placed on the plane of the fantasies of desire: "The analyst made me believe I could carry out my desire—that is, to be omnipotent" (projection).

The defence against insight of her own desire to commit a crime experienced through transference is expressed in the giving up of her desire for healing and, even earlier, for going mad. In fact, when she broke off the analysis before time, the patient considered her desire for healing absurd, because in her case it was not a question of illness but of real fault and remorse "to be kept" (allusion to her recent miscarriage). This position could be considered a special form of "flight into healing" or rather, "flight into psychosis". The lowest common denominator is the (flight into) "negation of illness", which coincides with a "flight into delinquency" (past), and which probably corresponds to the previous fantasy of acquisition of the husband–father's penis (the husband is lame); but it is also probably a flight from delinquency into analysis—that is, from the repetition of the crime in transference

This also partly recalls the patient's refusal to continue studying after beginning middle school, for which she justified herself by telling a lie—i.e. that the teacher had said: "You'd do better staying at home and plucking chickens." Her parents had a poultry shop, and she threw herself into her job. She associated this memory to another of having stolen a little ring when she was about eight and having given it back after listening to a priest's sermon. Even now, she does not feel happy until she has given a person what she owes them (see Patient F, who pays in advance and has the impression she does not "render" in analysis). When her father fell ill, she refused to prepare his medicines, so as not to be seized later by doubts about having made a mistake. Initially, concerning difficulties in analysis, she quotes one of her father's warnings: "He who speaks too much speaks badly."

Sometimes, when circumstances permitted, her masochistic position towards her father was inverted, and it was the patient who controlled her father, as in the following memory (which I mention in analogy with a previous element to the central episode of Case F). When she was about four or five, having crushed a finger, she was taken to hospital by her father on the crossbar of his bicycle. She bullied him, saying: "Now you won't send me to kindergarten any more, see how it hurts me!" The theme of being hurt—metaphorically—is taken up again in the lie she used in order to stay at home and kill and pluck her father's chickens.

That it might have been her phallic and lying mother who denied her the penis (see Patient F) and that she is the one the patient wished to castrate by becoming pregnant now also emerges, as in the following lapsus made in her reference to a young bride who is expecting a child: "Faustina, protect the Madonna!"

On the other hand, when her (paternal) grandmother died, she wanted to give herself up, to be put inside, to be delinquent and pay for the crime: to be the *penis captivus*, instead of having it. (As a child, in bed with her sister, she had been afraid of being shut up in a coffin). Later, however, she preferred being mad—that is, to lose her head–penis–faeces. This was exactly the opposite of what was happening in analysis at the time when she broke it off: delinquent option with negation of the recidivous psychopathology.

A propos recidivism, the aphorism "psychopathological" "*Semel mente [pene] captus, semper mente [pene] captus*" (see Zapparoli, 1967, p. 27) might find the "criminological" correspondent in "*Semel mentem [penem] capiens, semper mentem [penem] capiens*". Probably the patient's feeling herself to be delinquent and not mad shortly after the beginning of the analysis may have had a reassuring function in terms of the "prognosis": she will once again be "*capiens*" and not "*capta*". On this basis it seems to be the rationalization with which she breaks off the analysis: "It's not for me, because I am really guilty, not ill."

Not seeing any other way out than breaking off the analysis would, however, take place when the patient's desire to be delinquent [*capiens malum*] meets, in correspondence with the eroticization of the transference, with that of being mad [*a malo capta*]. This could also be seen in terms of the choice between the pregenital (anal) needs and those of an incipient genitalization.

These oscillations are expressed, for example, in the following dream which she had at the onset of menstruation: "My mother spoke with the doctor; I knew I had caught the illness [epilepsy], before puberty. The doctor said to me, "It's a nasty hereditary illness", but I wasn't displeased. Then I was in the outhouse [where the chickens were plucked] with my brother, and I was washing a dress in a basin." She recalls that in her episodes of sleepwalking, she would take some clothes and go into her parents' bedroom or—once—into her sister and her brother-in-law's bedroom (they had recently married and slept in the same room) and sit on her brother-in-law's head (see Patient F). Once during this period, arriving at the analyst's office and saying to the person who opened the door for her that she wanted to keep her overcoat, she thinks: "I'll stay and sleep here." The day prior to this dream, during his sermon, the priest had spoken of our insignificance and our need for God's help, giving the example of a mad woman who had killed her child. She also recalls that the first—morpheic—epileptic seizure took place the evening after she had overheard an argument between a husband and wife, during which the husband had pulled out a revolver. She adds that her sister—who has now entered menopause—has accepted her doctor's advice to go into hospital for sleep therapy; she thought that her sister was strong. It is the same doctor who in the past had recommended the patient's admittance to hospital, when she had had electroshock treatment.

In Case A mentioned above, the initial problem was the woman's unsatisfactory sexual life and an intense sado-masochistic relationship with her husband, with a prevalence of masochistic behaviour in the patient, who was virtually dominated by her husband. She is a borderline patient I accepted in analysis after having followed her in analytic group psychotherapy. During this analysis a gynaecological examination had revealed the presence of uterine fibroids, thus almost excluding the possibility of a pregnancy, with or without conservative surgery.

The patient claims she is sure the fibroma was formed psychogenically during the group therapy, and this is proof that she was deceived both by the analyst and by her parents. This point of view was reinforced by the opinion of a psychotherapist the patient had seen earlier, who offered her a short psychotherapy with a totally favourable prognosis.

Shortly before announcing her intention to break off the analysis—which she later reversed—she says she rather confusedly recalls a dream: "I had a malign mass as big as a fist in my abdomen, but not inside an organ. It was by now too late to begin anything new." Amongst other things, she associates that as a child she was told that she just had to wait to grow older to find the right man and have a family. Her mother was therefore responsible for her sterility and the analyst for her neoformations and thereby once again for her inability to have children, because they had not informed her, they had deceived her. According to her mother, by not knowing she would have had what was necessary at the right moment. "The fibroma is a false, but also destructive, fruit. I was unable to defend my femininity because I never knew it; I was never taught it by my mother or by my father, who kept me like a little girl to play with, also negatively, to tease me. I certainly expected analysis to be pleasant, to learn to appreciate my worth as a woman. Instead, any such moments I have had have destroyed themselves" (the patient had crises of "retroactive shame" in which she used to hit herself on the head, etc.).

"I also dreamt that there was to have been a play, but it didn't take place: I didn't even know my role. I thought the play was enough, but this isn't activity. When a man is not able to be active (with girls), he understands it immediately, but the girl doesn't. Even today I still don't know how to be active as a woman."

After ten days or so she starts off by saying:

Patient: "I have deceived as well. For example, ten days ago in my dream about the tumour: the way I put it into context was false. I'd like to continue talking about deception, but I feel it's a bit voluntaristic."

Analyst: "Like deceiving time."

Patient: "I have never deceived time: it is time that has deceived me. I have always struggled against time. At a certain point I trusted time. Wanting to use it well leads to false goals, but trusting time—in the sense of waiting passively—doesn't work. Struggling with time, here, was thinking I was doing, which wasn't true. I'm referring to when I thought I was going onwards. . . . My only sexual fantasy at puberty had nothing to do with a man or my genitals: I imagined myself naked in the middle of a stage. I forbade it to myself, saying: 'Stop playing.' In my dream last week I should have played a very precise role [but her memory is vague] in a play that didn't take place because I couldn't remember my role. In [group] therapy perhaps I thought it was enough to act without any contact. Even exhibition scared me, because it didn't go well: one always reveals one's weak side, presenting the wound that exists, which already hurts, on which the other person puts his finger. Touching a sore point means revealing it, recognizing the error. My brother really used to do this when someone hurt himself, and he enjoyed it. I remember my father who teased me, saying, for example: 'Oh, you think, you even know how to think!'"

In the next session she brings the following dream:

"I was on a kind of chair-lift made out of a board on which I was lying—like I am now—which went from the upper to the lower bank of a river. It was busy because my younger brother, who is a doctor, was also there, and he was holding onto the board on the lower side. I got off feet first because I didn't know how to help him. I tried to help by pushing with my right foot, resting it on his stomach. But the pressure of my foot didn't help him and he fell: at that point I woke up. The evening before I had been very absorbed with the previous session; my feeling however didn't correspond [to those in the dream]. The feelings about the session were of intense anger, but I also felt it was a good thing, that all I had to do was express the anger to free myself of it. My brother, whom I looked after when he was young, has also undertaken psychotherapy, which he started before me, and with it he has grown away from me. He referred me to the gynaecologist who touched on the sore spot without then trying to help me. I have the feeling that they [her father and brothers] still enjoy touching on a sore spot. Also with you, I'm still doubtful. Not so much lately, but earlier, with the group. On the other hand, it's easier to be understanding now that everything has been destroyed, or half destroyed!"

She recalls that her father teased her behind her back and she defended herself by identifying with him, the only figure she respects in her family. Now with the fibroma she could pay the analyst–father back in his same coin (teasing): "This is what you're capable of producing."

There thus emerged a vindictive attitude, which the patient traced back to her conviction that the analyst was responsible for the generation of the fibroma.

Using the material quoted above, we may try schematically to list a series of stages or phases or levels (which recall the procedure from appearance to reality in the sphere of the ironic vision) concerning "deception":

1. self-deception without being aware of it, which corresponds to the silent phase of the "illness";
2. anticipating the possibility of remaining self-deceived, which corresponds to the beginning of the "illness"—or rather its appearance; this is also the presupposition to the anticipation of the future possibility of an undeception, and therefore the beginning of healing;
3. the illusion of being able to return to the previous status quo, expressed in phrases like "Doctor, make me healthy again, I want to be like I was before"; the therapeutic commitment may at a certain level be perceived (see Patient G) as a promise by the analyst to give (back) the penis; in a certain sense the deception is recreated with the installation of the analytic relationship;
4. the successive disillusion, which may be experienced and made explicit this time as having been deceived (a certain "negative therapeutic reaction" may be temporarily felt on this basis);
5 finally (the analogy is therefore not with unstable infinite irony but with finite irony), the acceptance of the undeception, of reality, of the difference between the sexes as something that is not the result of a castration, and, moreover, the acceptance of the difference in age and therefore in generations.

On the other hand, as mentioned above, more generally, searching for and finding one's own truth is part of the goals of therapy and could be one of the criteria of the "end of the treatment" (Lagache, 1964), which may also be seen by placing the emphasis on the relational aspect. The finding once more of truth could therefore be contrasted with the images of deception or falsity experienced previously and could largely result from the analysis of the resistances and the consequent leaving aside of the repetitive defences, including certain means of attacking the analyst. In this sense, the clinical examples quoted above seem to me to show how a closer study of the phallic problems and the equivalences, which involves an adequate working through [*Durcharbeitung*], may be fundamental, even in the analysis of borderline cases or of patients with serious psychotic nuclei.

Regarding such a *Durcharbeitung*, it is useful to recall what Winnicott (1951) says about how important it is that the small child not be forced to give up too soon what he calls the area of illusion—in other words, to have to verify whether it is illusion or reality, to trace the defined boundaries between inner and outer reality. This may be transposed onto the technical plane in terms of timing, and also with respect for the *durchspielen* ["playing to the end", "playing through"].

Pairs of opposites and terminability of the analysis

In Cases F and G, it seems that when, even in the sphere of transference, especially on the plane of the libido, indifference is impossible, the "difference" must be self-produced, actively determined, castrating the other (delinquent solution) or in fact oneself (psychopathological solution). [In both clinical practice and theoretical elaboration, I find it is useful to keep in mind the literal, or even the strictly etymological meaning of a word used by the analysand when he refers (consciously) to its figurative meaning, and vice versa. This kind of rule is analogous—and not unconnected to—the well-known rule regarding the *hic et nunc/alibi et tunc*.]

The patients' initial position as concerns the past was: it is better to be (actively) a murderer, guilty of filicide, or a criminal abortioner than to submit (passively) impotently to the loss of the daughter or the new-born child.

This is also the initial position in the relationship with the analyst, but it becomes difficult to keep up later on with the eroticization of the transference. Thus G breaks off analysis, and F begins to have the problem of the "right kind of detachment", which is experienced both in her relationship with her husband and, albeit less openly, in that with the analyst. The "right" (which may also be "right in the head", i.e. psychically normal) is revealed to be the opposite of the "true" (and also of the mad), as can, for example, be seen in the following excerpt, which shows the problem of the distance in the interlacing of the aspects of space and time.

It was the desire to sit on the analyst's knee, that the patient had unsuccessfully tried to verbalize before the winter vacation. When analysis started up again, she now says she is able to do it. She was unable to in the previous session because it didn't seem right: then the fantasy was experienced with intense emotion, whilst now she no longer feels the same desire and thus can say it; it is now right to say it. Now, however, the desire is no longer felt to be true, unlike before. It almost seems false.

Therefore, what is real (that is, emotively meaningful, real on the plane of inner reality, but also mad) is not right and, vice versa, what is not true is right (that is, permitted, allowed, and therefore realizable and, perhaps even real on the plane of outer reality).

It is interesting to quote here the following quatrain by Pessoa (1942–1978, p. 14):

O poeta è un fingidor
Finge tão completamente
que chega a Fingir que é dor
a dor que deveras sente.

[The poet is a feigner.
He feigns so completely
that he even feigns that it is pain
the pain he really feels.]

The poet therefore starts from feeling, and he ends up (also) feigning. His pain, which is originally true (felt), becomes simultaneously also feigned: that is—according to the etymology of the term—modelled, formed, something towards which he is secondarily an agent ("feigner"), not only a percipient. We may now, symmetrically, represent the picture—for the sake of simplicity—of a hysterical pain thus:

> The hysteric is a feigner.
> He feigns so completely
> that he even feels that it is
> the pain he is feigning.

The hysteric is therefore the opposite of the poet; starting from his feigning, he (even) manages to feel. His *originally feigned*, modelled pain (according to an unconscious symbolic representation) *becomes simultaneously real* (felt). It therefore becomes something towards which he is secondarily a percipient, not only an agent ("feigner"). In the case of Patient F, we may observe the true/feigned succession at two different moments in the sphere of transference: the greater (more emotionally charged) the feigning or fiction the transference consists in, the truer do her fantasies seem (inner reality), which, vice versa, seem to her to be feigned, the smaller (less emotionally charged) the feigning or fiction of transference. There appears to be an ironic aspect in the manner in which the outside world—or, rather, the inner map of the outside world—is experienced in the transference (see Sacerdoti, 1976).

These considerations help to complete those set out in the previous section and connect the true/false antithesis to the active/passive antithesis through what is "feigned".

Returning to Patient F, she moves towards understanding truth, on the plane of inner reality through the transference, and on the plane of outer reality through acting out. She sees with her own eyes that the truth is being different and implies not being in-different, therefore loving and/or hating.

The conscious desire to know the truth (about the death of her daughter) temporarily coincides with her (re)discovery of her vagina—an experience that the patient is unable for the moment to integrate and which is accompanied by a manic state. The true–genital equivalence also emerges from an image that the patient claims to have drawn, which shows, amongst other things, the isolation of the genitals. [It is well known that in order to guarantee truthfulness in biblical oaths, for example, the hand was placed under the thighs (the genitals) and how this is connected, according to some, to the etymology of "testicles" (Latin: *testes* or "small witnesses").] It depicts three bands of colour, separated from each other by lines: from front to back, they are red, white, and brown, inscribed, respectively, with the words 'love', 'truth', and 'shit'.

On the other hand, the truth may lead to the acceptance of death (orgasm)—both one's own and that of others—that is not self-provoked; i.e. the rejection of narcissistic omnipotence. This rejection, and the depressive experience that accompanies it, probably contribute to the need to resort to a maniacal hyperactivity as a disavowing mechanism.

However, the changeover from the narcissistic, omnipotent attitude to the objectal choice (as well as the resistances to such a changeover) becomes evident.

This may, for example, be seen in the following material. The patient thinks that by not having her daughters, she cannot stay with her mother. And then her mother is never happy with what she has. She does not want to be (like her) mother. She herself notes that first she asks the analyst for advice and then does not listen to what he says, and she recalls similar behaviour in her mother towards her: excessive respect and its opposite. She sees images of her mother in bed, with her hand on her vagina, of her mother looking at her approvingly; associations: against nature, her dead daughter. She wished she had had a son. Her mother, too—as the patient has always known—wished she had been a boy; finally, the mother "had" to be a boy for her parents. She seems to recall that she had first had the idea of dying together with her daughter when she had made her bleed slightly when trimming her fingernails. She had felt unable to "pick her up" and had given her a bottle of milk containing one of her husband's sleeping pills. During this session, she scratches her face until it bleeds, and she sits up. Earlier she had said: "I am 'marked' for ever by what has happened: when someone has been mad and/or a murderer, everyone still expects them to be like that. I have recently been reading newspaper stories, looking for and often finding the phrase 'He has been committed to a lunatic asylum'." (She associates "marked" with the craftwork she does—engravings on hard stone. Previously she had overcome her perplexities concerning the planned transferral of her daughter's body into the family tomb by thinking that she could have placed the child's name there without engraving it.) She adds: "It is the same as for tuberculosis", just after the analyst has coughed. Whilst she was driving to the session, she was caught between two trucks; she thought about braking, but she would have been hit from behind. In the same session, making a *lapsus*, she says 'sister' instead of 'daughter', and she feels she has had the same experiences as her dead daughter. In the previous session she had asked to break off the analysis.

She asks if the analyst thinks that the analysis is useful. Faced with his silence, she says she does not know whether it is something she should understand, could realize herself, or whether it should be the analyst who tells her. Soon afterwards, she will no longer think about death, that is, about killing herself (by herself); only if it came (from God) would she accept it. She thinks about her gynaecological results, which might be positive for a tumour (she has had a vaginoscopy).

Her (own) death could therefore come from her vagina, and she would accept it, if the results from the gynaecologist–God–analyst–father were positive. She would in any case no longer give it to herself through her own hand. She will not be like her masturbating mother who managed to "pick her up" only to have her own penis and who has forced her until now either to remain her mother's penis or to feel guilty of murder (matricide, of which infanticide is merely another version). "If you get pregnant, I'll hang myself from a pole", her mother used to say to her after puberty.

A child's reaching a (certain degree of) mature objectal relationship and therefore autonomy may be experienced by some mothers—who see their children as being "the staff of their old age"—as a veritable murder. This sometimes coincides with the appearance in them of disturbances of a psychotic nature (the death of the psychic individuality) and even mortal cardiovascular incidents (inner reality that reaches the somatic level).

The idiot/murderer alternative therefore seems for Patient F to be closely conditioned by her phallic and lying mother's personality. [The understanding of the fluctuations and oscillations of the active and passive towards either parent may be useful in the understanding of the superego (Hart, 1961).] The possibility of the evolution towards an interminable analysis would here essentially be linked to the maternal transference.

The corresponding questions in Patient G seem, on the other hand, to be mainly centred around her relationship with her father. Here the temporary premature interruption of the analysis seems to have taken place under the influence of the anxiety that on the plane of the paternal transference arises at the moment in which eroticization takes over, and what therefore creeps in is a doubt about managing to maintain the omnipotent position. Later, after an attempt at clinging to the delinquent solution—in the dream in which the ceiling was falling in—or the psychopathologic solution (the fear of going mad), there is, finally, the dream about the false priest. These two dreams reflect quite a different inner reality: amongst other things, the first indicates the need to realize—on the plane of inner reality—the desire to have a penis, and the second, the abandoning of this desire.

* * *

I would now like to return to the pairs of opposites, to attempt both to frame further, from this point of view, the personal material, and to make use of it in the sphere of a connection between the themes developed by Freud concerning the terminability of analysis and concerning pairs of opposites [*Gegensatzpaare*].

The polarities put forward and discussed by Freud (1915c) as antitheses of loving (hating; being loved), as antitheses of loving and hating (being indifferent), and as polarities—real, economic, biological—that govern the whole of our mental life (subject/object or ego/outside world; pleasure/unpleasure; active/passive), could perhaps be widened and connected to elements that bring their usefulness to an operative level, so as to begin a valid discussion precisely on this plane. A conceptualization of this kind seems to have been thus far quite clearly formulated concerning reaction formation (Freud, 1926d [1925]), which could on this basis be defined as the ego's utilization of the inherent opposition to drive ambivalence.

Comparing the six pairs of opposites or Freud's antitheses concerning, respectively,

A. the opposites of love:
   1. love/hate
   2. love/to be loved (self-love: narcissism)
   3. love and hate/to be indifferent

B. the antitheses that govern the whole of mental life:
   1. subject (ego)/object (outer world)
   2. pleasure/unpleasure
   3. active/passive

we may immediately observe that antitheses in B are more general and that B(3) includes A(2).

Moreover, with regard to B(2) and its relationship to A(3), from the point of view that interests us of its operative utility in the field of psychoanalysis, we may recall with Lagache (1964) that defence mechanisms belong to the register of fantasy (inner world), even though we are used to contrasting them to the fantasies of desire. The fact is that they also express a desire: that of avoiding unpleasure, the preference for security and peace (cf. the concept of resistance).

Now, if in-difference is the opposite of love and hate (Freud, 1926d [1925]), the presupposition of love and hate is difference.

Considering the analytic situation, we may find that it is basically regulated as a situation of difference or inequality (see Greenson, 1967), although occasionally, and in the end, equality is (re)established (see also Lagache, 1964). Some resistances in analysis may translate the revival of the attempt to negate the differences, or at least the attempt to experience them actively, as if they were self-produced, on the transference plane, as far as the analyst is concerned (naturally including the child–adult difference). In the cases under scrutiny, we have seen the importance for the patients to experience actively (that is, as an active choice) even situations of loss, inferiority, and disparagement. Thus, for example, "better to be a murderer than mad" is, at the anal level, the affirmation of one's own will: "faeces are eliminated only when and because I want to"; it is, at the phallic level, "better to be autocastrated than heterocastrated", and so on.

As Gendrot (1968) says, our role as psychoanalysts is that of helping those who want to discover their fear of castration—a difficult task—but each person is free to use this awareness as they wish: his "healing" belongs to him, as does the sense he gives to this notion.

Gendrot's statement seems to refer mainly to men, and the term castration seems to be intended passively. The fear of castration intended actively—that is, the fear of castrating—must also be considered. Moreover, there is perhaps not always enough awareness in castration fantasies of the aspects of desire apart from that of fear, and vice versa. On the basis of the realization—at the level of inner reality—of fantasies that are typically characteristic of phallic problems in men and women, respectively, it is evidently possible that there exists the envy of what one has but fantasizes not having, and, respectively, the fear of losing what one does not have but what one fantasizes having.

As Lagache (1964) notes, more often than the defence against reality through fantasy, we may observe defence against fantasy through reality (in the personal cases, the miscarriage, the death of the child), or rather through a fantasized idea of reality (in the cases of the killing of the foetus and, respectively, of the daughter), and this attenuates the opposition of these two directions of defence. [With reference to the material presented, separating it from factual reality, I find it interesting, as far as inner reality is concerned, how the repression of the "delinquent" aspects of the image of self—see, for example, in the case of Patient F, "If my memory deceives me, I am not a murderer but mad"—may contain the way of finally realizing, through the return of the repressed, an (existential) "delinquent" project. This may also be equivalent to realizing, again through a return of the repressed (or a defence against a defence), a kind of male identity with, sadistic connotations. At the same time, the repression of the "psychopathological" aspects of the image of self—as, for example, in the case of Patient G, "It is not an illness to be cured but guilt to be held"—may be the way of finally realizing, through the return of the repressed, an (existential) psychopathological project. This may also be equivalent to realizing, again through the return of the repressed (or a defence against a defence), a kind of female identity (agreeing in the cases of Patients F and G with their biological sex), with masochistic connotations. Mechanisms of this kind, which we could call "tricks" for they serve to elude a defence system, are probably a kind of obligatory step for those who are unable to realize what the ego consciously takes as its design. These individuals sometimes observe, not without irony: "To succeed in something, I must not want it—or, rather, I must want its opposite."]

And (also) considering all that the analyst may manage to do to help someone who wishes to discover their fear of castration and to abandon the position of in-difference (negation of the differences), and that he may succeed in doing this at the moment in which the sense that the patient gives to these notions and differences is not such as to allow him to seek inadequate "solutions" (in Patient G the breaking-off of the analysis or the dream of the ceiling; in Patient F the dream of the professor) but, rather, "adequate" ones (see in Patient G the dream about the false priest, in Patient F the vaginoscopy). According to Freud's (1937c, p. 252) statement quoted above, it is a waste of breath trying to persuade a woman to give up her desire for a penis. It may, in fact, be equivalent to persuading her to submit to—or to inflict—an injustice (for Patient F, to being "not right in the head", going mad, or being a murderer) or a difference, when she is looking for justice and in-difference.

Freud's text could be extended, utilizing the equivalences established above, in the following way: a woman's resistance to abandoning her desire to have a penis may (amongst other things) correspond to the attempt to be indifferent (not to love and not to hate) concerning active/passive especially at the phallic level (antithesis: to have/not to have the penis, to castrate/to be castrated), but also at an anal level (antithesis: to control/to be controlled) and so on (see also Figure 1, on p. 72).

In men, on the other hand, the resistance to the possibility of tolerating a passive attitude towards other men may also be equivalent to the inability to tolerate a difference, that is, the opposite of in-difference, therefore to tolerate hating/loving.

In short, also in men the resistance Freud refers to is the expression, like in women, of the desire (defence) to be indifferent (not to love and not to hate) in terms of active/passive, perhaps especially with regard to the anal level (antithesis: to control/to be controlled).

If we wish to reformulate the question of opposites on the operative plane, centring its finalization on the considerations developed by Freud in "Analysis Terminable and Interminable" (1937c) with reference to the final barrier that has to be overcome in analysis, we might turn once more to Figure 1 as a reference point, taking into account what has emerged from the study of the personal cases.

Unconscious equivalences of the psychopathologic/delinquent antithesis: ironic aspects and prospectives

In the patients to whom Figure 1 refers, the comparison between the unconscious images and the conscious representations permits them to be considered equivalences: the former, referring to the body (and fitting therefore into the stages of the development of the libido), belong to the category of the "sensible", unlike the latter. There are, therefore, the presuppositions for a metaphor in the original sense of the term—that is, a transference of the sensible into the non-sensible. This configuration could correspond to an (unsuccessful) attempt at self-therapy, in the sense of seeking to re-establish a continuity between the two levels (see Kubie, 1951, regarding the link between the symbol and what it may represent).

It is here that the role of the analyst may intervene because it is on him that the analysand's transferences converge and by him (also because he is the depository of a continuity) that the analysand may be helped to overcome his splittings by modifying, in the sense of integrating aspects that were previously opposite, his self-image, in terms of the possible exchange of the relationships between different and even "opposite" objects (reaching the genital level).

In Figure 1, the relationships between the self and the object are formed in the sphere of:

1. (*Side of desire*): a pair of opposites that enter the polarity that Freud (1915c) calls biological (active/passive). This reveals itself to be equivalent (underlying, at the unconscious level) to the (conscious) images of the "truth", of "reality", and "injustice" or "not right" (terms used by Patient F, for whom "right" is also "right in the head", and vice versa), which correspond to the situation of the pair, whilst the individual components correspond, respectively, for the active, to (conscious) delinquent and psychically evil images (Patient G and Patient F), and for the passive, to images of victim and mad person (hence the impossibility of escaping to the psychopathological/delinquent alternative);
2. (*Side of defence*): a pair of equals (which is placed in antithesis to the pair of opposites): this is revealed to be equivalent (underlying, at the unconscious level) to the (conscious) images of the lie, which may be experienced as deception (also where the analysis is concerned—see Patient A), (inner) unreality and "justice". [It must be noted that "to lie" in Latin is "*mentior*, the verb most directly derived from "mens" or "mind", and therefore could be considered the most "normal" basic expression of the mind (compare the opposite: "mad people tell the truth"). Indeed, according to Bion (1970), Descartes' "*cogito ergo sum*" only holds true for lies. It is a radicalization of the above and a concrete and objectifying distortion of Descartes' saying, in which there is a gratuitous attribution of an equation between the "*sum*"—that is, the image of self in its aspects of identity—and the existence of a thinker, on the one hand, and the "*cogito*" that is, the image of self in its aspects of the deferment of the action—and the existence of thoughts, on the other.]

These images correspond to the pair situation (seen mainly from outside), whilst the individual components, which are, in

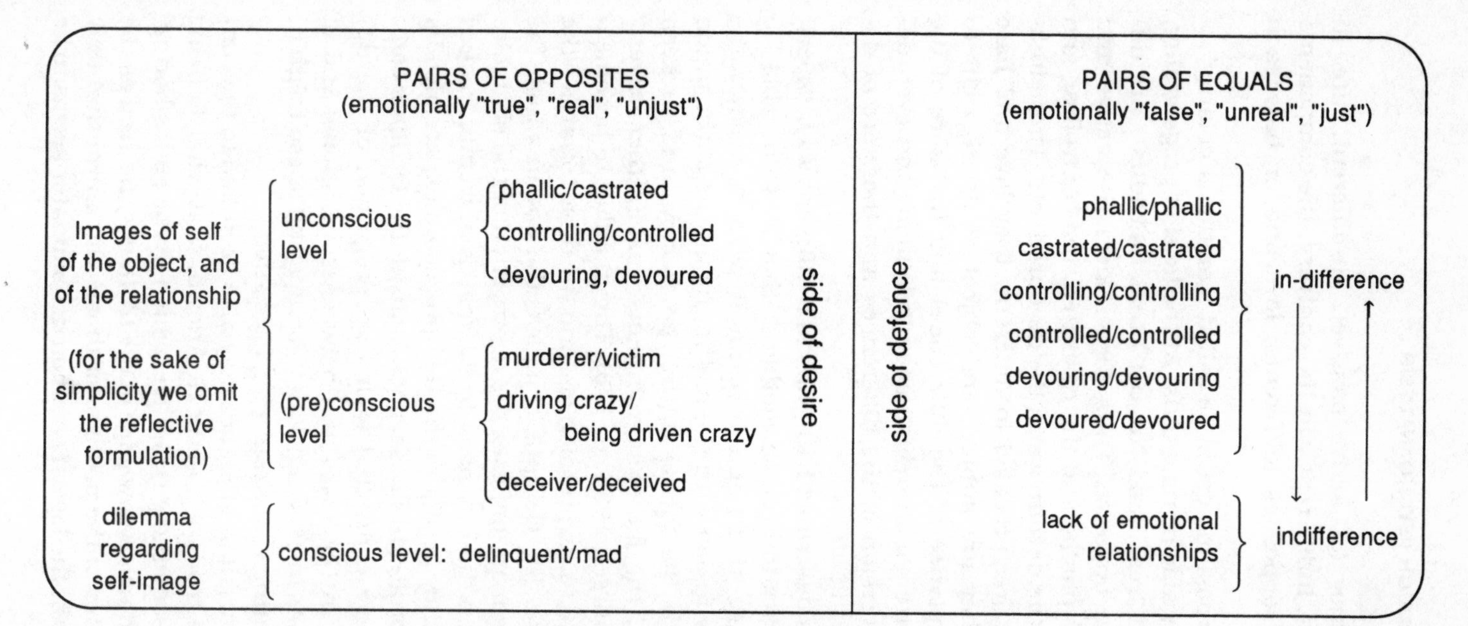

FIGURE 1

Relationships (deduced from the cases—pregenital stages) between conscious and unconscious images of self, of the object, and of the relationship on the one side, and the active/passive and emotionality/indifference polarities on the other "biological" terms (of active/passive), in-different, are in emotional terms, indifferent. On the contrary, the components of the pairs of opposites (differents) love and/or hate each other.

This counterposition could be called "emotional polarity".

Figure 1 may also be read thus: At the level of pregenitality, it is "true", and "real" (and "unjust") that individuals are different and even opposite. Thus there exists the active and the passive, the phallic and the castrated, the controlling and the controlled, the devourer and the devoured, etc. These individuals are not (reciprocally) in-different, they love and hate (themselves), they are subject and object of desire right to madness—acceptance of the differences and therefore of the (insatiable) desire—or to delinquency (rebellion, and even destruction or inversion of the differences and therefore of desire).

The patients described had, each in a different way, experienced an inability to become mothers—that is, to be able "to realize in fantasy [their] dual incestuous wish: to recover the state of primary fusion with the mother by means of the union established with the foetus during pregnancy, and to keep the love object, the father or his penis, inside [themselves]" (Chasseguet-Smirgel, 1984, p. 170). The inability to become a mother was once the expression of—and the drive towards—the archaic matrix of the Oedipus complex; the one in which the woman, like the man, imposes the destruction of the obstacles that intervene on the way back to the maternal womb. Desires of this kind, if they prefigure the Oedipus complex, are also its antithesis. According to Chasseguet-Smirgel, the Oedipus complex is intimately connected with the recognition of the differences (between the sexes and between generations) and of reality. It consists in clashing with it, comparing oneself with it, and not in negating it or destroying it as such.

Collective (social) indifference may also be linked to the conviction that the truth will never be known, that what is being experienced is something repetitive, which in the end is boring. Indifference and non-knowledge of the truth may be seen as the extreme opposites of the position of those who affirm that they possess the truth: the lowest common denominator seems to be the renouncing of the search for truth. In the first case, the indifference is obvious and manifest; in the second it is "hidden" or anticipated, avoided by apparent sureness, the rejection even of taking into consideration the possibility of identification with the other. This, in sexual terms, leads back to what Zaltzmann (1976) noted. In her opinion, Freud's procedure follows the guiding thread of a progressive distinction between the male and the female pole, through the successive stages of the evolution of the libido. At the end of the evolution, the difference between the sexes is generally established, assured in a sufficiently stable and decisive manner so that no further important rearrangement will take place, to bring about profound changes according to Freud. Nevertheless, when he takes up the question again from another point of view in "Analysis Terminable and Interminable" (1937c), it is in terms of *bisexuality common both to men and women, where the two poles exist side by side*, that he takes notice of the barrier of penis envy in the woman, and that of homosexual passiveness in the man. The sexual polarity that coincided with the male and female is now formulated in quite a different manner: *male–female/rejection of female*. This organization must not be confused with that of the phallic genital stage, where the male exists but not the female. Here, *the differentiation is established between the bisexual pole and a rejection of the female pole.* In analytic theory, the successive distinctions of the sexual polarity (subject/object, active/passive, penis/castrated organ, bisexuality/rejection of the female) are established in terms of differences. The difference is neither harmony nor opposition. Now, amongst the sexual genital theories, perhaps the most frequent theory is that of the war between the sexes, a theory in which the polarity is based on the *antagonism* that is more or less maintained within sexuality, from which one is liberated by attributing part of one's sexuality to the other. Its main insurance clause against uncertainty, therefore, becomes the process of the presumed identity of the other. Finally, and most importantly, this theory is directly induced and dominated by one of the poles of the unconscious structure of the sexual polarity: that of the "repudiation of femininity", of which Freud says in "Analysis Terminable and

Interminable" (1937c, p. 252): "[it] can be nothing else than a biological fact, a part of the great riddle of sex".

It is not, therefore, so much that the unconscious is femininephobic (on the other hand, the phobigenic object is not such because the unconscious is the artificer of avoidance conduct) but, rather, that the feminine [*das Weibliche*] is that part of sexuality, both for women and men (see what has been mentioned concerning bisexuality) that is closest to the unconscious. If anything, the unconscious is femininephylic, as the feminine may be associated with the representation of what is lacking, the lack of representation, with what cannot be formulated or represented. Hence the interest in collecting the representations equivalent to that of the feminine. Granoff (1976), having emphasized the central position that "the feminine" has for man whenever he tries to deal with it in terms of understanding, observes that Freud's construction of the castration complex, which could also be called his fantasy, was for him a necessary construction. But it is theoretical truth insofar as it is also necessary to the child's thought. The problem of knowledge has as a prototype that described by Freud in "On the Sexual Theories of Children" (1908c):

> But when the child thus seems to be well on the way to postulating the existence of the vagina and to concluding that an incursion of this kind by his father's penis into his mother is the act by means of which the baby is created in his mother's body—at this juncture his enquiry is broken off in helpless perplexity. For standing in its way is his theory that his mother possesses a penis just as a man does, and the existence of the cavity which receives the penis remains undiscovered by him. It is not hard to guess that the lack of success of his intellectual efforts makes it easier for him to reject and forget them. This brooding and doubting, becomes the prototype of all later intellectual work directed towards the solution of problems, and the first failure has a crippling effect on the child's whole future. [pp. 218–219]

On the other hand, we might continue, success may be feared as something that would lead, or which leads, to very serious consequences. These are represented in myths as: a voyage with no return (Ulysses); the loss of the earthly paradise (Adam and Eve), the loss of all property and especially sight, as well as the acquisition of a delinquent image of self (Oedipus). These images may be connected to what Freud recalls concerning what precedes and accompanies the "search for truth" in the child, especially in the male. Just before the passage quoted above, Freud says:

> If children could follow the hints given by the excitation of the penis they would get a little nearer to the solution of their problem. That the baby grows inside the mother's body is obviously not a sufficient explanation. How does it get inside? What starts its development? That the father has something to do with it seems likely; he says that the baby is his baby as well. Again, the penis has a share, for, in these mysterious happenings, the excitation in it which accompanies all these activities of the child's thoughts bears witness to this. Attached to this excitation are impulsions which the child cannot account for—obscure urges to do something violent, to press in, to knock to pieces, to tear open a hole somewhere. [p. 218]

The disavowal or the ignorance of the existence of the hole—that is, of the cavity that receives the father's penis—is exemplified in the image of the "Virgin mother, daughter of your son", and the splitting of the ego, which is the price to pay to sustain the disavowal, is accepted on the basis not of truth revealed [*non est mendacium*] but rather, of the truth re-veiled [*sed mysterium*]. [*Non est mendacium sed mysterium* is the phrase with which Saint Augustine "explains" Jacob's deception of his father by means of which he gains the primogeniture, eliminating Esau and all that his birth may signify.] On the other hand, participating in the mystery allows in a certain way the recovery, at a narcissistic level, of that from which one has been excluded. As Dante Alighieri wrote in the *Divine Comedy*: "Content ye, o human race, with the bare fact; /for had the power been yours to see the whole, /then Mary's childing was a needless act" (Purgatory, III, 37–39).

The disavowal (or ignorance of the existence) of the vagina as the welcoming cavity is also connected with fantasies and acts of violence and, in any case, with the sadistic image—for the male—and the masochistic image—for the female—of coitus.

The follow-up to a similar act is represented by the stories of Judith and Holofernes, Jael, and others, in which the reversal into the opposite also implies identification with the aggressor. (The prevention of such an evolution may be perceived in the customs of primitive populations, which deflower the bride in a way that does not involve the bridegroom.)

All these themes emerge also from the clinical material, especially in the cases of Patients G and F, in which the deaths of the child and the foetus were at the basis of the motivations for the analysis, which consciously centred around the search for "truth" concerning the alternative between a self-image as (psychically) ill or murderer (infanticide or criminal abortion procurer). There is only one way for the analyst to deal correctly with "what is lacking": the way that results from keeping in mind the aim indicated by Freud (1933a, p. 80): "Where id was, there ego shall be" [*Wo Es war, soll Ich werden*], which means, amongst other things, making it possible for the patient to become more open and lucid before his objects and before death (temporal incompleteness).

This also holds on the plane of scientific work: here "the feminine" holds a special position, insofar as femininity as a concept introduces a basic insecurity into theorization. It is no chance matter that Freud's writings on femininity are of an unfinished, enigmatic nature. The decision and also the *Urteilsakt* [act of judgement] were more difficult for him, because they are open to *Urteilsstreit* [conflict of judgement], as to knowing whether it concerned, as for the libido (of male essence) theoretical truth or theoretical fiction (Granoff, 1976). This theoretical challenge would, instead, be avoided in certain kinds of theoretical (and clinical) insight tending to dogmatism (see Sacerdoti, 1986b; Sacerdoti & Spačal, 1985).

I believe that these aspects of avoidance emphasized by Granoff could paradoxically reveal in mammocentric approaches an aspect of opposition towards the Freudian revolution, precisely because it centres on the unconscious and therefore also on the feminine [*das Weibliche*]. The attendant accusation of phallocentrism is basically due to the same mechanisms of avoidance that consider as central not the pair of opposites and complements that make up bisexuality but only its representable—male—pole.

The psychopathological/delinquent alternative, which is so easily forced on the psychiatrist by parents ("Doctor, you must tell me whether my child is ill or naughty!") or magistrates ("Let the expert say whether at the time of the fact the subject was, because of infirmity, in a mental condition such as to exclude or diminish his responsibility") or, even more, the lack of other alternatives, and that is, the dilemma, remains such even in the presence of egalitarian utopias.

The interchangeability of the psychopathological and the delinquent images is ironically represented in Samuel Butler's well-known *Erewhon* (1862), an imaginary mythical country (see Sacerdoti, 1971) in which the hero, at first completely disoriented, gradually discovers that those who are mentally ill are treated as delinquents and delinquents as mentally ill. The reversal, the *Verkehrung*, is also represented in the title, as *Erewhon* is nothing more than the anagram of *nowhere*. The title seems to contain all the irony of Butler's work: the anagram of utopia both reveals and re-veils (like all anagrams) that a utopia is precisely what it is.

But the reality that is hidden beneath the unknown appearance, or the knowledge of which has virtually been lost (there remained only traces about which fantastic tales were told), is not unambiguous. As *Erewhon* is "literally" the reversal of nowhere, that is, of utopia, it is also "everywhere", "common", and therefore non-utopistic, almost realistic.

Is it an unstable irony of the type Booth describes, perhaps even infinite? It does not seem to me that the indices of irony in *Erewhon* are of this nihilistic kind. Rather, I think that we could draw from them (going perhaps beyond the author's—conscious—intentions) the indication that resolving the problem of (mental) illness and/or that of delinquency by overturning one into the other is utopistic. This is, in fact, what happens when we assume (dis)avowing positions—as are now in fashion—towards mental illness and thus moving, in the collusion between "experts" and "politicians", from the "disavowed institution" of certain anti-psychiatrists to the "institutionalized disavowal" (see Sacerdoti, 1971). This would seem quite obvious if we recall the examples of equivalences and the vicissitudes contained in the material we have quoted above.

The capacity for ironic vision—in the sense of stable irony—concerning all that may therefore lead to an initial insight, avoiding facile and easy (for a while) preclusions. It is not surprising, therefore, that the worst anti-psychiatric trends, those based on (de)negatory positions (of the differences), (1) are successful (see demagogy); (2) are totally devoid of any humour and capacity for irony (at least "stable" irony); (3) are "serious"; (4) are "an easy game"; and (5) constitute a thrust towards the criminalization of the mentally ill and also of the so-called psychiatric operators (who are naturally all equal). What is thus encouraged is the ignorance of the psychiatric operators, disavowed and/or stimulated on the basis of clichés, which are also encouraged. A typical example is knowledge = power, with the disavowal of the desire for power through the attack on knowledge and/or the "smuggling" that naturally takes place on border areas.

I therefore believe that the manifest or latent approach, in terms of pairs of psychopathological/delinquent opposites [*Gegensatzpaare*], if we proceed beyond the conscious level, may be traced back to roots sunk in the image of the self. In addition to what I have tried to summarize in Figure 1, I would also add here that in the defences set up against insight, there also appears a game that may be seen in terms of the all/nothing *Gegensatzpaar* (not only at the oral level), which means that bisexuality may also be seen in negative terms: not having anything ("perfect" or unique), having lost everything ("psychopathological solution"), or, in positive terms: having everything (to take possession of it: "delinquent solution").

Both this position, which merely underlines the importance of having to the detriment of being, and the disavowal of the importance of having (and its related fears) preclude the (possibility of) dialectic reconciliation between being and having. It is a reconciliation that is, on the other hand, encouraged by humour and irony, insofar as they help to overcome the fears mentioned above (see the relationship between humour and fear of castration).

In short, the final barrier in analysis, about which Freud speaks in "Analysis Terminable and Interminable" (1937c), (also) seems to lead back, both in women and in men, to a lowest common denominator: the disavowal of the differences (between the two sexes, between the adult and the child, etc.), which is equivalent to the search for indifference—that is, in defence of both libidinal and aggressive objectal links (see Jacobson, 1965) (not loving and not hating).

This position corresponds to pre-genital levels and may easily lead to seeing, beyond in-difference, only the mad or delinquent alternative. This is expressed on the collective plane in a society that favours pre-genital manifestations to the detriment of genital ones, as is shown, for example, both in claims of equality or absolute justice, and in slogans of the kind "No-one here is a fool" or "The world belongs to the shrewd". [In Italian, "fool" (*fesso*) is the past participle of the verb "to cleave" (*fendere*) and may be associated with the feminine.] They reveal the fear of the "psychopathological" solution or, the preference for the "delinquent" solution, respectively.

The overcoming of this impasse and, in the same theme, the acceptability of the differences (both as "minus"—which more easily involves loving and hating—and as "plus"—which more easily involves being loved or hated) and, on the plane of clinical practice, the terminability of the analysis, seem linked to the reaching (of the supremacy) of genitality. This is what permits us, precisely through the genital object relation, to see in the differences—dialectic of what is distinct rather than of what is opposite (Lopez, 1970)—the possibility of self-realization, of reciprocal completion (in addition to that of instinctual satisfaction), which allows escape from the psychopathological/delinquent dilemma without falling into in-difference, the characteristic alternative of the pre-genital situation.

At a genital level, it is, in fact, possible—given the special kind of instinctual satisfaction this level permits—to reach, at least temporarily, satiety, the sense of completeness, a peace that is the opposite of hating (and perhaps also of loving), without being indifference. This, I believe, is expressed well in the biblical greeting *shalom*, which, as is well known, means peace and, on the other hand, as is perhaps less well known, derives from the root of three consonants *shin*, *lamed*, and *mem*, which means being complete.

The problem of completeness in the image of self and of the object (or in the combination of both)—that is, all that refers for example to the sense of completeness and incompleteness, the desire for completeness, the defences activated to disavow incompleteness, the acceptance and even the search for situations of incompleteness as a motivating element—all may be discussed here on the basis of the clinical material quoted.

I shall limit myself to certain comments that may serve as an approach to the problem. It is a theme that may act as a bridge between the intrapsychic—and even the intrastructural—viewpoint (see the splitting of the ego in the fetishist, etc.), and the interpersonal view point, between the sexual and the general aspects, between the libido and aggressiveness, between the primary and secondary process—all the more so if, or as, the completeness and incompleteness are considered according to the space and/or time dimension. In my opinion, the movement from one dimension to the other, as set out by Freud especially concerning dreams, has not been fully explored by psychoanalysts, either on the plane of conceptualization or, even earlier, on that of the clinical listening and the analytic technique (see Sacerdoti, 1976) as well as, in all probability, in so-called applied psychoanalysis.

In order to propose a further reading of the material along the same lines, I shall quote here some passages from an article by Abadi (1978):

> Naturally, the case of the Sphinx, of the phallic mother, has not been neglected. It seems more interesting to pose the problem of the Sphinx in terms of the incomplete and castrated mother, who is therefore unsatiably avid or jealously castrating. . . . Her symbol as a "terrifying mother" who will not allow birth, is also revealed by her name: Sphinx in Greek means "strangler", she who does not permit breath-

ing, which is birth; she therefore also closes her vagina in a sphincter-like manner to obstruct the birth of her child, whose complete possession she seeks in order to satisfy her desire for completeness". [pp. 405–406; translated for this edition]

[Two ways of aspiring, tending to completeness: the genital and the pre-genital, fusional, which does not stand for separation, as shown in the cases mentioned (see, for example, the mother of Patient F, who used to say to her, "If you get pregnant I'll hang myself from a pole". . . "You are no longer my penis, you have your own").]

According to Abadi (p. 409), castration as spatial incompleteness, by means of a mechanism of shifting the temporal incompleteness, symbolizes death, the always premature interruption of the life cycle (which, precisely because it is a cycle, a circle, presupposes and requires continuity, eternity).

Favouring the time aspect (signified?) over the space aspect (signifier?: but is that really "secondary", and this really "primary"?) corresponds to favouring becoming over being, and it is expressed also in the biblical prohibition of making (unchanging) images of self, which also perhaps indicates the way to reconcile being with becoming, given that the Being—that is, the Being *par excellence*—is itself unchanging (cf. Elohim and Yahweh in *Job*). [As Slochower (1970) observes, Elohim, to whom Job appears to be perfect, must be differentiated from the voice of Yahweh, who addresses himself to Job towards the end. Yahweh does not judge Job by the same standards by which he is declared to be upright at the beginning—in other words, the God of the Book, like his hero, faces a dramatic development.] This refers also to aspects and expressions of post-biblical Jewish literature related to a recovery of the psychological sense and the dynamic aspects—and, in fact, the *Midrash*, for example, may be seen as essentially directed to this. Thus, as far as active and passive are concerned, the Midrash explains by asking itself, not lacking in a certain irony: "Why did the Holy One (God), may He be blessed, choose Israel? Because . . . Israel chose the Holy One (God), may He be blessed, and His Torah." The vicissitudes of the drives in certain manifestations must have been at least widely preconscious to be within reach of the exegete and those who turned to him, and this is probably connected to the possibility of feeling also the passive formulations of a privileged relationship to be satisfactory. This is even truer as far as the equivalences and vicissitudes of the self-image, of the object, and of the so-called selfobject are concerned: it is not chance that the metaphor recurs with such frequency as to exclude its being "extinguished" (see Derrida, 1971, pp. 14–15). ("To the value of wear [*Abnützung*] . . . corresponds here [in Hegel] the opposition between effective and faded metaphors. . . . There would be inactive metaphors any interest in which may be rejected, because the author did not think of it and because the metaphoric effect is limited to the field of the conscious. To the difference between effective and extinguished metaphors corresponds the traditional opposition between living and dead metaphors.") If Abadi (1978) believes that castration symbolizes temporal incompleteness, death, the biblical "he died full of years" emphasizes how the "natural" acceptance of death defers to the physiological separation of a satisfying dual relationship, which is also the condition of terminability of the analysis

In conclusion, it may be said that the material quoted has offered us the possibility of establishing a series of equivalences between conscious and preconscious aspects of the image of self centred on pairs of opposites that match, at the unconscious level, other pairs of opposites included in the "biological" (active/passive) polarity and referable to biological models. Amongst these, the one that most serves to represent the psychological dynamics described is that in which the internalization, which is inseparable from fertility, leads originally precisely to the image of internalization, "the model for which is probably the penis which is retained to become a child, and not the nipple in the mouth" (Chasseguet-Smirgel, 1984, p. 169). This seems to be confirmed in the cases described, in which we have seen the insistence of the images relating to the abovementioned themes. The analysis of them and of their numerous equivalences in the sphere of transference has proved to be extremely fruitful, Abortion, the death of a child (infanticide?), sterility seem to have corresponded to an option for the male components of the image of the self with the associated criminogenous urges. ["It is probably this possibility of recovering in fantasy access to the mother's body via the capacity for motherhood which accounts for the lower rate of criminality amongst women, because the obstacles to this wish for a return to primary fusion assume a less absolute form in the light of this option, and consequently the need to remove them by destroying them does not manifest itself in so impervious a fashion" (Chasseguet-Smirgel, 1984, p. 170).] Starting from the antithesis between the pairs of opposites and the pairs of equals, we go back to the connection between the images of difference and in-difference from the points of view of the active/passive (biological polarity), on the one hand, and, on the other, of the libidinal–aggressive cathexis and the lack of cathexis (emotional polarity), respectively.

On this basis, the defensive meanings of the disavowal of the differences seem clearer, and it may be expected that they concern both men and women as a common element in the resistances that may make the analysis "interminable".

On the other hand, this also concerns the possibility of accepting and appreciating the limitations of the image of the self (which must be portrayed not only on the space plane but also on the time plane) and the (reciprocal) need of the object to reach completeness (genital level). Greater use may be made of the changeover between the space register and the time register—the latter characterizing and characterized (by) the dynamicity as well as (by) the irreversibility—in psychoanalysis.

On the theoretical and technical plane, a correct approach to the problem of language in psychoanalysis may thus be facilitated, Here, in a kind of pendant of the themes mentioned above, the risks may consist, on the one hand, of a reification that ceases to be aware and, on the other, a rejection of metaphorization. These are both possibilities that may lead to the obliteration of that (preconscious) depth within which the most productive movements in analysis may take place. In this regard it may, however, be preferable to speak, rather than of self, of the image (or representation) of self.

It is once again the clinical material quoted that offers us the possibility to discuss the opportunity of passing from the clinical concept of self-image to that—which remains more abstract—of "the Self", also following recent studies that seek to pinpoint its development and to catalogue its various clinical types. Referring again to the clinical examples in question, the term 'self-image' seems to be more appropriate than "the Self", also at the level of theorization. That the effort of "broadening", which seems to underlie the elaboration of the concept of "the Self", risks being in a position close to that of certain post-Freudians—that is, in fact, to pre-Freudian psychology—or straying onto a philosophical level, may be considered in the sphere of a stimulus to the use of a healthy (self-directed) irony —which was not lacking in Freud—also in proceeding at the different levels of theorization

One of the steps that reveals Freud's capacity concerning theorization—which is dealt with in chapter three—is to be found in "Analysis Terminable and Interminable". In this work, Freud (1937c, p. 252) speaks of the analyst's attempts to persuade the female patient to abandon the desire to have a penis and the male patient to accept the possibility of tolerating the passive attitude towards other men. On the other hand, Freud himself had often recommended, for example quite clearly as early as 1911, never to let oneself

> be misled into applying the standards of physical reality to repressed psychical structures, and on that account perhaps, into undervaluing the importance of phantasies in the formation of symptoms on the ground that they are not actualities, or into tracing a neurotic sense of guilt back to some other source because there is no evidence that any actual crime has been committed. [p. 225]

And in the sphere of this last position, what appear to be pertinent are not so much the attempts at persuasion but, rather, those at widening inner realities that are at the basis of the above mentioned difficulties.

The direction in which, for example, I believe the clinical examples quoted above to have been directed is that of the study of the detours through which "an organic correspondence . . . reappears in the psychic sphere as an unconscious identity" (Freud, 1917c, p. 133). This in the attempt (starting from the clinical material) to seek the classification and the equivalences of the phallic/"castrated" antithesis in the sphere of an examination of the problem of the pairs of opposites and the concept of self-image, which cannot be left out of consideration.

The clinical observations show, according to Freud (1915c, p. 126), that an instinctual impulse may undergo the following vicissitudes: (1) transformation into its opposite; (2) turning against oneself; (3) repression; (4) sublimation. To summarize, as far as the first two are concerned, Freud (1915c, p. 140) says that instinctual impulses [*Triebregungen*] are subject to the influence of the three great polarities dominating the psychic life, as we have mentioned above.

These three great polarities may be described as follows: active/passive, as in the biological polarity; ego/external world, as in the real polarity; pleasure/unpleasure [*Lust/Unlust*], as in the economic polarity. The first polarity is connected to a scale [*Reihe*] of emotions of extraordinary importance in the determining [*Entscheidung*] of our actions (our will).

Freud therefore introduces the concept of scale—that is, of a continuum between two poles, even if it refers less to the polarity itself than to what is connected with it. Also as far as the biological and real poles are concerned, if the two opposite poles are clearly distinct in the adult with a well-established identity, the same cannot be said of those in whom, for physiological reasons (age) or pathological reasons it is not so clear-cut, without a well-established identity.

This roughly corresponds to the problems of sexual identity and to those concerning self. Schafer (1976, p. 192) suggests that "the popularity of concepts of self-identity is symptomatic of a fundamental shift toward a modern conception of theory making" and that "Freudian analysis can only benefit from such a shift".

On the other hand, Schafer [1976, pp. 191–192] notes that, whilst there is a fall in the tendencies of reification and personification of the Freudian terms, this tendency has been reaffirmed, like a return to the repressed, in the concepts of self and of identity. But this seems closely connected precisely to the fact of wanting to make use of theoretical concepts "closer to subjective experience [of the analysand? of the analyst? of both?], which is the material of real clinical work". Thus it may happen to analysts, much more unintentionally than when referring to Freud's structural conceptualization, that they "import" these reports of adolescent experiences into their general theory. ["But these more orthodox Freudian authors seem not to recognize that once they go beyond self-representation and objection; once they begin to speak of self or identity as a determinant of behaviour and fantasy and feeling . . . they are in theoretical trouble" (Schafer, 1976, p. 192).] According to Schafer (1976, p. 193) this is to the detriment both of the explicative propositions and of the descriptive and phenomenological efforts. But perhaps worse may occur if this language infiltrates, in a kind of irreversible collusion with the patient, into the analyst's interpretative style. In a certain Kleinian interpretative language we may find something similar to what Schafer stigmatizes concerning the theory—in other words, the use of the adolescent way of thinking about self, identity and emotions, and the relationships they imply: infantile, concretistic, substantialized, i.e. with characteristics of the primary process.

On the other hand, when Schafer (1976, p. 194 ff.) considers the development of language based on the self and on identity as a transitional phase of the conceptual revolution that is replacing the metapsychology of the natural sciences (Freud's) with terms and explicative propositions that are more suitable to the methods and data of psychoanalytic study, and proposes his new language as the next promising step in this development, it seems that he is also mainly preoccupied with finding a theoretical language that may be superimposed on the operative (interpretative) one. Even though it is poles apart, in a certain sense, from the Kleinian language, I believe it corresponds, as does the latter (when at its worst it takes on grotesque aspects), to the analyst's need, which could resemble a kind of incontinence (from the "container"—irony of fate), in that it lacks depth, and it obliterates the (operative) space between the unconscious and conscious, between the primary and secondary process. Schafer notes that we may not use the primary process to observe, explain, and formulate propositions about the primary process (for example, anal theories to explain anal fantasies). But, on the other hand, his *action language* risks being a use of the secondary process that may reformulate only what is already in the sphere of the same process. Schafer seems to come close but does not grasp the possibility of avoiding this dilemma. He is very critical of "conventional metaphors" based on the primary process and of the subjective experiences modelled on it. But it is precisely the characteristics of the metaphor (see Rogers, 1978; Sacerdoti, 1976) that lend themselves, because of their intrinsic modal ambiguity, to the formulation of a theory that is consciously metaphoric and that lends itself to not being used *tout court* in the interpretative work but to being, from one time to the next, a model that allows the analyst to represent to himself (ana-logically) what takes place in the unconscious and, above all, in the preconscious of the patient, and to present the part of it that is representable at the conscious level in a likely way for the patient at that moment, directing it not through the metapsychological metaphors, but possibly through metaphors that spring from the context (see Sacerdoti, 1977a) and that are usable in the here and now as an "amphibious" means.

As regards what has been mentioned above, the concept of image of the self and image of object, based on the material centred on these representations and including their preconscious and unconscious equivalences, seems acceptable without the fears Schafer rightly points out concerning the use of self as a metapsychological concept.

Rapaport (1957, p. 693), on the other hand, whilst considering reasonable the use of the term "self-representation" notes that the self will have to be given a metapsychological definition before it can be used to clarify the concept of narcissism. He considers that the attempt to define it as the set of the relationships between the various psychic institutions is merely a poor beginning. Freud (see, for example, 1914d) speaks generally of *Selbstgefühl* and Jacobson (1965) of self-image. Numerous psychoanalytical works have since been written about the self;

but Rapaport's observation seems to remain for the main part valid.

Winnicott's description (see Gaddini de Benedetti, 1976) also emphasizes the connotations of representation or image that characterize his conception of self.

The term "image" refers mainly to the body, to the image of the body (see Schilder, 1935)—a reference that in Schafer's view would be criticizable as an undue adaptation to the natural sciences. However, it was Freud's originality also, or perhaps precisely because of the abandonment of the *Project* (1905a [1887–1902]), which classified psychoanalysis (see Rapaport, 1944; Ricoeur, 1969) as including the characteristics both of the ideographic and of the nomothetic sciences. [According to Rapaport (1944, p. 189), the consequence of our method, the clinical–historical method for our theory, is that the theory is of necessity built on the concepts of psychic continuity and meaning (and the postulate of continuity is implicit in every ideographic science); on the other hand, determinism (which is a distinctive characteristic of nomethetic science) proves to be, in the psychological sphere, a corollary of psychic continuity.]

This classification—and the importance of being well aware of it in the analyst's choice of interventions—is once again confirmed (as if there were really any need for this) by the study of the clinical examples cited. This has given us the opportunity of realizing that the unconscious equivalences referring to self-images that definitely belong to the anatomic–functional or biological register are the counterparts of the old psychopathological/delinquent dilemma, which refers to self-images that typically belong to the psychological and social register.

In this sphere, which recalls the double vision that is characteristic of irony, mention has been made of the greater operative adhesion of the expression "self-image" as compared to "the self". There is no attempt here to diminish the interest and the value of those studies, which, also through the agreement of the data of the clinical psychoanalysis with those of child observation, tend rigorously to collect elements for a metapsychological definition of the self (see, for example, Gaddini, 1981).

Summary

What we have attempted in this chapter is to verify the legitimacy of the concept of latent irony through several clinical illustrations, which are as specific as possible. They have shown the way in which this question is connected to that concerning the playful or serious aspect, which may also give rise to the combinations resulting from the way in which each of the terms of this pair intersects with each of the levels of the conscious/unconscious polarity in the analytic relationship. The fact that the analyst is aware of these themes increases his possibilities of provoking insight in the patient by working and playing with him, while it lessens the possibilities of "being played" by the patient as well as (*absit iniuria verbis*) "playing" the patient and in any case those of playing the success of the analysis (which may happen right from the first session with the patient).

This pair of opposites—or, rather, this dialectic pair (playful/serious and playful/working)—thus seems to be fundamental to a study of irony in the psychoanalytical field, also insofar as this pair may lie at the intersection of a series of dialectic themes and polarities or of pairs of opposites [*Gegensatzpaare*], which may be summarized, on the one hand, in the contrast between an appearance and a reality—characteristic of irony—and, on the other, in the "great polarities" that according to Freud "dominate psychic life".

Of the Freudian theme of bipolarity, the operative potentials have by and large not been used to their best advantage, for it has perhaps been classified as an abstract, aprioristic, idealistic, and static position (in a similar way as other aspects of metapsychology) instead of being recognized as what it was, in fact, for Freud—that is, a function of the praxis, in the sphere of a dynamic vision, aware of clinical vicissitudes, the ones of the instinctual drives being a conceptual corollary resulting from the (application of) psychoanalytical methodology (see Rapaport & Gill, 1959). Amongst the vicissitudes [*Schicksale*], particular attention has been paid to reversal in the specific examples of the ironic aspects, given the importance of reversal into the opposite [*Verkehrung ins Gegenteil*]. The *retournement* seems to be at the same root of Freudian dualism. Moreover, with the aim of exploring these (fundamental) aspects of irony that intersect and are set within the above-mentioned bipolar theme, other aspects of the same theme are also examined in the light of examples and a widened discussion. In particular, attempts are made to grasp, especially at the level of clinical theory, the implications of the psycho analytical material concerning borderline cases that have demonstrated more or less explicitly and always dramatically the oscillation, the dilemma between psychopathological and delinquent aspects of self-image. This bipolarity has been seen—at the conscious level—as antinomic and has accompanied a total lack of capacity for ironic vision. The association of these two characteristics has not been seen to be chance and has centred on questions related to libidinal development and sexual identity with insistence on the active/ passive dimension. The opportunity of grasping the unconscious equivalences and the vicissitudes of the psychopathological and delinquent aspects of self-image shown by the above-mentioned cases has proved to contain a wealth of possibilities concerning the study of fantasies underlying the representation of the mental illness, falling ill, recovery and therefore also healing oneself, being healed, and healing as well as self-deception, being deceived, and deceiving in analysis.

These—like other—"obscure" aspects may be studied thoroughly and made less troublesome in the analytical relationship (also) because of the clarity of the setting that makes up the free acceptance of an asymmetric situation, of recognition of a difference between the partners. In the material of the cases in question, this problem of the difference (and of its opposites, both reversal of the difference and its disavowal, i.e. in-difference), occurred and modulated in parallel and inversely in the (conscious) psychopathological and delinquent registers. About the theme of the (in)terminability of analysis there was thus offered the possibility—in the light of unconscious equivalents—of putting forward an additional unifying hypothesis that could join the two modalities through which, according to Freud, the analysis may be interminable in men and women, respectively.

Whilst the oscillation of the self-image between the two (psychopathological and delinquent) poles was conscious, that which took place in the sphere of the analytical relationship—especially at the transference level—remained as equally unconscious as the above-mentioned equivalences. Indeed, the equivalences appear to the preconscious relatively early on.

Already in the old mad/delinquent alternative, we saw a kind of irony of fate (see Butler, 1862) from which it was impossible to escape. In this situation, every approach by the analyst that is even cautiously ironic would be completely out of place, not being able to strengthen the experience of guilt (delinquent) or persecution (mad) and extending it *tout court* to the "unjust" relationship with the analyst (alternatively victim and persecutor). Extreme caution in the use of any ironic nuance by the analyst thus seems to remain the rule with psychotic and borderline patients.

CHAPTER 3

Ironic aspects in psychoanalytic theorization

It is well known that for many years the fundamental concepts of psychoanalysis have widely been the object of sarcasm in scientific circles, even if this attitude is today considerably attenuated. As to the nature of the resistances to psychoanalysis, it is sufficient to recall how the modalities have changed radically: what interests us here is that not only has sarcasm become exceptional, but even conscious irony has become relatively rare. Much more frequent is the kind of resistance to psychoanalysis that consists in highlighting its positive aspects and then, often concentrating on the context—or, rather, isolating the analysis from its context—changing the nature of its essence. This operation may only be considered ironic when, following on from what has been said in the previous chapters, the concept of irony is widened to the preconscious and unconscious levels.

What is more, a development of this kind may be found not only outside psychoanalysis but also within it and in a manner I consider increasingly less conscious. This may be facilitated (again as far as it interests us here) by the fact that as the "exploration" gradually deepens, it may become easier to lose sight of the "surface". Through a kind of irony of fate, the context in (the sphere of) which insight may take place is thus modified. On the other hand, it is a basic condition of conscious irony that the vision of the surface also co-exists with that of the interior. This is why at this level irony seems to be absent—lack of ironic vision—precisely in the developments mentioned above, where it may be present at the unconscious level. A closer examination of this situation might perhaps help to illuminate the recurring genesis of certain post-Freudian theoretical and methodological criticisms and revisions. It is thus necessary first to trace how Freud's receptivity to the ironic and self-directed ironic vision (in the sense of stable irony) has contributed to the creation and evolution of the psychoanalytic conceptual edifice, as well as to the invention of the setting and the analytic situation.

The work/play pair

Recalling once more what has been explained in the previous chapter, I shall start from the following three quotations from Freud:

> For we find that even after the ego has decided to relinquish its resistances it still has difficulty [*Schwierigkeiten*] in undoing the repressions; and we have called the period of strenuous effort which follows after its praiseworthy decision, the phase of "working-through" [*Durcharbeitung*]. [1926d, p. 159]

> This working-through of the resistances may in practice turn out to be an arduous task [*beschwerliche Aufgabe*] for the subject of the analysis and a trial of patience for the analyst. Nevertheless it is a part of the work [*Arbeit*] which effects the greatest changes in the patient and which distinguishes analytic treatment from any kind of treatment by suggestion. [1914g, pp. 155–156]

For it is not so easy to play upon the instrument of the mind. [1905a, p. 262]

In the first two extracts, speaking of *durcharbeiten*, Freud emphasizes, amongst other things, the difficult, arduous aspects [*Schwierigkeiten; beschwerliche Aufgabe*] for the analysand and the aspects of work [*Arbeit*] that try the analyst's patience. This distinguishes the analytic work from the influences of suggestion, which—we might say—are, relatively, a joke, an easy game. Furthermore, he refers not only to the laborious aspect [*Bemühung*], but also to the *serious* aspect. ["Serious" is probably derived from a Germanic and Baltic root *swer* (heavy), which is the same as the German *schwer*: Devoto, 1966, p. 388.] Here, therefore, the work/play pair is superseded by the serious/joking pair. [In Italian "play" is *gioco*, which comes from the Latin *jocus* (jest): Devoto, 1966, p. 189.]

On the other hand, speaking about difficulties, in the third quotation above Freud refers to the playing of a musical instrument, a metaphor taken from Shakespeare's *Hamlet*, which he then quotes on the following page. It seems to point to the need for a synthesis between the serious, professional, "scientific" elements on the one hand, and the "artistic" or playful elements on the other.

Following for a moment the linguistic thread that links the playful aspects to the illusory aspects, we may note how along this thread there runs a tendency to deterioration (see the analogous considerations made earlier about irony and parody). Thus the Latin *illusio* means "irony" and only later "derision". To illude, made up of the illative *in* and *ludere* [play], means "to insert in play" and only later "to play or sport with" (Devoto, 1966, p. 201). On the other hand, the pedagogical rule *maxima debetur puero reverentia* [the child deserves the greatest respect] may lead to—or be the expression of—attitudes whose effects turn out to be disastrous. Erikson (1968) calls attention to the tendency of worried, anxious adults to take adolescents too seriously.

Continuing to develop this theme, it would seem appropriate here to quote what Favez (1971) says:

> It is all a quantity of illusion and disillusion that each person brings to the psychoanalytic cure and it is what he carries—and transfers—most often unaware of it from the beginning of his life. . . . The disillusion grows with frustration . . ., a barrier that refers man to impotence, weakness, to child-like dependence. [p. 45]

And later:

> The cure does not concern itself with anything else other than perceiving and pointing out the infantile reactions and interpretations before frustration. [p. 47].

I would like to recall that it was precisely Freud's capacity to keep himself on a razor's edge between illusion and arduous work that allowed him to overcome the worst moments of professional crisis. It suffices to quote what he says in his *An Autobiographical Study* (1925d [1924]): ". . . an error [the theory of parental seduction] into which I fell for a while and which might well have had fatal consequences for the whole of my work" (p. 33).

Without "error" (illusion) there might not have been the "arduous work". On the other hand, if the truth rises from misunderstanding, as Lacan maintains (1954), it must also be added that, for it not to dissolve, this "truth", which has risen almost from play, must be subjected (as analysts learn every day) to a working operation, to *Durcharbeitung*.

We might here consider a specific kind of work in the psychoanalyst's activity, which has its *pendant* in certain maskings unconsciously operated by the patient (from which the analyst is in principle never totally immune) and indicated in analytical language as work, with reference principally to intrapsychic economy.

I intend to develop and specify the concept of work, both with regard to the analysand and the analyst, and therefore, obviously, the analytic relationship, following Freud's thought on the question. I shall also examine a more general concept of work, as well as the developments of it that certain authors have put forward.

The resistances to psychoanalysis within the setting, and in particular those Freud calls the resistances of the unconscious or of the id, which require *durcharbeiten*, are essentially resistances to work, which may (however) be realized in certain phases as resistances to—or rejection of—play. They may be seen as being responsible both for the shift of the analytic treatment to another kind of operation, which may take place despite the opposite laudable intention [*löblicher Vorsatz*] both of the analysand and of the analyst (at the level of conscious ego), and also for the opposition to the psychoanalysis from the exterior which, as mentioned earlier, has today taken different forms from those in the past (being less or not at all manifest, to a point of apparent support, which, in fact, changes its nature).

Very schematically, all these modifications go in the direction of the least effort. This is probably in agreement with a general tendency linked to improved conditions of life (also for the "psychotherapists"), which has led to the possibility of a widespread avoidance of effort, therefore of intense work in the original sense of the term; it has also resulted in the possibility of passing off as real work a series of pseudo-works, which are clearly expressions of needs of the id, which, conversely, are not manifested and satisfied in the appropriate situation.

According to Meltzer (1973), just as adult sexual behaviour often cannot be descriptively distinguished from infantile behaviour but only through analysis of the fantasy and unconscious motivation, thus work often cannot be distinguished from pseudo-work, from compulsion, from omnipotent control, and from other forms of non-play that emerge in behaviour when infantile rather than adult organization has taken control of motility. No descriptive criterion will help the analyst to recognize these aspects of his patient or, indeed, his own acting out and acting in. Only the analytic method of exploring the transference and countertransference may be of any help.

Meltzer proposes—perhaps with excessive schematization—that

> the infantile organization of the self places the ego in a primary relation to the Id, resulting in play, while the adult

organization of the self, through introjective identification, places the adult portion of the ego, in children and grown-ups alike, in a secondary relation to the Id via the super-ego-ideal, resulting behaviourally, in work.

As I have mentioned elsewhere (Sacerdoti, 1974), the psychoanalytic situation is structured in such a way that the experience that takes place within it is contemporaneously or alternatively often of a dramatic playful or working nature. Both these aspects are necessary for the good progress of the analysis (see also chapter two).

One of the analysts who has dedicated much thought to the conceptualization of play in the above-mentioned sense is Winnicott (1971), whose thesis is that psychotherapy takes place in the superimposition of two areas of play—that of the patient and that of the therapist. The corollary of this is that, where it is not possible to play, the therapist's work is directed at bringing the patient from a state in which he is unable to play to one in which this is possible. More comprehensively, it could be said that the psychoanalytic situation must be structured in such a way that the experience taking place there may be contemporaneously or alternatively playful and working in nature (for the most part with a dramatic progression that involves a decreasing trend for the former and an increasing trend for the latter).

It therefore appears to be vital that both may be realized and that the analyst has a conceptual scheme to which he may refer so as to picture the basis of the difficulties of explication on one or another of the registers. It is therefore important to be able to recognize pseudo-work and pseudo-play.

In the adaptation of psychoanalysis to the roles that society attributes to it, true play, in its serious effort, may seem to be suspect (as Morgenthaler 1977, 1978, states); and this is not contradicted by the use of play techniques in infantile psychoanalysis. Indeed, it must be asked what space remains, within these techniques, in which the child analyst may really play. Morgenthaler (1977) claims that in play, what is serious is considered less and less, because it no longer corresponds to the norms of social evaluation. Furthermore, psychoanalysis is the science of the unconscious. The seriousness with which it pursues the scientific understanding of the object should be mixed with the enjoyment for play, so as to be able to conceive fully the possible potentials of man and to relativize, widen, reformulate, and understand in a new manner what was previously considered certain. The results of a process of this kind would be equal to the seriousness that underlies all true play (p. 4).

With regard to the difficulties in making use of the playful and the working side, respectively, we must recall Meltzer's ideas. He considers that true play cannot be realized basically in two situations: (1) when, as a result of idealization, objects do not show much of that quality of clemency under which the infantile thought-in-action, which we know as play, may proceed, and, (2) when splitting and idealization are not adequate, when a clear distinction between good and bad, both in the self and in objects, is lacking (Meltzer, 1973):

> Under these circumstances, play is not able to proceed because of excesses of persecutory anxiety and is either inhibited or replaced by concrete behaviour which is play-like in form but joyless and compulsory in quality. [p. 129]

The play of the infantile structures is therefore conditioned by the benevolence of good objects which are tolerant and omnipotently reparative in the psychic reality.

> But just as psychic reality is primary and overwhelming in importance for the infantile structures, external reality and responsibility for the world becomes primary for the adult portion of personality in its introjective identification. [p. 129]

As far as work is concerned, Meltzer starts from a quotation by Freud (1930a):

> Professional activity is a source of special satisfaction if it is a freely chosen one—if, that is to say, by means of sublimation, it makes possible the use of existing inclinations, of

> persisting or constitutionally reinforced instinctual impulses. And yet, as a path to happiness, work is not highly prized by men. They do not strive after it as they do after other possibilities of satisfaction. The great majority of people only work under the stress of necessity, and this natural human aversion to work raises most difficult social problems. [p. 80n]

For Meltzer (1973), if taken in its fullest sense, Freud's quotation could acquire a meaning in which the pleasure of work no longer needs to be seen as desexualized in any sense. Through the operation of admiration and introjection, the "existing inclinations" and the "constitutionally reinforced instinctual impulses" will have found their correct place in the structure of the personality as qualities of the superego that is particular to that individual. In the implication that all work is sexual in its meaning, we should therefore fully recognize the libido-affective aspect; in other words, passion.

In an article published posthumously in 1977, Bahia dwells on the question of the simultaneousness of the principle of pleasure and that of reality, and emphasizes how Freud was aware of the fact that both neurotic and psychotic patients retire momentarily from reality and then return to it, each in his own way, once the modification that is desired—or at least the modification that has been possible—has been reached. (1924b [1923], 1924e). Furthermore, Freud (1911b, pp. 219–220) admitted that an organization that 'was a slave to the pleasure principle and neglected the reality of the external world could not maintain itself alive for the shortest time', and therefore, as Bahia notes (1977, pp. 354–355), the concept of sexual instinct that behaves in an auto-erotic manner, isolated from frustrating situations (which are what creates the institution of the principle of reality), may only be a fiction. The fact that the pleasure principle and the reality principle are therefore permanent parallel realities was until Bion's (1962) studies insufficiently considered.

Whatever the case, it may be of interest to recall here how the Talmudists have interpreted the Biblical commandment

(*Exodus*, XX, 9) concerning work: "Six days shalt thou labour, and do all thy work". They apply to it the technique that consists in attributing significance to the apparently pleonastic or the apparently tautological, considering the pleonasm or the tautology as something to be deciphered. Under and through the apparent tautology, the divine prescription (which combines superego, reality-ego and pleasure-ego) refers—and this is the interpretation—both to means of subsistence and to pleasure. Man therefore—in psychoanalytical terms—will in his work satisfy the needs both of the principles of reality and of pleasure.

Next to the conception that considers work as utilizing desexualized libidinal energy and the conception that considers it as a fully sexualized libidinal expression, we must recall the conception of Hendrick, who distances himself from both. In a paper given in 1942 to the annual meeting of the American Psychoanalytical Association, he discussed certain links between work and the pleasure principle, noting that the principles of reality and pleasure do not fully take into account psychosocial activities. He suggested that work is not primarily motivated by sexual need or by associated aggression, but by the need for efficient use of muscular and intellectual means for the performance of functions of the ego that allow the individual to control or alter his environment. He called this thesis "work principle" (ibid., p. 311). Whilst the fulfilment of the reality principle is basically a defence mechanism, the work principle is not a temporary disavowal of instinct but, rather, the satisfying of an instinct, the instinct to master (which refers to Freud's *Bemächtigungstrieb*), through a well-organized activity. For example: an amateur's art is dominated by the pleasure principle, that of the professional artist by the work principle (ibid., pp. 316–317).

It therefore emerges that regarding this important theme of work (following Freud, the capacity for work is considered by analysts, to be a basic requisite, next to the capacity for loving, of mental sanity)—in other words, its definition, classification, and importance—psychoanalytical literature shows a range of widely differing opinions.

Irony, insight, and the repressed/repressing pair

The lack of perception of the simultaneousness of the principles of pleasure and reality could (see Bahia, 1977) even contribute to the loss of contact with reality. The capacity for ironic vision (especially in the sense of a stable irony, which permits a psychic elaboration and a mastering of unpleasant and discongruent or conflictual situations) is linked to the possibility for two simultaneous perceptions, which are (classically) indicated by ironologists as the perception of surface and depth, of opacity and transparency (see Muecke, 1970). I believe it is worthwhile to take the visual metaphor further by making it concrete. Thus, for example, a sheet of water recalls the existence of a submerged world that has both an appearance (that of the reflection) and a reality. The reflection (the appearance) is visualized through a "lucid opacity", whereas the submerged reality is visualized through the transparency of the water (which thus reveals its real contents). In Dedekind's phenomenon, what is highlighted (see the Myth of Narcissus) is the contrast between appearance and reality (also) as regards the view of the whole made up of both the "worlds"—or, more precisely, as regards an object that lies partly in one world and partly in the other. The stick appears to be broken where it enters the water, whereas in reality it is continuous but may only appear so if seen totally emerged or totally submerged. Dedekind's break is therefore "mobile"—between these two extremes—with the degree of immersion. The analogy between this mobility and that of the "localization of perception" achieved when an object is explored with a stick has been noted (Besançon, 1975, p. 69). The perception lies at the end of the stick if held rigidly or at the other end, where the hand is, if held lightly. [The "light" or "heavy" hand also differentiates between two ways of establishing contact with the horse in riding. That this "art" lends itself to metaphorizing the contact with one's own (and the other's) instinctuality is strengthened amongst other things by the classical image Freud proposes to represent relations between the ego (the rider) and the Id (the horse).]

This image has also been used as a metaphor for the possible different placement of the place of division between observer and observed in the so-called behavioural sciences. The method of psychoanalytic enquiry would thus seem to belong to the family of the explorations carried out with a stick held lightly.

Continuing this kind of metaphor, we could again emphasize the analyst's need to have a graduality of lightness or of a mobility of focus at his disposal in order to be able to move between the two extremes of the sensitive or sensorial perception; in other words, between the two possible extreme visions. The depth of focus will then permit the contemporary vision, within certain limits, both of what lies on the surface and what lies under it.

The width of the visual field could allow the inclusion of what emerges and its reflection without the risk of considering the reflection as really existing, and thus meeting the same end as Narcissus.

Along the thread of these metaphors, it is worth briefly examining the concept of insight and comparing it with that of the return of the repressed. Today, the term "insight" is defined (Webster, 1970, p. 437) as:

1. the power or act of seeing into a situation: penetration;
2. the act of apprehending the inner nature of things or of seeing intuitively.

In both these meanings it is implicit that the vision of the interior is added to that of the surface and coexists with it. We are therefore very close here to the concept of double vision, which, according to Muecke, defines irony; we are, on the other hand, far from those explorations that lose sight of the surface.

As far as the return of the repressed (in the repressing force) is concerned, the best thing is to quote here the following passage from Freud (1907a):

> In such cases the old Latin saying holds true, though it may have been coined first to apply to expulsion by external influences and not to internal conflicts: "*Naturam*

> *expellas furca, tamen usque recurret*". But it does not tell us everything. It only informs us of the *fact* of the return of the piece of nature that has been repressed: it does not describe the highly remarkable *manner* of that return, which is accomplished by what seems like a piece of malicious treachery. It is precisely what was chosen as the instrument of repression—like the *furca* of the Latin saying—that becomes the vehicle for the return: in and behind the repressing force, what is repressed proves itself victor in the end. This fact, which has been so little noticed and deserves much consideration, is illustrated—more impressively than it could be by many examples—in a well-known etching by Félicien Rop. . . . An ascetic monk has fled, no doubt from the temptations of the world, to the image of the crucified Saviour. And now the cross sinks down like a shadow, and in its place, radiant, there rises instead the image of a voluptuous, naked woman, in the same crucified attitude. [1907a, p. 35]

In this case, therefore, there is no double vision: the repressing force disappears, and in its place rises what is repressed.

Given that the repressing force and what is repressed generally have contrasting characters, the progress may be not a double ironic vision but at most an "irony of fate", a "betrayal" (as Freud says), or a "revenge", according to the point of view, or a victory of the pleasure principle, which, however, chases away that of reality—almost an intrapsychic nemesis. It must be recalled that the word némesis first meant "to deal out what is due", according to justice and merit, and only later did it take on the meaning of "the goddess who avenges or punishes". This evolution, in a deteriorated sense, seems to be a common destiny—as mentioned above—to other concepts in which reference is made to connections between the primary and the secondary process.

Furthermore, we may note that:

- the repressing force and what is repressed represent a pair of opposites in the sphere of the active/passive polarity;
- apart from return of what is repressed (which, although comparable, is different from the acquisition of insight),

the return of the repressing force may also take place—that is, the return of repression (which is, although comparable, different from the loss of insight) [Weiss (1970) has this to say with regard to the technique Federn used with psychotics: "I knew that Federn had tried to have his psychotic patients repress some impulses in order to encourage the integrating capacity of their Ego. In these cases, I believe, Federn's principle is "where the Ego is there should be the Id" and not "where the Id is should be the Ego"" Perhaps some similar considerations could also be made—if we look more closely—for some modern therapies, which are claimed to be not only analytical but "superdeep"];

- (only) when the repression takes place through a transformation into the opposite [*Verkehrung ins Gegenteil*], does the *retour* [return] of what is repressed in the repressing force coincide with the *retournement*, i.e. with the inversion;
- in this last case, the possibility of repetition *ad infinitum* of the *retournements* recalls the operations of infinite unstable irony, even if the description of it given by Booth deliberately concerns the conscious level.

Ironic work

From what we have tried to define up to this point, it may be seen that, precisely in the events we usually catalogue as playful, there is an entire psychic activity that takes place at various levels, and which merits being considered and indicated as a certain kind of work. Let us now return to the concept of work within the psychoanalytic practice and theorization that has been made about it, so as to deal specifically with the work connected to ironic play.

It is significant that a philosopher who is one of the few to have really come close to the understanding of analytic work, Ricoeur (1974), clearly mentioned this, starting precisely from the quotation of one of the rare passages by Freud in which he mentions the relation [*Verhältnis*] (Freud, 1919a [1918]):

> Cruel though it may *sound*, we must see to it that the patient's suffering, to a degree that is in some way or other effective, does not come to an end prematurely. If, owing to the symptoms having been taken apart and having lost their value, his suffering becomes mitigated, we must reinstate it elsewhere in the form of some appreciable privation; otherwise we run the danger of never achieving any improvements except quite insignificant and transitory ones . . . activity on the part of the physician must take the form of energetic opposition to premature substitutive satisfactions. . . . As far as his relations with the physician are concerned, the patient must be left with unfulfilled wishes in abundance". [pp. 163–164; italics added]

["Cruel though it may *sound*", could be seen as a constitutive element of an ironic situation; compare, instead, in the sphere of public assistance, the demagogic orientation in the theme of psychotherapy. As regards the substitutive satisfaction, it may be one of the aspects of the playful situation. The reference to the unfulfilled wishes with which the patient must be left characterizes at the same time the playful and the working aspects of the analytic relation; that a part of desire, in its realistic (serious) component, remains unrealized is characteristic of play.]

Ricoeur (1974) notes that these themes are of an exemplary clarity; they are sufficient to create an abyss between what reflection can obtain from itself and what may be taught only by a trade. He adds that he would gladly see in these observations by Freud on the manipulation of transference, the final irreducible difference between the more existential phenomenology and psychoanalysis.

Considering how rarely Freud uses the word *Verhältnis* [relation] with reference to analysis, it makes us think that this happened because Freud abhorred the pleonastic. On the other hand, all the talk there is today about relation could be ascribed to the fact that the "logical subject" (which, by definition, is not named) has remained in a certain sense too distant. To name "in vain" is also connected with "idolization" (as has been known since the times of Moses)—in other words, with *Ersatz*, the substitution of the good (inner) object, the constant object with the idealized object. One might think here of existential phenomenology, of *Daseinanalyse*, where the relation (which takes on the connotations of the idealized object) is named at every step, and also of the sterility (to say the least) of the "daseinsanalytic psychotherapy"—that is, of the coupling between a certain word and a certain action, a sterility that can be explained on the basis of a lack of depth (see the considerations concerning the self-image as an operatively more valid concept than that of self), or, if one so wishes, of a lack of differentiation between the speaking of a relation and the speaking in a relation, so that the second situation ends up by becoming equivalent to the first. This may also be expressed in terms of avoiding necessary clarifications: for example, where it is a question of speaking about a relation and where it is one of setting it up: up to what point can (and must) we play, and when, instead, must (and can) we work (do seriously). The problem of "where to stop" in ironic play is developed by Booth (1974) with regard to stable irony as a characterizing element that distinguishes it from unstable irony.

Ricoeur (1974) again takes the concept of work as a guide when considering the metapsychological apparatus, and he notes that

> the work in which analysis consists (under the double figure of the analyst's work and the analysand's work) reveals the psychic functioning itself as work. The Freudian energetics is without doubt metaphoric, but it is the metaphor that protects the specificity of the metapsychology in relation to any phenomenology of intentionality, sense and motivation.

This does not seem to have been well understood by many "modernizing" critics of Freud—precisely those who speak so much about relation, "discovering", for example, that the economic point of view is scientifically untenable. The fact that within psychoanalysis these critics are perhaps more numerous amongst those who deal with psychotic patients, borderline patients, and children could make us suspect that, in their refusal or lack of capacity to utilize Freudian metapsychological constructs metaphorically—especially the "economic" constructs—they are in some way feeling the effects of the concretistic thought of their patients, which usually accompanies the lack of capacity for ironic vision. In one of the clinical examples described in chapter two (Case A), it was through attaching herself to the literal aspect of the analyst's comment, taking it out of context, that the patient distorted its meaning in a superegoic key, using it to convey a victimist and at the same time caricatural nature to the relation with the analyst (the comic effect remained, however, unconscious).

Certain analogies could be summarized between:

1. *caricaturing the rules by taking them literally* (see working to rule): in analysis this is particularly frequent in obsessive patients (see Sacerdoti, 1979); caricaturing the consequences of the rules—or, rather, drawing caricaturized conclusions from them possibly in unconscious collusion with the analyst; for example, the excess of anonymity may encourage projective identification and hinder introjective identification;
2. *caricaturing theory*: by the patient on a conscious and/or unconscious level, by the analyst, by fanatics of psychoanalysis, and by popularizers of psychoanalysis (analysts and others), at an unconscious level.

Isolation is one of the mechanisms that most often concern caricaturing, as Freud had already noted for example with regard to pathological caricatures (see latent, unconscious irony) of philosophy and religion (see also the concept of unstable infinite irony and the problem of "where to stop").

Beres (1980, p. 17) recalls that the obsessive patient and the philosopher may isolate abstract thought from the thought of common sense, which leads to scepticism and doubt.

Through this isolation, philosophers are able to function more or less adequately in their everyday life and, at the same time, to "prove" the non-existence of inanimate objects, of others, and even of themselves (see again unstable infinite irony). Is this nothing but the isolation (see also Sacerdoti,

1977b) that is at work in certain criticisms of metapsychology? [This is basically what Brenner (1980) observes when, using the example of the concept of psychic energy and the way it is attacked (almost in an obsessive manner), he illustrates "the impropriety of criticizing and/or rejecting psychoanalytical concepts without reference to the data on which they are based. It is not the name of a concept that is important nor the derivation of the name, it is the meaning and the consonance with and/or relevance to available data of observation" (p. 213).]

An example of how isolation may contribute to the creation of ironic and caricatural situations and to their remaining latent has already been reported in Case B.

The symptom with which the patient had managed—confirming himself in his omnipotence—to play the neuropsychiatrists was, as we have seen, his "absences". As the patient himself described them, they had curious analogies with the manner in which the origins of the world are prospected in the representation of the Lurian *Cabbala*.

This representation rests on two large composite tropes (Bloom, 1975), *zimzum* and *tikkun*, and on the concept of the connection between them. Bloom notes that

> zimzum is initially a rhetoric irony for the act of creation, in that it means the opposite of what it appears to say. It says "withdrawal" and means "concentration". God withdraws from a point only to concentrate Himself upon it. The image of His absence becomes one of the greatest images ever found for His presence, a presence that is intensified by the original metaphor of *mezamzen*, His holding in of His breath. [p. 74]

It is precisely through his held breath that the patient mentioned brought on these states of "absence" that had led the neuropsychiatrists astray: absence was the greatest image of his presence, which had left them no diagnostic space. In the case of this patient, latent irony was aimed against the doctors (and, in the end, his parents).

In the case of the first Cabbalistic emanation of God—as Bloom notes (1975, p. 28)—it is an entity that rhetorically begins as simple self-centred irony. Indeed, *Keter* (the first attribute or emanative principle), as the infinite God, is contemporaneously *ayin* or "nothingness" and *ehyeh* or I AM, absolute absence and absolute presence. [This might refer both to the logic of the unconscious and also to how the presence/absence pair may be played at the same time on the register of inner reality and on that of outer reality (for this latter point, see Sacerdoti, 1986a).]

Cabbalistic irony concerning the first emanation of God has a socio-historical precedent in a passage from *Exodus*. Moses objects to God: "Behold, when I come unto the children of Israel, and shall say unto them, The God of your fathers hath sent me unto you; and they shall say to me, What is his name? what shall I say unto them?" (III, 13) and God replies: "I AM THAT I AM". Then He says: "Thus shalt thou say unto the children of Israel, I AM hath sent me unto you" (III, 14). Commenting on this passage, Fromm (1966), noticing that the God in the story, the "living" God, can have no name, says that in *ehyeh* there is an ironic compromise between God's concession to the ignorance of the people and his conviction that he must be a God with no name.

If of the stable type, according to Booth (1974), self-directed irony goes against the tide as far as pseudocreative narcissistic indulgences are concerned and is thus not defensive but collaborative regarding true creativity, of which it may be an essential ingredient. Booth claims that by no means does it lead to the serious losses that take place instead in the case of unstable irony and especially infinite unstable irony.

I believe this to be such an important point and so pertinent to the theme that I shall develop further considerations, taking a cue from the comparison between a passage by Freud and some verses by Heine quoted by Freud

In the above-mentioned "Lines of Advance in Psychoanalytic Therapy", Freud (1919a [1918]) expressed the following ideas:

> Any analyst who out of the fullness of his heart, perhaps, and his readiness to help, extends to the patient all that one human being may hope to receive from another, commits the same economic error as that of which our non-

analytic institutions for nervous patients are guilty. [p. 164]

In *On Narcissism: An Introduction*, Freud (1914c, p. 85) quotes the following verse from *Neue Gedichte, Schöpfungslieder*, by Heine:

> Illness was no doubt the final cause
> of the whole urge to create;
> By creating, I could recover;
> By creating, I became healthy.

In the perspective that interests us here, I believe that the two quotations may be seen as representing, respectively, the negative (even destructive) aspects and the positive (even creative, or, in any case, constructive) ones of the "action" in the treatment of psychic disturbances. In the first case, what is implicitly emphasized is the danger that, under the appearance of oblativity, for reasons of incapacity—we might say—the narcissistic–omnipotent aspects of the therapist's *action* are unacknowledged because one lacks the capacity to view one's own work ironically. The need to hold in due consideration the economic aspects is explicitly recalled.

In the second case, Heine's verses—so full of self-directed irony—are used by Freud for general considerations on the need to love in order to be psychically sane. In any case, they exemplify a situation in which the narcissistic–omnipotent aspects are clearly assumed, together with the awareness of one's own need. It is the Omnipotent in person who, precisely through the recognition of His own unease, acts in such a way as to create man and also to heal himself at the same time. In Heine's quotation, we may therefore perceive the (self-directed) ironic aspect inherent in showing that the existence of the object created by the Omnipotent becomes a necessary condition—and therefore a limitation for the Omnipotent himself.

Comparing the rhetorically ironic representation of the Creator in the Cabbala with the prohibition to make graven images, we may observe that also the characteristics of the Cabbalistic representation obey a kind of regard for non-representability [*Rücksicht auf Undarstellbarkeit*], almost as if to avoid confusion between different levels and between inner reality (fantasy) and outer reality, between representation and perception, between the primary process that allows contradiction and the secondary process that does not allow it, even though (or precisely because) it takes into account both terms of the pair.

The creation—or, rather, the miraculous image of it—may lend itself to similar confusion insofar as from projectual representability (desire) we move to perceptibility (realization of desire), which is similar to, but also unlike (lack of gestation and labour) what happens in procreation, where the representable "inner object" becomes the concrete, perceptible inner (and then outer) object.

These themes concerning the dynamic and even dialectic aspects of the image of the object, of self, and of the relation, to which the prohibition to make images—i.e. to fix the image in a static representation—is connected, may be linked with the vicissitudes of impulses. It is under this aspect of the vicissitudes—and therefore of the equivalences and oppositions—that it was possible to grasp the preconscious and unconscious significance of old pairs of dilemmas such as psychopathological/delinquent, deceiver/deceived, in the cases reported in chapter two, which were centred on the lack of procreation and the death of the child, respectively.

Keeping in mind these perspectives, we may now return to Ricoeur (1969). He concludes his reflections on the work of analysis with the quotation from *Hamlet* (which Patient B also recalled) that Freud enjoys repeating: "'Sblood, do you think I am easier to be played than a pipe? Call me what instrument you will, though you can fret me, you cannot play upon me" (Act III, Scene 2) (1905a, p. 62).

"The psychic instrument . . . to be played": Ricoeur believes that this expression opens up to a fundamental aspect of the psychoanalytic technique (including free-floating attention)—in other words, that the theory that corresponds to it (including the availability of more or less fantastic constructions—see "Constructions in Analysis" 1937d), which Freud (1937c, p. 225) calls the Witch Metapsychology [*die Hexe Metapsychologie*], is itself a function of praxis and also of the fantasy aspects of praxis, which are paradoxically ever more necessary, the closer we get to the so-called rocky layer or underlying bedrock [*unterliegender gewachsener Felsen*] (Freud, 1937c, p. 252).

According to Ricoeur, in the metapsychological apparatus of psychoanalysis, the concept of work is at the centre of the interpretation of dreams: if the dream can be considered "the fulfillment" of a wish [*Wunscherfüllung*] it is because unconscious thoughts are "distorted". This "distortion" [*Entstellung*], interpreted by Freud as work, is the work of the dream [*Traumarbeit*] and the processes that take part in it are ways of working: condensation work [*Verdichtungsarbeit*], displacement work [*Verschiebungsarbeit*]. The sites of the topic expressly take account of "distancing" [*Entfernung*] and "distortion" [*Entstellung*], which separate [*Ent-*] and render unrecognizable the other question that comes to light in the discourse of the analysis. Distancing and distortion of what derives from the unconscious are at the root of these resistances, and they require the recognition of self through self to become work. Metapsychology attempts to take account of misdeed, of a work of refusal to recognize, which gives rise to recognition as work. If there is a problem of interpretation, that is because the wish is fulfilled in a masked and substitutive manner. The work dealt with under the term *dream work* is the manoeuvre with which psychism realizes this *Entstellung*, this distortion of the sense by which the wish is rendered unrecognizable to itself.

At the end of the chapter on the technique of *Witz*, Freud (1905c) has this to say:

> So far-reaching an agreement between the methods of the joke-work and those of the dream-work can scarcely be a matter of chance [*Eine so weitgehende Ubereinstimmung wie die zwischen den Mitteln der Witzarbeit und dessen der Traumarbeit wird kaum eine zufällige sein können*]. [p. 89]

We might wonder why, whilst tracing the *Traumarbeit* is an integral and often important part of the analytic work, something similar cannot even distantly be said of *Witzarbeit*. We could put forward the justification that the *witzig* material brought by the patients is incomparably rarer (or even absent) as regards oneiric material. However, at least two kinds of objection may be made to this consideration: the first is that the analyst's (real or supposed) expectations are in any case experienced by the patient as far as dream, but not *Witz*, is concerned; the second is that, whilst the analyst's attention is ready to grasp the oneiric aspects of the patient's experiences and communications (as long as, for example, we speak of the sessions as a dream, the space of a dream, etc. even when no dream in a true sense exists), the same thing cannot be said of the *witzig* aspects of the patient's (verbal and extraverbal) behaviour. Moreover, also in the sphere of countertransference, the analyst is particularly attentive to his dreams in the true sense and also to his "dreams" during the session as part of the analytic relationship, whereas his sensibility to his own ironic visions (see Schafer, 1976) or movements in the analytic process are probably not so much part of his free-floating attention as a cue for tracing his own witty or ironic work and the related countertransferential implications.

By analogy with oneiric work, also ironic work (like the work of *Witz*) may be seen as something that, based as it is on the consideration of verbalizability and not, as with dreams, on the consideration of representability—*Rücksicht auf Darstellbarkeit* (Freud, 1900a)—reaches an acceptable verbal (rather than prevalently figurative) form.

The condition of verbalizability (at least for verbal irony) involves some differences from the conditions of representability. We may say that representability even limits the possibilities of representation of an ironic theme. Indeed, whilst in linguistic terms irony is in principle *in absentia*, [according to Kerbrat-Orecchioni (1977, p. 139), like allusion, "irony does not exist but *in absentia*: under the risk of losing all its salt, the signifier corresponding to its intentional signified must remain implicit"] it seems that the image makes of irony rather a figure *in praesentia*. As Dubois and collaborators (Groupe μ, 1976, p. 430) note, this holds only for the process of reading the ironic message: the co-presence of contradictory elements does not in fact exist for the decodifier of the image. And it is in the reading of the image as a whole that the (ironic) connection of the antinomic poles takes place. In a study entitled "Ironique et iconique", the authors of the above-mentioned group highlight how the ironic ethos basically intervenes at the level of the communication between the enunciator of the design and the reader of the image and not at the level of the character or characters represented (Groupe μ, 1976, p. 435).

"It [irony] is not carried out in the act of discourse. Because it is only the position of the enunciation that allows the *simultaneous* grasping of the two antonimic significances. It is here that the famous 'ambiguity', the celebrated 'balance' defining the figure are realized" (p. 435). We thus have confirmation of what Kerbrat-Orecchioni (1976, p. 15) stresses: that is, that irony is made to be perceived but in an increasingly doubtful way; it should make use of certain indices, which, however, remain only presumptive and always uncertain.

From all this it appears that we may approximately see in verbal irony—or, rather, in some of its forms—a finished product that is analogous to the manifest aspect of the dream, and we may suggest that through ironic work, inner censure is "played". Furthermore, as irony is social, like *Witz* (Freud) [unlike dream, which is asocial (Freud)], it is possible that censure of the other (in its common or analytical meaning) is also "played". To my knowledge, Muecke is the only (non-analytical) author who, inspired by Freud's work, has tried to outline the rhetoric and the hermeneutics of *verbal irony* by speaking of "ironic work" and using this expression in analogy with "dream work". Three types of operations are involved: the first establishes the degree of likelihood that can be attributed to the literal meaning, the second transforms the intention into literal meaning, and the third supplies any signals that indicate the presence of irony. To clarify briefly how and where Muecke (1978, pp. 491–493) classifies ironic work, two of his diagrams are reproduced in Figure 2.

Figure 2, Diagram A, shows the analogy of (Muecke's) concept of "ironic work" with the Freudian concept of "dream work", and Diagram B shows a similarity of "ironic work" to analytic work. Moreover, Diagram B refers (mainly) to the *situational*

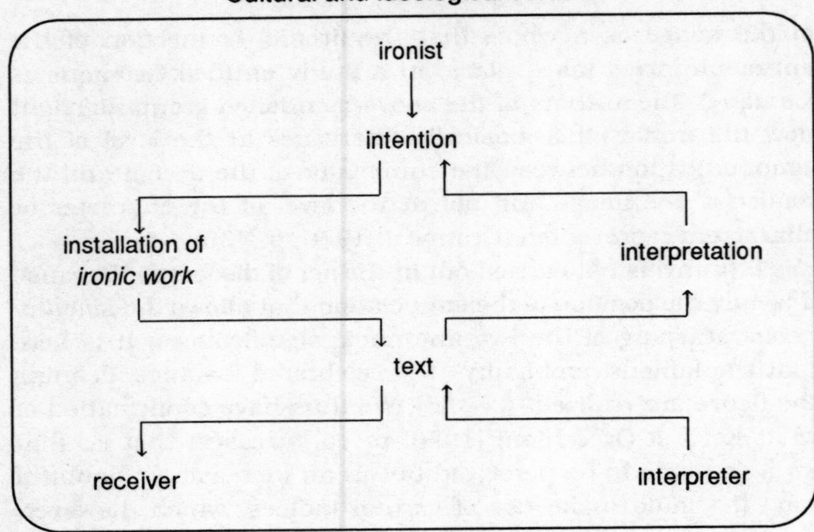

DIAGRAM A

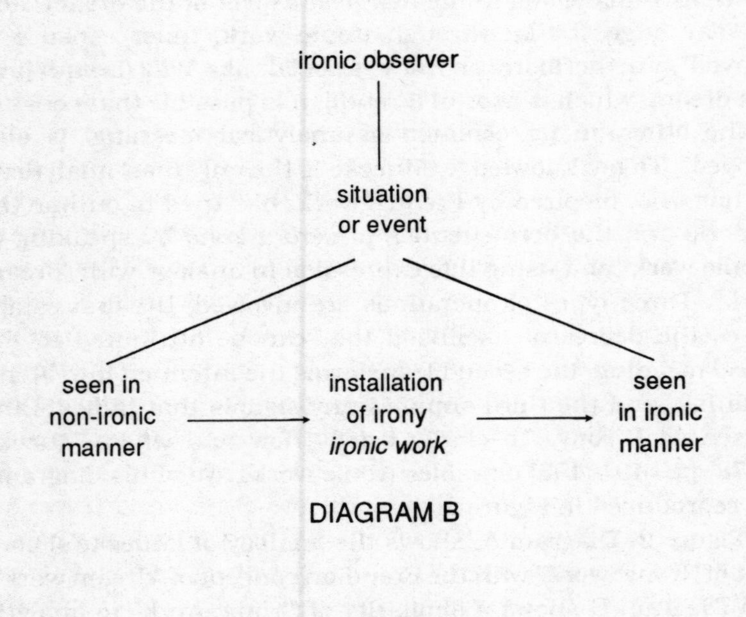

DIAGRAM B

FIGURE 2

irony that Muecke—unlike, for example, Knox—tends to keep separate from verbal irony. In the simplest case, there is someone who has a sufficient sense of irony (the ironic observer) and who realizes that a certain situation or a certain event could be perceived in a different light. In this case, the "ironic work" would not be coding a text, but the setting up of a new illumination that transforms the non-ironic comprehension into ironic comprehension. The question that arises immediately is: at what point can the nature of the "ironic work" be specified?

However, Meucke (1978) goes no further than hoping for a classification of the

> operations of "ironic work". But even here there is a problem, for the different ways of describing the same operation may easily give the wrong impression that several operations exist. [pp. 493–494]

I would say that this same problem exists also in psychoanalysis, but it may be better clarified and, ideally, split into two orders of phenomena: one is the phenomenon described by Muecke, which takes place periodically when the thirst for originality leads analysts who, although experienced, have the character of smugglers rather than of conquerors, to mistake what is more properly a different way of describing, for example, the same operation described by Freud (which may also have its importance) for (the "discovery" of) new psychic operations. The other order of problem—which is not, however, insuperable, and which indeed may indicate a path to follow—is the fact that for one operation there may be (and, indeed, there usually are) unconscious equivalents, and precisely on this basis they may be, on the one hand, co-determinant and, on the other, over-determined. This is undoubtably a complication that must be reckoned with *a priori*. Perhaps two examples given by Muecke (1978, p. 494) may illustrate the two orders of difficulty I have tried to explain. On the other hand, even he expresses himself differently as regards the two following pairs, saying that "keeping a distance" and "setting aside" (Pair A) may "simply be *two ways of saying the same thing*", whilst "placing a situation in a new context" and "juxtaposing oppositions" (Pair B) "*may cover the same operation*" [my italics]. The two terms in this second pair seem to me, however, to be linked in a manner that is intricate rather than a simple "covering". It is therefore probably no matter of chance that the considerations referred to above come just before the conclusion to Muecke's complex article (1978, p. 494), in which he hypothesizes that the fact that irony has been subject to a much smaller theoretical analysis than metaphor may be because

> Aristotle dealt very little with verbal irony and dealt not much more with those "intrigues" (situational irony) in which "fortuitous facts appear to have been taken from a drawing—when for example the statue of Mitys at Argus kills the man who has caused the death of Mitys, by falling on him during a public spectacle".

This extract is reminiscent of certain patients with strong character defences especially with regard to aggressiveness, who, when their defences crumble, commit a series of behavioural *lapsus* (both within the relationship and outside it), of hetero- and self-inflicted wounding acts (quite differently from the patients mentioned previously)—acts that in extreme defence they tend to consider chance facts that do not follow any intrapsychic pattern. When they see an "irony of fate", these patients are not in fact as far as one might think from being able to take the step by which the events, instead of the "appearance" of having been guided by an external pattern, become, in their eyes, the "reality" of having basically been guided by an inner pattern. On this basis, I believe that the distinction between verbal and situational irony weakens according to the relations that take place between inner and outer reality and the co-determination of the latter by the former.

The analytical relationship as eirōneía

The considerations set out above could induce us to consider the analytical relationship—seen longitudinally in the characteristics according to which the analysand/analyst relationship forms, progresses, and resolves—as being "ironic" in two senses. On the one hand, the analytic situation may be seen, as regards the evolution of the most common interpersonal relations, as a kind of representation through the opposite, insofar as what is initially emphasized is the "appearance" of the analyst in the world of the analysand, whilst the "being" is highlighted with analysis and the resolution of transference, which signals the end of the relation. On the other hand, the progression of the analytical relationship from appearance towards reality brings us close to the way irony proceeds which—according to Knox (1973)—may be defined as the conflict of two meanings that possess a specific dramatic structure, especially a significance, an appearance, presenting itself as truth of evidence. But when the context of this significance develops, in depth or over time, it reveals, to the reader's surprise, an unexpected conflictual meaning, reality, by the measure of which the first meaning now appears false and limited and, in its very sureness, blinded by its situation. [The analogy between analysis and reading (a text) may be even more fitting if we see the analysand as being simultaneously (or alternatively) the author and the reader, and the analyst as he who, on the one hand—almost a muse *sui generis*—(co)determines a situation favourable to the production of a certain "text" and, on the other, referring widely to the context ("*hic et nunc*") of which he himself is an integral part, guides the "reader" towards grasping the "reality" underlying the "appearance" of the text. Often the two meanings are conflictual (even opposite), and the "real" one is experienced as surprising by the patient–reader, who has difficulty in identifying with the patient–author.]

Let us compare this with what Rapaport (1944) says regarding the "true interpersonal relationship" [the "true" relationship must often move through a phase in which it is experienced as "feigned" or deceiving (see chapter two)]:

> When I use the phrase interpersonal relationship I will mean the relationship between the analyst and the analysand. About the other procedures which seem to be interpersonal relationships, I will endeavour to show that they are "pseudo interpersonal relationships" in this specific sense of the phrase, because they do not carry the interper-

> sonal relationship to its last consequences as psychoanalysis does. [p. 196]

And further on:

> One cannot talk to another person without reservations, one cannot build a "conversation"—in the specific meaning of the word—if one is not sure that the other person will accept one in spite of all that an unrestrained and sincere exchange would lead to. . . . Let us suppose that a person is proud. When you have a conversation with that person, at what moment will he be ready to discuss matters which may cut into his pride? Only when he knows that he has at least as good a defense in you of what he defends with his pride as he has in himself. [p. 201]

In his studies on the scientific methodology of psychoanalysis from which this passage is taken, Rapaport tends to throw a bridge (at the same time stressing the differences), between the psychoanalytical situation and that of a conversation *tout court* in the specific meaning of the word as far as the methodological aspect is concerned, and, between unconscious and conscious, between the primary and the secondary process as far as the metapsychological aspect is concerned (see also Sacerdoti, 1977a).

As regards the first point, Rapaport (1944) himself notes:

> The importance of "appearing and existing in the world of the other" is quite different in everyday life and in the psychoanalytic situation. In everyday life we operate as if we were in a world that is objectively existing and common to us. But the more consistently the "method of interpersonal relationship" is carried to its last consequences, the more the private world of the individual becomes accepted, and the further away we get from the significance of the objectively existing world. [p. 295n]

The psychoanalytic fiction (*eirōneía*), partially declaring itself as such at the beginning, may be seen longitudinally as the reverse of many situations of everyday life (see chapter one). Indeed, in everyday life we work as if we were in a world that is objectively existing and common to all of us, at least until the "as if" becomes "too" conscious, the moment that may signal the end of the relationship.

It must be recalled that the ironist's fiction is merely the first of two stages, the one in which one is placed before the appearance. In the second stage it is, instead, reality that emerges and draws its incisiveness from what precedes it—that is, from the first stage.

In this sense, the analysis, if it is considered a process that mainly rotates around the "anonymity" of the analyst, could be seen as *eirōneía* in its double meaning of fiction and irony.

Perhaps precisely because it stands at the intersection between fiction and reality and because it affects the analyst's attitude, his elasticity or his rigidity, and, above all, his timing, not only in the usual sense but also in the sense of an evolution with particular regard for the measure of appearance and existing, the question of the analyst's anonymity is one of the least clarified conceptually, one of the most equivocal, and one of those in which the discrepancies are most defensively attributed to the differences in technique or the theories of technique of the different schools. Furthermore, starting from Freud, the analyst's behaviour in widely reported clinical examples is often quite different from the picture we might draw from the same analyst's theoretical notes.

For what interests us here, I shall briefly examine certain points. One of these (about which almost no-one has spoken, perhaps because it is so obvious—but, as we know, obvious things often risk being "forgotten" in favour of more sophisticated things, which is not always in favour of the good progress of the analysis) is the fact that the "anonymity", the "benevolent neutrality", of the analyst is often used by patients to "justify" their difficulty in associating "freely" or even their excessive caution in "letting themselves go", or their embarrassment or "anger" about the "asymmetrical" aspect of the analytical relationship.

One of the few authors who has examined what I believe is a central aspect of this question is Singer (1977, p. 187 ff). He notes that a patient's "ignorance" about the analyst, unless it is an unconscious loophole, counterfeiting or psychopathic imposture, or a pretext used for manipulating purposes, reflects precisely what is wrong in him, it describes precisely the nucleus of every psychopathology. But the possibility the patient might arrive at an insight of this kind is conditioned—we might say—by his "taking to extremes", encouraged by the analyst's "anonymity", his psychopathologic tendency to abandon a birth right and a fundamentally given human capacity, to use Singer's words. In other words, to hear what can be heard, to see what can be seen, and to grasp what can be grasped (cf. *stupidité névrotique*).

This "taking to extremes" mentioned above seems to be part of the "carrying the interpersonal relationship to its last consequences" that Rapaport (1944) classifies as being characteristic of the psychoanalytic relationship. It is part of it, as the first phase, as fiction, like the other side of the coin, which is made up, on the other hand, of the analyst's reliability, of his total availability and trustworthiness within the contract.

To trustworthiness, in the sense in which Rapaport uses the word, must be added the reverse of "anonymity", which takes shape as the analysis progresses. The analyst's "anonymity", therefore, in addition to activating the transference dynamics, stimulates the patient to grasp, through experience and/or inference, the aspects of the analyst's character (besides those of his own). The situation in this regard is asymmetrical mainly quantitatively; qualitatively also the patient has at his disposal important information regarding the analyst: in order for him to use it, he must be "brave" enough. In fact, knowing the other deeply requires a penetrating comparison with self: the knowledge of the other moves through the knowledge of self. This is what the patient learns from the analyst, so long as he is not entrenched behind the exclusive interpretation of the transference. It is no chance matter that the entrenched position leads (irony of fate!) to often practically interminable analyses and is sometimes supported by conceptualizations in which primitive narcissistic indulgences abound, almost as if, held out the window of the analytical situation, they come back in through the door of the theoretical–clinical work. It is small wonder that Freud's style in "Dora", the "Rat Man", and the "Wolf Man" may be seen as the style of an analyst who is too easily "acting in".

Freud was certainly never an "anonymous" analyst. On the other hand, with his incisiveness and his ironic capacity, he must also have understood that the very effort to be anonymous is the most self-revealing. Here we return to a pair of opposites (anonymity/self-revelation) and therefore to the irony of the situation, of the relationship, and of the analytic process.

To sum up, we might say that the analyst's "anonymity", which mainly concerns his outer reality, is part of the analytic "fiction". As far as the analyst's inner reality is concerned, in the history of psychoanalysis it has moved almost from one extreme to the other: from "benevolent neutrality" and from countertransference seen as a disturbing factor, to maximum utilization of the latter, but, also to the analyst's availability to be the object of the patient's "projective identification". This last orientation, if pushed to excess (caricatured, we might say), especially when it limits or slows down the awareness of what is happening in the relationship, may, paradoxically, along another path, bring about the analyst's "anonymity", to the extent that he allows himself to be invaded and/or manipulated by the patient precisely in virtue of the aptitudes and the attitudes that should best qualify him. This case could be seen to contain situational irony, but obviously only by those who have the capacity for ironic vision.

The awareness of these aspects is not so far from—or is in any case connected to—what Schafer (1976, pp. 50 ff) indicates as the ironic component of the psychoanalytic vision of reality. He stresses (p. 56) that the life story that emerges from the analysis must be seen as a joint creation of the patient and the analyst and not an invention of the imagination or something that is simply factual. Indeed, the story depends to a certain degree on the limitations, the individuality, and the vision of the two participants and therefore—we might add—on the peculiarity of the analytical relationship, which, in turn, depends to a certain degree on the story actually experienced by the patient (and to a lesser extent the analyst). Schafer directs our attention to certain evaluative implications of the psychoanalytic vision, especially those concerning the "love of truth". In this regard the analytic standard of objectiveness appeals to the tragic and ironic visions of reality. The ironic vision, which is principally characterized as the readiness to search for inner contradictions, ambiguities, and paradoxes, might seem—as Schafer (1976, p. 51) notes—to be in the service of the withdrawal of experience and the disavowal of its significance, of the not taking anything seriously (in this way it can be used as a kind of resistance in psychoanalysis). Nevertheless, it is essentially a serious matter. The ironic and the tragic visions are similar in the relative emphasis they place on reflective thought and on the inner articulation of emotion. When it is not "resistant in intention", the ironic vision facilitates, according to Schafer (p. 53), the exploration of the analysis. It permits the patient better to enter the regressive process and especially transference, through the assurance that the experiences he meets, although they are not unreal nor of little importance, are part of a program of research and treatment; that they include a component of "as if" as well as a "true" quality, and that they are not a total, absolute nor overwhelmingly new reality. Schafer notes that psychotic patients undergoing treatment cannot use ironic capacities. As far as the analyst is concerned, "his capacity for irony makes it more possible to appreciate that, on the average, the crises, retreats, and advances to be dealt with are great and not so great at the same time" (p. 53). In Schafer's opinion, Freud expressed an ironic vision, for example when he says that psychoanalysis shows how individuals are more moral and also more immoral than they think.

Finally, whether or not the ironic tone is used, the ironic vision is essential for the psychoanalytic interpretation. Schafer's observations basically place the general problem of the ironic vision in psychoanalysis next to tragic vision, giving these visions a preeminent position with regard to comic and romantic vision. As for the relationships between tragic and ironic vision, Schafer notes that ironic vision tempers tragic vision by becoming integrated with it. We might add that this happens also, and especially, thanks to the surprising aspect of irony (we already know how tragedy ends!). Putting forward the relationship and the analytic process once more as *eirōneia*, this allows us to place the surprising aspect of irony next to that of the analysis. In both we may say that things evolve differently from the way they are expected to. A new awareness is created: in the case of irony, through a leap, a discontinuity with regard to what was known—whilst, in the case of metaphor, this happens through the creation of connections, of an unsuspected continuity (see Sacerdoti, 1986a, pp. 196, 200). Also in psychoanalysis, as in general, the attention given to irony has been much less than that given to metaphor. And yet it is also along the path of "ironic surprise" that the patient may reacquire the pleasure of moving off the tracks of repetitiveness and that the analyst may find an ever-renewed interest in his work.

Ironic considerations on the position of metapsychology

In the "impossible profession"—that is, psychoanalysis—the need to be able to stay on the razor's edge, oscillating between the positions of work and play and integrating them, is central not only, as is obvious, in the practical field, but also in that of clinical theory and metapsychology. For the sake of clarity, I would like to specify that I believe the term "clinical theory" to be understood in the sense Rapaport (1969, p. 8) uses it as "special theory", which is different from—in continuity with—the "general" theory of psychoanalysis. The use of the notion of *Gegensatzpaare* [pairs of opposites], of *Polarität* [polarities] etc.—which is found both at the clinical level and in theorization—offers one of the most meaningful examples of continuity, which Freud aimed for, amongst the "descriptive" aspects, their conceptualization ("clinical theory") and metapsychological theorization

That being said, we shall now examine a passage from "Analysis Terminable and Interminable" (Freud, 1937c) to exemplify how it is possible to grasp, in the manner that Freud had of proceeding in theorization (starting always from the clinical experience), a vision and even a development of thought closely tracing what we have seen is typical of ironic procedure and, more precisely, of (self-directed) "stable" irony.

Freud (1937c) asks himself:

> Is it possible by means of analytic therapy to dispose of a conflict between an instinct and the ego, or of a pathogenic instinctual demand upon the ego, permanently and definitively?

And he explains:

> To avoid misunderstanding it is not unnecessary, perhaps, to explain more exactly *what is meant* by "*permanently disposing* of an instinctual demand". *Certainly not* "causing the demand to *disappear* so that nothing more is ever heard from it again". This is in general impossible, nor is it at all to be desired. *No, we mean something else*, something which may be *roughly* as "*taming*" *of the instinct*. That is to say, the instinct is brought completely into the harmony of the ego, becomes accessible to all the influences of the other trends in the ego and no longer seeks to go its independent ways of satisfaction. If we are asked by what methods and means this result is achieved, *it is not easy to find an answer*. We can only say: "So muss denn doch die Hexe dran! the *Witch Metapsychology*". Without *metapsychological* speculation and *theorizing*—I had almost said *phantasying*—we shall not get another step forward. Unfortunately, here as elsewhere, *what our Witch reveals* is *neither very clear nor very detailed.* We have only a single *clue to start from—though* it is a clue *of the highest value*—namely, the *antithesis between the primary and secondary process*. [1937c, pp. 224–225, italics added]

The object of the irony is first one of Freud's hypotheses, together with one of his expressions about the nature of the economic–structural objective that can be reached with analysis (the "permanent disposing of an instinctual demand"). In fact, Freud warns the reader, and even a part of himself, not to let himself be deceived by "*appearance*"—certainly not disappearance: we mean something else.

Given the field of research, "reality", or at least all the reality of things, is evidently not the other side of appearance. On the other hand, this does not induce Freud to take the path of "unstable infinite" irony; rather, it makes him go, step by step, along the path—we might say—of stable irony. The first step is that the real object may be roughly defined: it is a taming of the instinct, and this has its significance. What remains to be explored are the path and the means by which this takes place. This is by no means easy, but here, too, Freud evades both the Scylla of the all-inclusive reply and the Charybdis of the nihilistic position, by being careful, as an experienced stable ironist (Booth, 1974), "where to stop". He is not afraid of invoking the "Witch Metapsychology", of using fantasy in theorization, in short of coupling an availability, a fantastic "artistic" attitude—which is why he uses a quotation from Goethe—with scientific research. [This coupling was considered scandalous in his time, and continues to be so to a certain degree, even today, and even amongst some analysts.] And he contents himself with stopping at a point of reference made up of a *pair of contrasts* (primary and secondary process) "of the highest value".

In this context, his ironization (always in the sense of stable irony) concerning clinical and historical limits and a certain conception of the scientific nature (serious, working aspect) of psychoanalysis seems, in general, to be evident. This scientific nature cannot be separated from his capacity and willingness to move from the serious to the playful register as a moment of invention and also of expectation, aware of the possibility of describing further, of setting, of representing, of expressing in the language of the conscious mind other unconscious instinctual dynamics (operating in analysis) and in the meantime supporting the uncertainty (see Beres, 1980).

This does not seem to have been fully understood—or at least insufficiently worked through—by many of the psychoanalysts who have examined this article by Freud.

As we are dealing here with self-directed irony—which concerns a common objective (scientific ideal) of the group—the difficulty in grasping its signals may be linked to the yielding to a kind of narcissistic indulgence that does not seem extraneous to certain radical criticisms concerning this text by Freud.

It suffices here to quote from a detailed study by Gill (1976):

> It is noteworthy how often Freud refers to metapsychology as "speculation"; the most oft-quoted example of this is in the references to the "witch metapsychology". . . . I suggest that Freud so often referred to metapsychology as speculative, and seemed so much more ready to abandon or change it than most psychoanalysts, because it does not include his purely psychological hypotheses, but does include the propositions which, despite his disavowals, are based on neurological and biological assumptions. [pp. 82–83]

Gill seems totally unaware of the metaphoric aspect of these assumptions, even though he also quotes the following extract from Freud (1925d [1924]) as an example:

> The subdivision of the unconscious is part of an attempt to picture the apparatus of the mind as being built up of a number of *agencies* or *systems* whose relations to one another are expressed in spatial terms without, however, implying any connection with the actual anatomy of the brain (I have described this as the *topographical* method of approach). Such ideas as these are part of a speculative superstructure of psycho-analysis, any portion of which can be abandoned or changed without loss or regret the moment its inadequacy has been proved. [pp. 32–33]

Quite unlike Gill's proposition is the position, for example, of Brenner (1980) who, with regard to the above-quoted extract from "Analysis Terminable and Interminable", by no means emphasizes the scandal or the contradiction of giving an important position to metapsychology and considering it at the same time equal to fantasizing.

What, according to Gill and others, would be a deplorable ambiguity on the part of Freud—that is, continuing to use a language suitable for biology—is only part of the free use of hypothetical constructs borrowed from various different sources, with "neutral" significance, without reference to any final form of "reality" or substance (see Madsen, 1969; Sacerdoti, 1974). If it is true that the psychoanalyst belongs to those psychologists who perceive such constructs as conventional or heuristic models, it is also true that the use of biological models also has the function of helping the researcher never to lose sight of the fact that he is dealing with an object whose structure is biological, even though, because of methodological choice and praxis, his field of research is a different one. To re-call (in the original meaning of the word) this "banal" reality may lie at the basis both of more general methods of schematization of its interactions, as in the theory of the "complemental series" (Freud, 1916–1917, pp. 362, 364), and also of attempts to identify biological elements that in some way condition the progress of the analysis. But, above all, it may help the analyst to avoid emotional positions of omnipotence (and impotence).

Granoff (1975, p. 213) notes that when Freud expresses himself through the use of a language that is for him that of the biologist, it is the surest signal that he has the impression that at that point the analysis is clashing with what he is no longer able to mobilize.

But—Granoff (1975) asks—it is, more precisely, an example of what?

> Very precisely of the fact that the levers of transference may, on certain psychic dispositions, remain without effect. . . . In fact, we must wait until 1937 for Freud to discover . . . what until then he had ignored about bisexuality, about which he had already said so much. Even earlier Freud had placed bisexuality on the side he called constitutional. . . . Compared with the question in the most dramatic form it can be put to the analyst, i.e. the woman suffering from serious hysterical neurosis, Ferenczi yields, gives way. At what level? We have already begun to review it at the practical level: with humour, Freud brings the shift back to being a trifle [*vétille*]. At the theoretical level, there is material for splitting. [p. 216]
>
> "Analysis Terminable and Interminable" (Freud, 1937c) is one of those texts whose nature is eminently that of revealing to the analyst that, if he clashes [*bute*] there with something that is impossible for him, it is perhaps —without his knowledge—often because all his Freudian reference (or reverence) rested on a misunderstanding. And this text has the merit that, if after reading it we are able to say "we

weren't brought up like that", then we are able to realize that our upbringing, no matter how admirable, diverges from Freudism, not so much in the style that has generated the practice but in the fundamental relationship of doctrine. [pp. 222–224]

The "underlying bedrock" (which has as a corollary the possibility or the probability of interminable analysis) and, in short, bisexuality is, therefore, a *shibboleth* of psychoanalysis. Freud mentions as such the unconscious (1923b, p. 13) and the dream (1914d, p. 57; 1933a, p. 7).

It remains to ask ourselves why today the basic (doctrinal) divergences regarding the few *shibboleths* of psychoanalysis are taken much less seriously than in the past—and not on the basis of the capacities for humour shown by Freud at a practical level.

This said, let us return to the question of the pathogenic reinforcement of the external danger by the addition of the inner instinctual danger: the fear of a feminine attitude. Reconnecting himself to Freud, Granoff (1975) adds:

> It is in this sense that a strong bisexuality, introducing the representation of something unsuspectedly constitutional, is a precondition to the strengthening of neurosis. . . . Therefore, to the accusation of not having analysed negative transference, paternal hatred, Freud replied that, in order for this to be possible, it would be necessary for him to intervene in external reality. That to activate a theme (*ein Thema, ein Komplex*) he would be forced to adopt, in reality, a hostile attitude towards his analysand. And that on the side of something that the transference does not necessarily mobilize, for it is to be found under the dependence of the factors that support bisexuality, which he saw as the cause of their discordance. [p. 225]

I believe that the pessimistic label attached by various analysts to "Analysis Terminable and Interminable" reveals in them not only a *furor therapeuticus* and an aspiration to omnipotence, but also their incapacity to grasp Freud's spirit of theorization, which expresses the fantasy (and we might also say fantastic or even fantasmatic) aspect—here we could think of the bisexuality of the witch, in connection with the above-mentioned quotation from Granoff—starting, however, always from the clinical material: directly proportional convergent seriousness and playfulness

All this implies (see also Brenner, 1980) a good capacity for irony—which is evidently not available to all—as well as the capacity to tolerate consciously the contradiction, ambiguity and uncertainty that make up (Beres, 1980, p. 2) Keats' "Negative Capability" ("When a man is capable of being in uncertainties, mysteries, doubts, without any irritable reaching after fact and reason" [see Keats, 1935, p. 72]) and which are "characteristics already denoting the unconscious mind". They therefore denote (and this is what interests us most here) the conscious ego's capacity to tolerate these characteristics. In psychoanalysis, this capacity is particularly important precisely because of the further complication caused by the distinction between knowledge at the conscious level and knowledge at the unconscious level, which evidently increases the ambiguity of the term "knowledge". Nevertheless, this has led neither to scepticism nor to nihilism.

When it becomes obsessive, in psychological and metapsychological theorization, the pursuit of truth may follow various trends, that are, in theory, aimed at the greatest effectiveness. Now if effectiveness, or operationality, may become inversely proportional to psychological significance (Gibson & Isaac, 1978) and if it is realized at best through mathematical formulae, it follows that, through these formulae, ironically we may see psychological significance realized at its worst. I think this may be connected with (emotional) separation and therefore with the discontinuity between the symbolizer and the symbolized, between the abstract and the concrete, which is realized in the use of formulae and symbols resembling those in mathematics in psychoanalytic theorization.

Of the paths scientific claims may take, when dealing with conceptualization, we might here recall the use of unnecessary neologisms or words taken from dead languages—see, for example, the observations of Bettelheim (1982) and Ornston (1982) on the English translation of Freud—when dealing with the clinical use of affected or slang or scientific words, of abstract and general terms, and of stereotyped "formulae" and clichés (see also Sacerdoti, 1977a). This is common of obsessive or even only poorly educated patients. It is known that these patients often give us the impression of being not very lively, deathly boring, and, at the same time, not emotionally true—a little like the *Golem* (the creature of Rabbi Lõw of Prague) to whom the fall of the *alef* from the phrase on his forehead is fatal because it changes from "*emet*" [truth] to "*met*" [death].

This is the opposite, we might observe, of what happens with an analogous operation (the fall of an "a", this time at the end) to the Czech word *robota*, "drudgery", which thus changes from something abstract, and therefore inanimate, to something concrete: *robot*—Čapek's creature (Ripellino, 1973)—which is animate, even though in the form of a caricature. And it is characteristic of both these Prague "doubles" that they do more than is required of them, caricaturing themselves and caricaturing thus also their creators—in other words, the Omnipotent (omnipotence). This might refer to an excess work, with the risk that everything will be submerged, that it will occur when the "sorcerer's apprentice" forgets the formula without which what has magically been set in motion cannot be undone.

As analysts well know, it is through memory, the dissolution [*Aufhebung*] of repression, that the patient (and the analyst) may escape from the demon of repetitiveness. With oblivion we risk instead setting off in the opposite direction, that of the (omnipotent) fantasy of being able magically to undo the past [*ungeschehenmachen*]: therefore, nothing irreversible can happen. It may be of interest here to recall the denouncing of the illusory nature of this fantasy in the Cabbala (which is, as we have seen, full of ironic figures). According to it, the anagram is death, as if the image (double fruit) of the literal possibility of reversibility were, at the same time, the image of the irreversible event *par excellence*—death—which is precisely what is wished to be disavowed. *Nier le rien* is the (impossible) task that Jabès (1980), with the awareness of what has been expressed above, has undertaken. And along the thread of the impossible move the clinical work and the analyst's theoretical work (Freud, 1937c), as well as, obviously, their integration.

Following Beres (1980, p. 16) once more, we may observe that in psychoanalysis, as regards the integration of theory and practice, the question of certainty involves two different yet connected aspects—one the confirmation of the theoretical positions, the other the verification of the specific interpretations the analyst presents to the analysand. With regard to the second aspect, we must function at a level of "operative truth"—"pragmatic truth"—which is made possible by the "psychoanalytic situation" (Beres, 1980):

> The psychoanalyst and the analysand intercommunicate to achieve a degree of conviction that permits recognition of unconscious fantasies, that leads to renunciation of infantile wishes, and that integrates past and present, the irrational and the rational. These are considerable accomplishments. [p. 15]

These "accomplishments" do not always succeed. Here we could compare what Beres has described (successful analysis) to the procedure of "stable irony", whilst at least a certain kind of failure could be compared with Booth's "infinite irony". I recall an analysand who compared me to Socrates, seeing me as being seductive and unseduceable; he felt he was an orphan. He gave me a collection of poetry he had published under a pseudonym, which was full of irony, with the dedication "while the mirrors perhaps multiply". In all likelihood, his image of Socrates corresponded to that of the German Romanticists and Kierkegaard ("absolute infinite negativity", according to Booth). Whilst expressing an excellent opinion of the analyst and the analysis, this image had led him to a turning in his existence in a direction that he thought I, as an analyst, judged negatively. I must add that he was a patient I had been inclined to take particularly seriously right from the beginning.

We know that Freud generally took his patients very seriously, and this is the analyst's role. However, it cannot be excluded that sometimes this attitude may have a blocking effect similar to the one described by Erikson (1968) in the premature reply of adults who are overly worried ("fatal seriousness") about certain adolescent behaviour.

It is possible that in such cases the analyst is burdened, through a projective operation, with "serious" aspects by the patient, and that a complementary countertransference in Racker's (1968) sense of the word is established, which may render the therapeutic relationship difficult in one way or another (see Sacerdoti, 1979). For example, returning once again to the case in question, something of the kind might have been activated by the analysand also seeing the analyst as a kind of Socrates, the "absolute infinite negativity" of the Romantic Germans and Kierkegaard we find in Booth (1974, pp. 273–274).

Despite what they made of Socrates, we may find a platform on which Socrates, Phaedrus, Plato, and the reader may stand while meditating on the rich ironies of the dialogue. And this meditation may lead to hearing that Socrates believed in something so much that he gave his life for it: the value of the city and its laws, the value of conversation with its citizens, the value of truth itself, which is definitively inaccessible (see the Messianic idea).

We should recall here some of Kierkegaard's positions (1841, p. 348), which have been fixed so memorably in as many theses, attached to his dissertation on "The concept of irony with constant reference to Socrates".

The Thesis V reads:

> *Apologia Socratis, quam exhibuit Plato, aut spuria est, aut tota ironice explicanda*
>
> [Socrates' apology, as presented by Plato, is either spurious, or else to be explained wholly ironically]

And if (Thesis VIII)

> *Ironia, ut infinita et absoluta negativitas, est levissima et maxime exigua subjectivitatis significatio*
>
> [Irony as infinite and absolute negativity is the lightest and weakest intimation of subjectivity]

Thesis XV states:

> *Ut a dubitatione philosophia sic ab ironia vita digna, quae humana vocetur, incipit*
>
> [As philosophy begins with doubt, so also that life which may be called worthy of man begins with irony]

Let us also examine another of Kierkegaard's (1843) ideas—that this intense desperate remembering is the eternal manifestation of dawning love; it is the sign of true love. Nevertheless, the elasticity of irony is necessary to be able to make use of it; he whose soul is too tender for irony lacks this elasticity.

We might think that, unlike Freud, Kierkegaard, that great ironologist, was a mediocre ironist who came close to what he says of Socrates in Thesis VI:

> *Socrates non solum ironia usus est, sed adeo fuit ironiae deditus, ut ipse illi succumberet*
>
> [Socrates did not merely use irony, but was also so completely dedicated to irony that he himself succumbed to it]

In any case, Kierkegaard cannot perhaps be so closely compared to the German Romanticists as Booth would like. In Booth's (1974) opinion, Plato believes that it is possible to master Socrates' irony by fighting through it until a comprehensive ironic vision which will encompass all disavowals is reached (p. 274). The common image of Socrates in the sense of the Romantic Germans is evidently part of a (more) general destiny of irony, which could be represented in the difficulties of moving through the Pillars of Hercules without getting lost, and which could be close, in psychoanalytic terms, to the difficulty or the dangers of the insight and the regression this may involve (which does not always remain at the service of the ego).

The "negative destiny" of such operations, and therefore also of the concept of irony, could correspond to a kind of deterrent for which the alternative would be renunciation or perdition. Both these positions, however, empty the human adventure in general, the scientific adventure in particular, and the psychoanalytical adventure even more specifically. Booth (1974, p. 274) notes that the natural sciences, for example, could be called infinitely ironical because every honest scientist knows that his formulations will certainly be reviewed by the scientists who follow. Goethe (quoted by Muecke, 1969), claimed that a good scientist must have a good sense of irony. On the other hand, Muecke (1969) stresses the limits the irony of science must have:

> For although the dialectics of science accepts the possibility of contradiction, its eye is fixed more firmly on that other possibility, the possibility of reunification. It continually looks beyond the possible antithesis to the possible synthesis; its ideals are simplicity and unity. Irony on the other hand needs, and looks for, contradictions and duality. [p. 129]

For psychoanalysis in particular, the contradictions and dualities are even part of the observation material, certainly in relation to its double position (Rapaport, 1944, p. 189) in the nomothetic sciences and in the ideographic sciences

This matches what Eugenio D'Ors (quoted in Muecke, 1969, p. 129) states: "Science is irony: science is in a sense aesthetic like art. At every point of its progress, science accepts implicitly, notes in its own margin, the possibility of contradiction, the progress to come." And for progress to come, it is necessary to be able to make free use of fantasy.

This concept (which might correspond to the analyst's everyday clinical work) may help us to understand, on the one hand, why Freud turned to the "Witch Metapsychology" and, on the other, how this operation has been and still remains the object of misunderstanding by means of which certain criticisms seem to contain (or seem to imply) a previous operation that could be defined as a kind of unconscious caricaturing of the object of the criticism—caricaturing that has its pendant in the incapacity for ironic vision.

Summary

In this chapter we have sought the presence—and the absence—of ironic aspects more specifically in psychoanalytic theorization. For this purpose, at the conceptual level we have turned our attention from the clinical examples and discussion to the interlacing of work and play aspects. Considering this pair once again, from the theoretical point of view, we have dwelt on their reconcilability rather than on their opposition, on the complementary nature of the two aspects (which should not be confused with the concepts of pseudo-play and pseudo-work) that may be grasped in the "stable" irony that also involves a certain kind of self-directed irony. These considerations have been developed on the basis of the acknowledgement of preconscious and unconscious levels in irony and therefore of latent irony—an acknowledgement that derives, above all, from the examination of the clinical material presented in chapter two. This also offers us the opportunity—developing a scheme by Muecke (1978)—to consider, following on from the "work of *Witz*" (1905c) Freud speaks of, the existence of "ironic work". This leads us to consider the ironic perspective, both in the sphere of conceptualization of the analytic situation and process, and in the sphere of the debate on the birth, evolution, and position of metapsychology.

As regards the first point, we may schematically consider the analytical situation—seen longitudinally in the characteristics according to which the analysand/analyst relationship is formed, progresses, and is resolved—as being "ironic", in two senses. On the one hand, the analytical situation may be seen, as regards the evolution of common interpersonal relations, as a kind of representation through its opposite, insofar as initially it is the analyst's "appearance" in the world of the analysand that is most important, whilst the "existing" comes to the forefront with the analysis and the resolution of the transference, which signals the end of the analysis. On the other hand, the progression of the analytical relationship from appearance towards reality resembles the way irony proceeds, which may be defined (Knox, 1973) as the conflict between two significances with a dramatic structure that is specific to them.

As regards the debate on metapsychology, we may consider that it derives, in part, from a kind of seriousness in some analysts, from an avoidance of the danger of letting themselves go in certain sectors to a free(er) use of fantasy, of ("stable") ironic and self-directed ironic play. Self-directed ironic play may oppose narcissistic indulgences—without falling (back), into nihilism and masochism, as is the case with "unstable" irony.

Freud's reception to a similar vision and behaviour has already been prospected here with regard to his method of proceeding in analytic conceptualization. The consideration of ironic aspects in metapsychology, which could be heard as an iconoclastic act, therefore seems to fall within the spirit of the founder of psychoanalysis.

In chapter four, we shall see Freud as an ironist in different circumstances, where his contribution is more notable than what we may see *en passant* as an ironologist. In particular, in addition to his manifestly ironic expressions, he clearly concentrates also on the latent and preconscious aspects regarding both the emission and the reception of irony and self-directed irony. Self-directed irony seems to have an anything but negligible importance for Freud, and this is also the case in the construction of the conceptual edifice of psychoanalysis. Freud was very open to the unexpected and the surprising in this construction, as for the "constructions" in any analysis.

The surprising aspects of irony and of the analysis are compared. To be able to count on things that evolve differently from what is expected seems to be necessary to both protagonists of the analytical relationship—to the patient so that, in and through the analysis, he may (re)gain the pleasure of leaving the tracks of repetitiveness, and to the analyst so that his interest in his work with the patients will not diminish with the accumulation of experience. Furthermore, with his work of conceptualization, the analyst contributes to unexpected developments of theory, proving wrong certain scientific criticism that, from the outside, denies the possibility of development based on an alleged intrinsic unverifiability–unfalsifiability of psychoanalytic hypotheses.

CHAPTER FOUR

Stable irony and genitality: an historical perspective

A Jewish theme in Freud's day

I have critically discussed the restrictive Freudian definition of irony and attributed to it, instead—as also for *Witz*—unconscious levels or mechanisms of production and reception. In this final chapter, which also examines historical aspects, I shall quote references, particularly literary ones, that may not specifically concern irony, but can be extended to cover it, following the broader definition we have already given.

The question of why Freud returned to his work on *Witz* only in his 1927 essay on humour (in which he applies structural theory) and why he never up-dated it, as was his habit, especially with the writings that had a certain organic unity, has never been answered satisfactorily. In addition to being evidently of cultural interest, this question is also important because Freud never took the step to a greater theoretical, clinical, and even technical use of many of the elements his work contained, which would have lent themselves to this kind of application, as we have attempted to demonstrate here merely for irony (one of the least specific arguments developed by Freud on the basis of a restrictive definition of it).

One contributing factor for the limited use of irony in the historical development of psychoanalysis might be due to the particular nature of the material that made Freud's study on *Witz* possible. Basing his comment on personal research, Musatti (1982) comments:

> . . . the Jewish joke, on which Freud built his theory for this kind of production, seemed to me to be virtually unique, and could only with difficulty be repeated in different literatures and cultures. . . . Obviously this does not signify that there are no other kinds of jokes, but only that Freud was able to write his book on Witz referring solely to his own environment of origin and demonstrating in the most open fashion that he belonged to a Jewish background. [pp. 124–125]

Freud, on the other hand, was concerned for a long time that psychoanalysis would remain "a Jewish matter", with all the disadvantages and limitations this would entail. And even though he had chosen for himself the way of Hannibal, the Phoenician commander assimilated for the occasion into Jewishness, for his creature, psychoanalysis, he had chosen right from the start the path that in his old age, and probably driven by the swift turn of political events, he was to follow in his own fantasy: that of the Jewish leader, Moses, assimilated for the occasion to an Egyptian.

We might, therefore, say that, whilst his work on Witz is probably the greatest affirmation of the Jewish roots of psychoanalysis, *Moses and Monotheism* (1939a [1937–39]) is the rejection of the idea that the tree bearing the psychoanalytical fruit has (only) Jewish roots.

Wanting to accept the interpretation of Freud's last book as his true testament, Marthe Robert (1974) expresses the theory that

> when the moment came to leave the stage where he had so bravely played his role, he could say that he was no longer

> Jewish, nor German, nor anything that still had a name: he does not want to be the child of any person or place, but the child of his works and of his work that, like the assassinated prophet, leaves generations perplexed before the mystery of his identity. [p. 278]

This thesis seems to me to be a somewhat extreme interpretation, in a narcissistic key, and, in any case, too all-inclusive a hypothesis to be anything more than just that. However, in all probability it pinpoints one of Freud's basic preoccupations, which had their root in the general and personal historical circumstances and which (now) basically concern—as mentioned earlier—his creature (psychoanalysis) and also, obviously, those who were to be responsible for its future development.

It is no chance matter that, from this point of view, *Witz* and *Der Mann Moses* stand in mutual contrast; and, furthermore, in the latter we can see a kind of unconscious irony, but not so much and not only of the kind mentioned by Robert (which may be more or less linked to "unstable" irony), but rather of the kind activated by Koestler (1976) in *The Thirteenth Tribe* or by Freud himself in a piece that obviously has quite different limits, but with somewhat similar circumstances, which imposed on him a protective operation—an operation he conducted with such subtle irony that it was missed by Jones, a fact that is probably not unimportant in the distortion of the episode (Weiss, pp. 42–43) that Jones himself effected (1957, pp. 180–181). It is the dedication of *Why War?* (Freud, 1933b [1932]) to Benito Mussolini ("from an old man who greets in the ruler the hero of culture" [*mit dem ergebenen Gruss eines alten Mannes der im Machthaber den Kultur Hero erkennt. Wien, 26 April 1933*] added by Freud in 1933, on the occasion of a consultation about one of Weiss' patients, the daughter of a close friend of Mussolini. The patient's father asked Freud to present Mussolini with a book with a dedication. Weiss was extremely embarrassed because he knew that Freud could not refuse. For his sake and for the sake of the Italian Society of Psychoanalysts, Freud was forced to agree.

Freud as ironist

Even on the basis of these considerations, I still do not believe in separating the most strictly personal moments from Freud's work—nor, in his work, separating the clinical from the theoretical, even though—or perhaps precisely because—my exposition is aimed at clarifying aspects that are generally neglected when considering the latter. In this brief *excursus* of Freud's ironic expressions, I will follow an order going roughly from the most manifest to those that are least (or not completely) so—in other words, those in which the unconscious and/or the preconscious may be involved. These are the levels that interest us perhaps most here, as we intend to examine again, from a different angle, how and to what degree the capacity for ironic vision has contributed to the creation and evolution of the psychoanalytic conceptual edifice (apart from the invention of the setting and the analytic situation), and therefore also possibly to what degree certain misunderstandings, criticisms, and theoretical and methodological revisions are linked to the incapacity for such vision.

1. In many ways, a good example is what took place in a tragic moment between the German Gestapo and Freud, who, although old, ill, and literally in their hands, did not cease to be the true conqueror, even in terms of politics (at a level of inner reality, and—we can today say retrospectively—of historical and cultural reality). As in his account of the "revolutionary" dream (which I will mention later), in the tragic circumstances of his departure from Vienna, Freud did not fail to make the excessive power of his adversaries the target of his irony with a passion that is today easily underestimated. He was perhaps also strengthened by the conviction, mentioned earlier, that irony "easily risks being misunderstood", even though the signals that characterize it "clearly indicate that one thinks the opposite of what one says".

However, despite the indubitable courage implied in this decision to run even a calculated risk in such circumstances, there are two things that most interest us here. On the one hand, in both episodes (the other being the publication of the revolutionary dream, and above all, what preceded it), we may observe again, albeit in different ways, in and through the irony, Freud's love of and need for truth, which leads him to run a risk—in this case, the risk that the irony will be understood.

It is well known (Jones, 1957, p. 241) that, before leaving occupied Austria, Freud had to sign the following document:

> I, Prof. Freud, hereby confirm that after the Anschluss of Austria to the German Reich I have been treated by the German authorities and particularly by the Gestapo with all the respect and consideration due to my scientific reputation, that I could live and work in full freedom, that I could continue to pursue my activities in every way I desired, that I found full support from all concerned in this respect, and that I have not the slightest reason for any complaint.

Jones relates that when the Nazi Commissar presented the declaration to him, Freud signed it without compunction. He did ask, however, that he might be allowed to add a sentence, which was:

> I can heartily recommend the Gestapo to anyone.

Irony here becomes the means by which he stood firm in the reaffirmation of the truth (which, in the episode of the Gestapo, seems to prevail over the expression of aggressiveness) without exposing himself—except for a "calculated risk"—to more serious consequences. [See the non-masochistic aspect of the best Jewish irony as emphasized by Schlesinger (1979).] As regards this "calculation", I think it might be somewhat of the same kind (but reversed) as the one that makes the analyst decide to intervene. In this case, the decision is based on the feeling that it might lead to insight, preferably in the here and now. In the exchange of courtesies between the Gestapo and Freud, his decision to intervene is, in all likelihood, based on the feeling that no insight will be produced in the SS, at least in the here and now; at best, it will be suffocated as the disavowal arises.

In the perversion and perversity of certain behaviour, there comes a moment at which the denial in the service of the need to survive of which Geelerd (1965) speaks becomes pervasive, and if this ceases to take place, it may overwhelm the individual even physically when he becomes (once again) an individual. An example of this is the death of Stangl at the end of the "interview" by Sereny (1974). [Regarding the kind of irony Freud uses in the episode reported, see Sperling's (1963) "Exaggeration as a Defense"]. This ironic modality lends itself—through exaggeration—particularly to written "communications" that start from a theme proposed by the other, probably allowing a satisfying alternative: or that—at least at the level of fantasy—the irony is doubtfully understood, or, if not understood, that there is at least the confirmation of the adversary's "stupidity", or even the conferring of this label by the ironist.

2. When—according to Schorske (1973, p. 309)—at the age of 45 Freud, a "lover of jests", was finally nominated Associate Professor [*ausserordentlicher Professor*], he reports the episode in a parody of journalistic style, describing his nomination as if it were a "political triumph".

In his letter to Fliess of 11 March 1902 we read:

> Public acclaim was immense. Congratulations and bouquets already are pouring in, *as though* the role of sexuality has suddenly been officially recognized by His Majesty, the significance of the dream certified by the Council of Ministers, and the necessity of a psychoanalytic therapy of hysteria carried by a two-thirds majority in Parliament [Freud, 1887–1904; italics are added]

His "as though" and his unmistakably parodistic tone prevent any confusion between fantasy and reality, and Freud's similarity to a politician remains a play of fantasy and, more precisely, a (single) side of this play, whilst the other, ironically, is that of a contraposition linked precisely to the display of that humour the politician either does not possess or must set aside (in managing his role) in favour of attitudes that are more or less paranoiac. Freud quotes Goethe, who said: "Where he [a witty satirist] makes a jest a problem lies concealed", and he adds: "Sometimes the jest brings the solution to the problem to light as well" (1916–17, p. 38).

In the "play" mentioned above, Freud evokes the exact inversion of the political reality of the time. Indeed,

> the Reichstag of 1902 had in fact fallen so low that it was unable to bring together a simple majority. This did not mean that political paralysis as such was an important preoccupation for Freud. His uneasiness had at the same time a more precise and more vague object: his relationship with the whole political system as well as its components and consequences within the university. Hence his jest fulfilled his desire—the desire to have the political authorities [to whom he had to yield] fall into line. [Schorske, 1973, p. 310]

In the above-mentioned letter to Fliess, we may read further:

> I myself would still gladly exchange every five congratulations for one decent case suitable for extensive treatment. I have learnt that the old world is ruled by authority, as the new one is by the dollar. I have made my first bow to authority.

3. According to Schorske, following the material in *The Interpretation of Dreams* in the order in which it is presented, we may note that

> the psychoarchaeological section is divided into three levels: professional, political and personal. Furthermore, the three levels approximately correspond to the three phases of Freud's life. [p. 311]

Certainly the political level is the one that, as a result of its connection with elements of present reality, provides Freud with the greatest amount of ironic and parodic material. I shall dwell for a moment on these aspects of Freud's irony, particularly because they provide us with a reference to the general considerations that follow. As Schorske notes, he could not fail to feel the recrudescence of anti-semitism. Promotion within the university for Jews became more difficult in the faculty of

Medicine in the course of the years of crisis that followed 1897. Freud *ironically* reports the reply that one of his Jewish colleagues, who was also awaiting promotion, received from a high-ranking person.

> The reply had been that, in view of the present state of feeling, it was no doubt true that, for the moment, His Excellency [the Minister of Religion and Education] was not in a position etc. etc. . . . The same denominational considerations applied to my own case. [Freud, 1900a, p. 137]

Freud's psychological crisis on the death of his father had, according to Schorske (1973), taken on the form of a crisis of professional failure and impotence, then of political guilt:

> To exorcize the ghost of his father, he had, like Hamlet, both to affirm the supremacy of politics by expelling what is rotten in the State of Denmark (which is a civil task) and also to neutralize the politics by reducing it to psychological categories (intellectual task). [p. 314]

Freud hides from the reader, but not from himself, an important truth regarding the subject of his problem of political guilt as a scientist and as a son.

> The Rome of his dreams and his adult desires is clearly a love object. It is not the Rome of Hannibal but that of Johann Joachim Winckelmann . . . the Rome of pleasure, of maternity, of integration, of fulfilment. Science had to defeat politics and exorcize the paternal ghost. [Schorske, 1973, pp. 318–319]

4. Freud (1900a, pp. 208–218) managed these tasks with the help of another dream, which he called a "revolutionary" dream. It is somewhat ironic—notes Schorske (1973, p. 320)—that 1898 (when Freud had his revolutionary dream), a year of paralysis and chaos, was also characterized by the fiftieth anniversary of the coronation of Emperor Franz Josef, after the revolution of 1848. What preceded the dream is the following: whilst he was waiting for a train, Freud recognized Count Thun, who, striding with long steps towards the platform, moved past the guard and entered a luxurious compartment.

The Count's arrogant behaviour unleashed all Freud's social bitterness against the aristocracy. He found himself humming an aria from Mozart's *The Marriage of Figaro*:

> *Se vuol ballare, signor contino*
> *Se vuol ballare, signor contino,*
> *Il chitarrino Le suonerò.*
>
> [If my Lord Count is inclined to go dancing,
> If my Lord Count is inclined to go dancing,
> I'll be quite ready to play him a tune.]

The "revolutionary dream" produces a work of elimination of Freud's aspirations and political awareness. While in the dream he fulfills the political aspirations he has long repressed by bringing to light in the analysis the persons that prove that his desire for a political role could actually have been fulfilled, he refuses to draw all the conclusions from it (Schorske, 1973):

> In his "revolutionary dream", his last explosive farewell to politics, Freud entered the campaign as a liberal–scientific David against a wholly real political Goliath, the then Prime Minister. He revealed his political and social opinions in no uncertain terms. But on the pavement, as in the dream, the meeting between the small Jewish doctor and the fearful aristocrat seems like a quixotic duel, both ironic and absurd. In his analysis, Freud did not see it as being civil courage but rather an "absurd megalomania, eliminated for some time from my everyday life" and a rejection both of aristocratic authority (Thun–Taafee) and the authority of socialism (Adler, his older and more daring brother). The "political" problem was dissolved in the final scene, when the dream substituted the living count with his dying father. . . . Freud had finally become "minister" not in the political, but in the medical sense. Not Hannibal the general, but Winckelmann the man of science.

The reversal of the infantile situation in the final scene of the "revolutionary dream" has ironic aspects:

> My father let fall the words: "The boy will come to nothing". This must have been a frightful blow to my ambition, for references to this scene are still constantly recurring in my

> dreams and are always linked with an enumeration of my achievements and success, as though I wanted to say: "You see, I have come to something". . . . The older man . . . was now micturating in front of me, just as I had in front of him in my childhood. [Freud, 1900a, p. 216)]

Schorske observes that an intellectual vendetta thus takes place not against Rome, nor against Count Thun, but against his father. Just as his father replaces the Prime Minister on the platform of the station, so patricide replaces politics (1973). This remains valid even if, at a more general and primitive level, the order is reversed.

Schorske's interesting and well-documented analysis allows us to see how the ironic aspects present in the "revolutionary dream" (and in the day's residues) are not isolated (see Sacerdoti, 1977b), but, rather, connected with other elements that may be traced back both to other dreams—like, for example, the one about Hungary, in which Freud (1900a, p. 427) attributes to his father the important role of political conciliator—and to one aspect of the way in which Freud presents Oedipus—which, according to Schorske, is linked to his undertaking to neutralize politics: indeed, he pays no attention whatsoever to the fact that Oedipus was King (Schorske, 1973):

> Sophocles' play *Oedipus Rex* is inconceivable outside the *res publica*, with its royal hero driven by a political imperative: to remove the plague from Thebes. Although Oedipus' guilt is personal, his search for self-discovery and his self-punishment are a public matter, and it establishes public order once more. Freud's Oedipus is not a king, but a thinker in search of his identity and its meaning. Reducing politics to personal psychological categories, he establishes order once more at the personal level, but not public order. Doctor Freud abandoned Thebes to the plague of politics, whilst he lifted the spirit of his dead father to regalness in his Hungarian dream. [pp. 324–326]

And Schorske wonders: "Was nothing left of Freud–Hannibal, of Freud–Figaro, of the Freud who challenged the count in the 'revolutionary dream'?" With regard to this question, the following observations may be of interest. One of Lassalle's most brilliant pamphlets (*La guerre d'Italie et la tâche de la Prussie*, 1859) portrays *en exergue* on the title page: "*Flectere si nequeo Superos, Acheronta movebo*". In the same letter of 13 July 1899 in which Freud (1887–1904) announces to Fliess that he has chosen this phrase as the epigraph for *The Interpretation of Dreams*, he writes, without making any connection, that he was taking Lassalle's book on holiday with him to read during the summer. (And *La guerre d'Italie*—notes Schorske—appeared in several editions of selected works that were then available, unlike many others.)

In Schorske's view, the great similarity between Lassalle's pamphlet and Freud's summary of his youthful political persuasions and the political anguish of the 1890s indicates that it is likely that Freud had read *La guerre d'Italie*, which contains themes and ideas that are also to be found in *The Interpretation of Dreams* (the hatred of Catholic Rome and the monarchy of the Habsburgs as bastions of reaction, the link between Garibaldi and the Hungarians as liberal protagonists, the support of German nationalistic sentiments—as in the revolutionary dream).

Schorske notes that Lassalle threatened "those in high places" with unleashing a political Acheron through the latent forces of the national revolution. It would have been easy for Freud to appropriate Lassalle's epigraph, transferring the insinuation of subversion, through the return of the repressed, from the political sphere to the reign of the psyche. All this must have been consciously done by Freud; therefore—as Schorske claims—in the last pages of *The Interpretation of Dreams* he is trying to dispel fears. With reference to a Roman legend, Freud (1900a) expresses the opinion that

> the Roman emperor was in the wrong when he had one of his subjects executed because he had dreamt of murdering the emperor. . . . most probably its meaning was not what it appeared to be. . . . would it not be right to bear in mind Plato's dictum that the virtuous man is content to dream what a wicked man really does? I think it is the best, therefore, to acquit dreams. [p. 620]

Once again this extract also shows—beyond "political" prudence—how the seriousness with which Freud treated a question (and without doubt that of dreams) was never separated from his capacity to ironize about it where there was a need for reappraisal, perhaps to check the behaviour of someone more realistic than the king (and it is possible that this species is hidden also amongst the analysts, with the risk, as then, of Freud's being "arrested" rather than exceeded).

5. One of the most important documents in the assessment of the determinant role played by Freud's capacity for irony and self-directed irony (of the kind Booth calls "stable") on the development of his thought, is his letter to Fliess of 21 September 1897 (Freud, 1887–1904).

This letter also shows the dramatic aspects of the turning-point that led him to "abandon" traumatic theory, to recognize that the "reality" he had been counting on was appearance, and to discover that it was hiding another reality, that of fantasy. To move from the formulation of the appearance ("Jocasta sexually desired Oedipus") to the one of psychic reality (inverting the statement to: "Oedipus sexually desired Jocasta") was certainly not a simple step. It involved a series of rejections and a series of acquisitions, which, however, did not stand out either immediately or automatically. Thus—as Freud writes to Fliess—

> I could indeed feel quite content. The expectation of eternal fame was so beautiful. . . . Everything depended on whether or not hysteria would come out right. Now I can once again remain quiet and modest, go on worrying and saving. A little story from my collection occurs to me: "Rebecca, take off your gown, you are no longer a bride!"

His capacity for self-directed irony on "this general catastrophe" appears to be closely linked to his state of mind described above ("If I were depressed, confused, exhausted, such doubts would surely have to be interpreted as signs of weakness. Since I am in an opposite state . . ."). A state of mind he finds surprising: "It is strange, too, that no feeling of shame, appeared—for which, after all, there could well be occasion. Of course I shall not tell it in Dan, nor speak of it in Askelon, in the land of the Philistines, but, in your eyes and my own, I have more the feeling of a victory than a defeat (which is surely not right)". Here his surprise seems determined by the possibility to grasp as reality his state of mind and as appearance the "catastrophe", which appears to him at a rational level ("Can it be that this doubt merely represents an episode in the advance toward further insight?"). As we have seen, surprise, contrast between appearance and reality, and indications about reality are all ingredients of "stable" irony. The possibility of bearing a situation in which we already know how things are not (to which we may apply irony: "it is not as it seems") without there being indications of how things are, about what is not appearance but reality without, however, this producing a nihilistic attitude (Booth's "unstable infinite" irony), all depends on individual gifts. It is basically the position of the researcher, who is creative precisely because he knows how to bear not knowing even though he does not reject the goal of knowledge. All this is a *conditio sine qua non* for the investigation (if not indeed the conception) of the unconscious, that place with regard to which Freud had been developing—as he says in the same letter to Fliess—"the certain insight that there are no indications of reality in the unconscious so that one cannot distinguish between truth and fiction that has been cathected with affect". This concerns the development of theory; but, basically, also the position of the clinical analyst, of the one who accepts the "impossible" yet creative profession, the work that may help an individual to come closer to completeness and that will always be incomplete. In the same letter, with reference to clinical work, Freud observes: "If one thus sees that the unconscious never overcomes the resistance of the conscious, the expectation that in treatment, the opposite is bound to happen, to the point where the unconscious is *completely* tamed by the conscious, also diminishes" [italics added].

I have dealt at some length with this letter, because it is an example of how Freud's capacities for a certain ironic vision were inextricably connected with his capacities as a researcher. It shows him in the intimacy of correspondence with a friend, in a particularly difficult exchange that is critical but also particularly fruitful.

As in the situation that brings him up against crude social reality in the contemptuous, arrogant behaviour of Count Thun, Freud reacts by humming Figaro's aria and then by having the revolutionary dream. So, when his implacable criticism and his clinical and scientific honesty bring him face to face with the untenability of his theoretical construction and the prospect of the destruction of the hopes connected with it, he reacts with a variation of Hamlet's words, "to be in readiness"—good humour is everything—and with Jewish jokes.

Whilst the first situation highlights the connection between Freud's generally combative personality and his capacity to direct irony outwards, towards the person who at that moment represented injustice (and, we have seen, which paths this allowed him to follow), in the second situation Freud's personality and capacities act in such a way as to direct irony towards himself, not to destroy his work but to permit it to take a much more incisive turn. In the first case, it was essentially social and political difficulties the ironizing of which became the starting point for the oneiric and later the self-analytical work and also for the affirmation of the supremacy of psychology over politics. In the second case, it was a question of scientific and clinical difficulties, and the self-directed irony was interlaced with the emotional and rational reaction, the former becoming the starting point for the latter in the sphere of a (re)constructive movement. In both cases, what seemed to be insuperable was no longer so thanks to a modification, a reversal of perspective.

The jüdische Witz

What has been described above basically forms part of the early years of psychoanalysis, when, as a result of the revolutionary nature of the new science, a seemingly insurmountable barrier was created around it by part of the academic world. Freud was well aware of the fact that in the possible segregation of psychoanalysis other elements might play a part, and he took the matter so seriously that he sought an association with Jung for reasons that went beyond those of simple friendship.

On the other hand, his freedom from prejudice, his aptitude and his ability, which came from his being Jewish (Freud, 1941e [1926], p. 274) (the loneliness in opposition [*Vereinsamung in der Opposition*] permitted him to defend intrepidly his identity and originality as a scholar also through the use of humour, irony, and self-directed irony, which were also part of his Jewish inheritance. [Freud's position seems quite different from Bion's need for "insulation from the group in order to work" (Bion, 1970). As Scholem (1972) notes, Freud, together with Kafka, Benjamin, and a few others, certainly remained unscathed by the German phraseology—indeed by the expression "we Germans"—and they all wrote with great awareness of the distance that divided them as Jews from their German readers. They are the finest of the so-called German–Jewish writers, and their lives bear witness to this distance, its pathos, and the creative qualities or possibilities that ensued for them, as do their writings, in which Judaism is only occasionally mentioned. They do not deceive themselves. They know they are writing in German, but that they are not Germans. Although they know they are strongly linked to the German language and its spiritual world, they have never fallen victim to the illusion that they are in their homeland. Scholem (1972) adds: "I do not know if they would have felt at home in Israel. I doubt it. They were, in the true sense of the word, men from another country: and they knew it.]

In his "Address to the Members of the *B'nai B'rith*" Freud (1941e [1926]), expressed the opinion that

> Because I was a Jew I found myself free from many prejudices which restricted others in the use of their intellect; and as a Jew I was prepared to join the Opposition and to do without agreement with the "compact majority".

I would say that the irony and self-directed irony—which clearly emerge from the letter to Fliess quoted above—were important ingredients, both of Freud's capacity to be free from prejudices and to join the Opposition, and also of his capacity to be free from "paranoiac" temptations and of his readiness to modify his theoretical constructions and also to leave the Opposition, naturally where this did not cost him the renunciation of his own identity as a scholar of the unconscious [see the more general Jewish dilemma, after the opening of the ghettos, between the persistence of isolation and the rejection of identity (see also Sacerdoti, 1986c)].

Musatti (1982) notes that, in Jewish jokes,

> the humorous cover that overlays the critical content ennobles, also in terms of the listener, the author who is making fun of himself, or the people he identifies with, by exaggerating certain typical, or recurrent, aspects of the Jewish world. By being the one to highlight these critical elements, he thus renders the aggressiveness of the others superfluous and reaches a certain form of superiority. [p. 123]

Now we must take into account that this final result is not purely narcissistic, but really ennobling (Musatti) and that it concerns not only the ironist, but also the people with whom he identifies, more affectionately than aggressively (see what Booth says about the communicative and even community aspects of irony). Moreover, we must also consider that Jewish humour is at its best almost always ironic. This has probably not been taken sufficiently into account, for the elements mentioned here, even when they have been noted, have (often) been relegated to a marginal position, whilst in ironic contrast they constitute the pole of reality (albeit often inner reality). Vice versa, it is generally the element of appearance that is highlighted when we state that Jewish jokes are all masochistic and self-abasing (albeit gently, as Musatti says).

Certainly this danger exists; it is one of the risks the ironist runs, especially when he uses self-directed irony, but it is one he must run precisely so as to be able to avoid narcissistic and masochistic indulgences in situations that tend to facilitate them: this is exactly the success of irony. It was no chance matter that with *Three Essays on the Theory of Sexuality* (1905d) and *Jokes* (1905c) Freud seemed to conclude a period of his activity. And what comes after is already influenced by a widening of horizons and interests, which coincides with the broadening of the scientific sphere in which psychoanalysis was welcome (Musatti, 1972, p. IX). This (relative) change in the environment is an element to be considered (and it summarizes—and is the expression of—other elements discussed earlier) when we wonder why Freud's work on *Witz* remained virtually isolated—with the exception of *Humour* (1927d)—from his later writings. But in part the question remains.

In the letter to Fliess of 22 June 1897, Freud (1887–1904) indicates both his interest in jokes (and it is the first time he does this explicitly) and his having recently made a collection of significant Jewish jokes. He does this by starting from the quotation of one of the jokes that he applies *ironically* to Fliess and himself ("We parcel things out like beggars [*Schnorrer*], one of whom gets the province of Posen, you, the biological; I, the psychological"). As we have already observed in chapter one, as Freud's work on *Witz* specifically deals with unconscious dynamisms, with the relationships between the preconscious and unconscious (and energy saving), and as Freud believes that irony does not need the involvement of the unconscious, he is only marginally interested in irony.

One element that might have contributed to the above-mentioned "isolation" of *Witz* and its inadequate utilization (as we have, for example, seen at the technical level) is that in its nascent state—and therefore with an insuperable vitality—it harbours intuitions and interests that are later developed by Freud in more systematized—and therefore, in a certain sense, less vital—theory, which probably permits easier, albeit less fruitful, references. I am basically alluding to his distinction between licentious and aggressive tendencies (which anticipates the dualistic doctrine of instinctual drives) and his interest in the social, of which *Witz* is the expression, in which it is interwoven. Moreover, in *Witz* (which is social, unlike dreams), and through it, we may grasp the drive and defence, unconscious and preconscious dynamics, that underlie the conscious, manifest aspects of the social—dynamics that were certainly not systematically analysed, as for example in *Group Psychology and the Analysis of the Ego* (1921c), *The Future of an Illusion* (1927c), and *Civilization and its Discontents* (1930a).

Another element that might have contributed to Freud's relative loss of interest in *Witz* may be found—as Musatti

(1972) again notes—in the fact that the joke material Freud uses

> mainly derives from a rather special sphere. Heine's jokes, those contained in the jokes of Galician or Polish Jews (originally in Yiddish), or those circulating in the sphere of the often-Jewish Viennese bourgeoisie Freud frequented, or generally in the countries of central Europe before the First World War, require a certain familiarity and a capacity for identification in order to be emotionally intelligible. [p. 5]

According to Schmid (1960), many of these *jüdische Witze* contain something specific, which leads to dimensions before which the *Witze* of other countries comes to a halt. Here is a law that is rigorous, meticulous in its prescriptions, penetrating the whole of life, like no other thing. No letter may be removed if the world is not to shatter. But here is also life with its pretensions and necessities; here is the weakness of man, who is unable to experience both life and the law without the help of compassion. Here nothing else may help except irony, which is reflected in all the small transgressions before the law, and, since it considers necessary an enormous use of *Witz*—using here the term in a Medieval sense of the word—it truly confirms the rule to bring together in the word the law, life, and itself. And there, beside the "law", the knowledge that life has its probabilities, which may and must be recognized and, for one's behaviour, made into rules.

What is expressed here is an underlying knowledge united with a profound wisdom, which realistically tempers *anánkē* and possible freedom. The knowledge concerns *ante litteram* the fact that, as Baudrillard (1979) explains, what in reality opposes the law is not the absence of law, but the rule. The rule plays on an immanent concatenation of arbitrary signs, whilst the law is founded on a transcendent concatenation of necessary signs. The law, be it that of the signifying, of castration or social prohibition, installs everywhere prohibition, repression, and therefore the partition between manifest and latent discourse, since it occurs as a discursive sign of a legal petition, of a hidden truth. The rule, on the other hand, being conventional, arbitrary, and without hidden truths, does not know repression; the reversible, endless cycle of the rule opposes the linear, final concatenation of the law.

Wisdom regards the utilization of the rule to oppose the law—not, however, in a direct confrontation, in a fight to the death, but in order to play with the law and also to play it or rather to play its *pièges* in which otherwise we risk being caught by a following-to-the-letter that may kill the spirit of the Law ("letter killeth", writes Blake in his comment to the *Book of Job*); that spirit which the *Midrash* incessantly, often on the edge of irony, seeks not outside but within the very study of the Law. We cannot therefore say, "Once the law is made, the loophole is found", but, rather, "Once the law is made, the way not to be deceived by idolizing it is found". Schmid (1960) recalls a *Witz* that tells of the scandalized wonder of a man who, knowing that on Saturdays a certain Rabbi rose into heaven, met him in the forest cutting firewood for a widow. He had risen even higher (than heaven)! But autonomy in the original meaning of the word may and must transcend not only the Law but also the Rule, otherwise this, too, risks idolization, or dogmatization, or, at least, transformation into clichés. Indeed, as Schmid continues, what good are knowledge and rules when nature forgets to deliver the concrete situation according to the rules? Does one not deceive oneself when, before the spontaneity that lives within every living being, the probable and the true are made equal? Certainly, "barking dogs don't bite", but do I know that the dogs know this? Some people are so wrapped up in logic that they forget to use their own senses. Schmid continues by stressing the antonimic pairs whose poles are from time to time laid bare by the *jüdische Witz*, and he asks: Is there perhaps any more delicious irony in the belief in the omnipotence of thought than that in the story about the Rabbi who is looking for his glasses, which are on the end of his nose? And, on the other hand, as in the story about the little *Schnorrer* who "calculates" the name of the person sitting opposite him in the train compartment, in all self-directed irony is there not a strong sense of pride as regards the power of the spirit on the sure ways to arrive at the contingent thing, starting from the maximum fallaciousness of meaning regarding the most abstract thing? Schmid again dwells on a vicissitude (which is well known to us, for we dealt with it when we discussed instincts and their vicissitudes) that is often highlighted by the *jüdische Witz*: the transformation into the opposite. He notes that in addition to the knowledge about paradox, there is another: that from a specific measurement of an event we have its reversal into its opposite, which can in no way be understood metaphysically; that if we owe a banker a million, he has us in his hand, and, vice versa, if the debt is of twenty million, it is the debtor who has the banker in his hand. Schmid concludes his brief but significant preface to Landmann's collection by stating that if one wished to reduce one's opinion on the *jüdische Witz* to a formula that might in some way be essential, one would say that the *Witz* always demonstrates anew that, in a world understood in the most precise way through the device of logic, it is precisely those equations that are resolved without a remainder that cannot be right. The *jüdische Witz* is the serenely-accepted mourning of the antinomies and apories of being.

A universal theme today

The question mentioned above concerning the difficulty of a true understanding of the *jüdische Witz* may certainly have its validity, insofar as an identity of psychological structure similar to that of those who coined such jokes—a requisite Freud stresses, as Musatti (1982) recalls—has obviously become increasingly rare. Despite this, each element risks being overvalued today. Indeed, if a series of incongruities and antitheses, starting from the "objective" (social–political) situation, were then associated into dualistic and opposite mental schemes [*geistige Gegensatzpaare*], which stimulated the development of the *jüdische Witz, mutatis mutandis* conditions in many ways analogous and related dilemmas have in a certain way become ubiquitous and universal today. Schlesinger (1979, pp. 328–329) notes that the dilemmas the Jews in the ghettos had to deal with have in a certain sense broadened "to girdle the great globe itself", and thus the Jewish identity, with its incongruities, has fused with the incongruent issues faced by human identity. In particular he considers a series of *geistige Gegensatzpaare*, which—we might add—although part of the three great Freudian polarities, transcend them: "Specialness opposed to shameful vilification; powerful thinking against powerlessness in action; the potential for great rage checked by the realistic consequences of its overt, direct expression; cohesive communal closeness opposed by segregation and isolation." All this is susceptible to the production of scepticism, which, in turn, may or may not be a point of arrival.

The Lemberg–Cracow story that Freud (1905c, p. 115) quotes as an example of the "sceptic" joke is famous. ["Two Jews meet in a train at a station in Galicia. 'Where are you going?' asks the first. 'To Cracow', replies the other. 'What a liar you are', grumbles the first. 'If you say you're going to Cracow, you want me to think you're going to Lemberg. But I know you're going to Cracow. Why lie to me then?'"] The effect is obtained by coupling the technique of absurdity to that of representation through the opposite. However, the more serious substance of this joke—Freud notes—is the problem of what the criterion of truth is. "The joke is once again pointing to a problem and is making use of the uncertainty of one of our commonest concepts. Is it the truth if we describe things as they are without troubling to consider how our hearer will understand what we say? Or is this only jesuitical truth, and does not genuine truth consist in taking the hearer into account and giving him a faithful picture of our knowledge?" If, as Freud claims, "What they are attacking is not a person or an institution but the certainty of our knowledge itself, one of our speculative possessions", they also pose the problem, discussed in chapter three, of the capacity to tolerate the uncertainty necessary to discover the truth, especially at the level of inner reality, distinguishing appearance, which may be true at the level of outer reality considered separately—"jesuitical truth"—from reality—reality that in the story is grasped precisely by the one who, being able to understand the almost imperceptible signals of a double ironic sequence, makes use of the dismantling of the double representation through the opposite to "unmask" the other, classifying him once again as one who (according to Freud's interpretation) does not care whether he is understood or even cares not to be understood, counting on the fact that the signals of irony are perceptible only at the level of the first sequence. But by whom does he not care to be understood? Not by whoever is in the same boat, but by those from whom not only has he everything to lose by offering a faithful picture of his knowledge, as well as, in the circularity that is established between the persecuted and persecutors, from whoever is expected to be a liar: only they will be the ones to fall into the trap of the "jesuitical truth".

There are, in fact, two slightly different versions of this story: one is Freud's "Lemberg–Cracow" story, in which one Jew meets another. The other is the "Minsk–Pinsk" version told by Erikson (1968, p. 29 [in his version of the story these replace the cities of Lemberg and Cracow]), in which the two main Jewish characters are also business rivals. In terms of communication, I would say that in the first version, the ("unstable" but not "infinite") irony is conscious (or preconscious) at the level of both sequences for the character who gives the information and knows that his companion will grasp the reality beyond the deceptive appearance of the truth; and, all things considered, this is what happens. In the second version, on the other hand, the irony is conscious in the character who gives the information, at the level of the first sequence, in which the truth is presented as appearance leading to the error, whilst it is unconscious (latent) at the level of the second sequence, in which the error leads back to the truth. The Jew consciously wants to lead his co-religionist—towards whom he is ambivalent—astray, and it is his unconscious that makes him express things in such a way that the other (who generally, although he is a business rival, is in the same boat) manages to understand anyway by grasping the almost imperceptible signals of the double ironic sequence. Therefore Erikson—who uses the second version—considers the story "one of the more timeless contributions of the Jewish wit to the understanding of the tricks of the unconscious".

According to Erikson, many young people seem to have a slightly more malicious identity crisis compared with the "Minsk–Pinsk mechanism". He adds: "It helps to know, however, that this at least is the crisis appropriate to their age, and also that some are now having it more openly because they know that they are supposed to have it." The ironic aspect of these dynamics seems to revolve around the attempt to transform passiveness into activeness, which may fail through a kind of collusion and transform activeness once more into passiveness. According to Erikson, young people often use this old game as a new kind of experimentation: he sees it also as being a new form of adaptation "to psychiatric enlightenment which in the past has employed seemingly less dangerous because mostly verbal forms" (1968, p. 28). We may observe, for example, that in the field of social psychiatry the proclamation of the rights of the ill, of the disabled, and of the social outcast, is too often (indeed, it has become the rule) translated (or se-duced) in practice in having to remain a mere proclamation. The term "mentally ill" is even dispensed with in order to avoid having to deal with therapy (Sacerdoti, 1971). This is an example of how the incongruity between theory (ideology) and praxis may border on what Adorno (1951) calls the "radical lie". At this point, we are interested in confirmation of the present spread of incongruities, concerning which there have been briefly registered two or three kinds of reaction. In wide sections of the population they may be accepted supinely, with resignation, or disavowed, as we have seen, through ideologization. In others, however, according to Schlesinger (1979),

> these incongruities are all productive of great anxiety. They also produce a tolerance for ambiguity, and increased capacity to alternate rapidly the frames of reference applied to inner and outer reality, while at the same time maintaining the ego's control. The ego-identity which grows out of the need to reconcile these tensions is both individually and collectively prepared to use a humour which allows the covert expression of rage, which raises to perfection the play with words and concepts and finally infuses these processes with the content of its life and values. [p. 328]

The double vision characteristic of irony (and self-directed irony) is often present in the *jüdische Witz*; it constructs the framework of authentic insight and, at the same time, a kind of defence against the defence, especially in the field of aggressiveness, the manifest expressions of which are circumscribed by large outer restrictions. Of particular significance here is the story quoted by Schlesinger as an example of satire, through the *reductio ad absurdum*, of the intellectualized anti-force attitude.

> Two Jews are riding along a country path in a small horse and wagon. A large tree has fallen across the road blocking their progress. They get out to contemplate, and discuss their predicament. Two peasants come along, get out of their wagon, heave, pull, tug and clear the tree trunk from the roadway, get back into their vehicle and keep on going. The Jews look at each other and shrug. "*Mit Gewalt?*" ["With brute force?"].

Schlesinger (1979) comments with great relevance:

> The peasants are not the target of the joke. Their direct mode is alien to East-European Jewish style. The joke arises out of the incongruity that is experienced when self-assertion and direct action is contra-indicated for survival reasons and where as a consequence rather simple problems have to be approached obliquely and intellectually instead of directly engaged. The incongruity is resolved with the expressed abhorrence of brute force and we are moved to laughter. This joke gets a relatively weak response from American Jewish audiences where there is no shared presumption of the alien character of direct action. Among those with East-European backgrounds it begets great laughter. [pp. 319–320]

Laughter therefore testifies both to the existence of incongruity and the capacity to resolve it, at the level of inner reality, with a broadening of the insight that understands, through laughing at it, the outer reality.

There is still much to be studied concerning the search for the correlations, in both directions, between the development of this kind of attitude and a certain culture that may be facilitating–facilitated or rather hindering–hindered by it. What Horkheimer and Adorno (1947) have written on the matter comes to mind: the half culture which, unlike simple lack of culture, with limited knowledge hypostaticized to truth, does not support the fracture—pushed to intolerable lengths—of inner and outer, individual destiny and social law, phenomenon and essence. Reconciliation is the supreme concept of Judaism and its whole meaning is waiting: the paranoid reaction derives from the inability to wait.

We might at this point begin a discussion in which the philosopher, the historian, and the psychologist easily tend to go beyond their respective fields, with results that are often confused or even simply dishonest. Remaining with what clinical psychoanalysis teaches us, we may emphasize the importance of the possibility of deferring judgement. Within clinical psychoanalysis, we might examine the relationships (in both directions) with the so-called *Wisstrieb* or *Forschertrieb* [instinct for knowledge or research] that Freud (1905a, p. 194) does not classify amongst the elementary instinctual components but, rather, as something that is carried out as a kind of sublimation of the *Bemächtigungstrieb* [instinct to master] that makes use of the energy of *Schaulust* [scopophilia]. We might perhaps say that the *homo psychoanalyticus* makes broad and continued use of these elements, and the greater his ability to wait, the smaller his pretension to be *illico et immediate* a *Menschenkenner* [a knower of men], the greater the depth of knowledge he is able to reach. This is facilitated by the setting, which should ensure also that the analyst has sufficient protection on the side of outer reality.

Certainly, the inflation of the means of "communication" (which gives the communication ironic connotations) and their "cold" seduction (Baudrillard, 1979) may have removed meaningfulness, bite, and efficacy from the word of those who hold power and, even more—albeit for different reasons—those who are subject to it. This is also perhaps one of the reasons why, especially for those who are subject to power, behavioural playfulness gradually replaces verbal playfulness. Many actions of today's young people belong, at least initially (perhaps at an unconscious or preconscious level) to the former category, and the answer to them might be more adequate—especially before the tragic evolution—if it were possible to develop not a greater *Menschenkenntniss* but a greater insight as to the ironic dynamics (especially the preconscious and unconscious ones) that underlie them, thus avoiding and mitigating the formation of vicious circles which in a certain way recall those that may be established in analysis between acting and counter-acting (Erikson, 1968; Sacerdoti, 1979).

The apparent disappearance of the medium of irony

It is the non-consideration of the preconscious and unconscious dynamics and the slant that results concerning the social—as well as, perhaps, the excessive preoccupation with not making the smallest concession to the deteriorated aspects of social interest, not recognizing even its seductiveness—that leads Adorno (1951) to say that today the very means of irony has entered into contradiction with the truth. Irony confutes the object insofar as it represents it as what it claims to be and compares it—without judgement, almost without the intervention of the observing subject—with its being-in-itself. It grasps the negative by comparing the positive with its same claim of positiveness. As soon as a word of explanation is added, the irony is destroyed. It therefore presupposes the idea of what is in itself evident and—originally—of social interest. With regard to "the current impossibility of satire", Adorno rightly belittles the importance of the relativism of values, of the absence of binding rules, but in his opinion, the understanding itself, the formal *a priori* of irony, has become a universal understanding in its very content. That which, as such, would be the only object worthy of irony cuts the ground from under its feet. The medium of irony, the difference between ideology and reality, has disappeared. Ideology resigns itself to confirming reality through a pure and simple duplication of the same. Irony used to say about a thing: "This is what it claims to be, but this is what it is in reality." However, today, even in the radical lie, the world draws its strength from the fact that things are just like that, and this simple observation is the equivalent, for it, of what is good. There is no fissure in the rock of what is, on which the talon of irony may take hold. Behind the one who is falling echoes the mocking laughter of the perfidious object that has made him impotent. The gesture of the irrational "that's how it is" is the one the world turns against each of its victims, and transcendental understanding, which is immanent to irony, becomes ridiculous before the real understanding of those it should attack. Against the "bloody seriousness" of total society, which has absorbed its appeal—the impotent objection that once was the precipitate of irony—there is nothing more than "bloody seriousness", including truth.

Certainly, limiting ourselves to the plane of outer reality, to the conscious level, Adorno's analysis may be considered exact and thorough, even if centred—it would seem—on "unstable" irony. However, Adorno himself, noting for example that "the world draws its strength", allows us to perceive here a defensive aspect, the masking of a weakness through the "simple observation" of the "fact that things are just like that". Adorno even notes that this takes place "even in the radical lie". Nevertheless, he ends up by playing along with (the "bloody seriousness") of "total society", therefore admitting that "there is no fissure in the rock of what is" and thus aligning himself with this position, against which—he concludes—"there is nothing more than bloody seriousness, including truth".

We might say, to use his own words, that Adorno also limits himself to confirming reality by triplicating it with resignation after it has already been purely and simply duplicated by ideology.

But the analyst, with his professional mistrust of clichés (Sacerdoti, 1977a), cannot in turn collaborate by purely and simply quadruplicating reality. I shall therefore, impurely and complicatedly (modalities that might, on the other hand, reveal themselves to be reversible), attempt to examine what reality we are dealing with. Rather than complicatedly, I shall make a detour or a leap, as might be considered suitable to exit playfully from "bloody seriousness" in order to return to consider the historical–social perspective, after having delved once again into clinical psychoanalysis and the theoretical–doctrinal developments derived from it.

A clinical detour

To begin with, I shall quote a very simple passage from an article by Nunberg (1926), which is child's play in comparison with the serious sophistications (perhaps because of the need to maintain the distance from the group, according to Bion) of most of today's psychoanalysis.

> Perhaps the best illustration of the fact that physician and patient mean two different things by "cures" is a case related by Ferenczi. . . . Here the patient's object was to have the nose cured by psycho-analysis, while he was really suffering from an affection of the penis. I had experience of a similar case. . . . A patient imagined that there was something wrong with her teeth, although they were perfectly sound. At the bottom of this tendency was a marked unconscious cannibalistic tendency and a powerful castration-complex. She was quite right in seeking to be cured by mental therapy, but she was not clear about the motives which impelled her to undergo it. Her conscious wish was: "I want to have sound teeth", but the content of the unconscious wish was: "I want to have a penis". [p. 67]

I may add, *ad abundantiam*, two personal clinical references. Remaining in the context of castrating themes, one of my hysterical patients brought as associative oneiric material, a scholastic memory concerning a poem by Giacomo Leopardi entitled "To Silvia", of which the verse that most struck her was "Oh nature, oh nature, why do you not now reveal what you once promised? Why do you so deceive your children?" And Patient F (whom we have extensively quoted in chapter two), who had begun analysis for the impelling conscious need to know the truth about the death of her daughter, let fall this need at the moment in which she rediscovered her vagina. The true–genital equivalence was expressed explicitly by a fantasy fixed graphically by the patient herself.

We can therefore add to Adorno's argumentation the parallel arguments that result (see the clinical material above) from the equivalences, at an unconscious level, of the "fissure in the rock"—and therefore also from its disavowal—of the "bloody seriousness", of "truth", etc.

But let us see what useful elements for our discussion may be derived also from theoretical or doctrinal perspectives opened up by clinical psychoanalysis, concentrating our attention on one of the historically most important themes for theory, that of seduction, which is also, as we shall see, one of the most misunderstood.

The relative misunderstandings are pertinent to what interests us here—that is, the insufficient utilization of psychoanalytical knowledge in the visions of present-day social reality and the affirmation that a space for irony does not exist there

Let us therefore begin by examining at some length the work of Baudrillard, an author with a good knowledge of psychoanalysis, who has subtly contributed to the misunderstandings concerning psychoanalytical thought on the theme of seduction.

Seduction as a form of unstable irony

Baudrillard (1979) claims that there is nothing less seductive than the social. But Adorno's ideas provide us with additional elements that lead us to doubt Baudrillard's claim. According to his etymon, seduction is a diversion, a deviation, a leading astray (*se* indicates, precisely, separation). But from what? From its own (true) path; it is therefore a matter of truth. Being seduced means being led astray from one's own truth.

If we substitute "truth" with "genitality", the account may be balanced with the considerations made above. As further confirmation, we know that it is mainly from the pregenital instincts that "sociality"—and "anti-sociality"—are drawn, given that the reversibility is, as we have seen in chapter two, one of the most characteristic vicissitudes of those instincts. The "social" will therefore perhaps be a "cold" seduction, play that is not recognized as such, but in the sense accepted above I do not believe it can be categorized as anything but seductive.

Baudrillard's study on seduction, although subtle, clumsily ignores the genital–pregenital distinction and, in a pre-Freudian manner, seems to identify sex with the genital and, roughly, seduction with the pre-genital (of which no mention is made), contrasting the two registers in an irreducible antagonism, defending the latter which is, both in its content and in the style with which it is dealt, quite similar to infinite unstable irony.

If in many ways a re-evaluation of seduction may today be opportune and timely, the path chosen by Baudrillard—although stimulating—does not seem to be the most constructive; moreover, in its (frequent) incursions into psychoanalysis, it is characterized by a casual academicism.

In Baudrillard's (1979) opinion, as seduction is something that removes the meaning from discourse and leads it away from truth, we might see in it the opposite of the psychoanalytical distinction between manifest discourse and latent discourse. Indeed, latent discourse leads manifest discourse not *away from* its truth but *towards* its truth. The interpretation is something that, *shattering into pieces appearances* and the play of manifest discourse, will free the meaning and re-establish the relations with latent discourse. In seduction, on the contrary, it is in some way the manifest, the discourse at its most 'superficial', that overturns on the profound order so as to *cancel* it, and substitute for it fascination and the trap of the appearances—appearances that are by no means frivolous, but are the site of play and bringing into play of a passion of the deviation—seducing the signs is more important than the emergence of any truth—that the interpretation neglects and destroys in its search for a hidden meaning. [It would therefore seem that between interpretation and seduction—as between "profound" and "superficial"—there must be a kind of massacring play: who will shatter whom into pieces? If we keep to the definition of irony as being made up of double vision, we already highlight the distance that separates it from seduction. There might, rather, be both a seduction of (especially unstable) irony and an (especially situational) irony of seduction.] Thus the interpretation is something that opposes seduction *par excellence*, and therefore every interpretative discourse is the least seductive there is.

Baudrillard thus declares himself against any discussion of meaning that wishes to put an end to appearances, and, more specifically, against psychoanalysis, which is responsible for the fact that, for some time, we have managed to eliminate this playing the stakes of seduction, which has as its space the horizon of the appearances, and substituted it with the stakes of profundity: the unconscious playing the stakes, the stakes of interpretation. He suggests that for a moment we be psychoanalysts and say that at the origin of the emergence of psychoanalysis as a "science", at the very origin of Freud's research, lies the revival of an original repression, *the repression of seduction.*

It is difficult to understand how such an authoritative and subtle author, who in a previous book (Baudrillard, 1976) had already examined the articulation between economic aspects and the play of meanings in psychoanalytic thought, could have fallen into such gross error. Perhaps as a result of his excessive attention to the trap, he stumbled into a rudimentary snare (irony of fate).

On the theme of seduction, both in the field of praxis and in theory, and—as Granoff would say—also in that of doctrine, repression and defence (as the history of psychoanalysis and the history of every individual psychoanalysis teaches us), do not go in the direction of the defence from reality by means of fantasy, but in the opposite direction of the defence from (primal) fantasy by means of reality, either real or, in turn, fantasized.

Baudrillard's error is evidently that of mistaking for the repressing precisely that which has been torn from repression (fantasy: Oedipal desire) and for what is repressed that which has been so recognizable as the repressing (the seduction by Jocasta).

From what follows, it would seem that Baudrillard also confuses theory and praxis and that, especially where the latter is concerned, the "disavowal" is basically not playing the patient's seductive game, not even counter-reacting seductively. He states that Freud suppressed seduction so as to activate an eminently operative mechanism of *interpretation*. He also believes that no delight can be taken in seeing the seduction break through in the psychoanalysis of Lacan, in the hallucinated form of a play of meanings: as a result of this, psychoanalysis, in its forms and its rigorous demands, in the form that Freud wished, dies equally certainly—even more certainly than it does because of its institutional banalization.

Psychoanalysis seems therefore doomed to die, by a kind of nemesis, through the return of the repressed (or of the foreclosed), as this is made up precisely of seduction.

Irony of seduction in the age of surrogates

If we were to abandon ourselves to the seduction of the infinite unstable irony Baudrillard (1979) develops concerning psychoanalysis—a cycle is completed and on it perhaps opens the possibility of other seductive forms of interrogation—we would lose sight of the irony of seduction in particular. Baudrillard's fantasy consists basically of a sophisticated transposition in general theoretical terms of an analytic treatment that has failed through seduction. This takes place by means of an inversion of the analytical path—"from terms pregnant in meaning to the artifices of a seduction", says Baudrillard—whilst the analyst, starting from artifices (the setting) that encourage regression and the repetition in the transference of, amongst other things, seductive games, manages to show their meaning. It is the artifices that become artificers, not vice versa. In the repetition that the artifices encourage there lies the tendency for the patient to silence needs and desires with surrogates, a tendency that is intensified in modern society and that is channelled in analysis into the neurosis of transference. As the two lines of tendency—the patient's and the analyst's—are different, we might even represent the process in terms of who se-duces whom.

To illustrate how things end up when it is the analyst who is seduced, Freud (1915a, pp. 165–166) tells the story of an insurance agent who is seriously-ill and who remains a firm unbeliever and manages to sell a policy to the priest who has come to convert him. The case of transference-love in analysis is the one that most clearly shows the irony of the seduction—at least, a certain seduction. After relating the anecdote mentioned above, Freud (1915a) writes,

> If the patient's advances were returned, it would be a great triumph for her, but a complete defeat for the treatment. . . . It is, therefore, just as disastrous for the analysis if the patient's craving for love is gratified as if it is suppressed. The course the analyst must pursue is neither of these; it is one for which there is no model in real life.

The impasse from which the analysis may be allowed to exit can also be seen as a barricade to the access to genitality through the tendency to activate a pseudo-genitality, to seek a surrogate for the genital relationship that seems authentic in the eyes of the patient.

It might be objected that this is relative, that it is a question of points of view, that it depends on the context. For example, where is the genitality in the analysis Freud (1907a, p. 35) makes of the etching by Rops (see chapter three)—in drawing the due consequences from the return of what is repressed, in repressing it, in co-existing with it by laying aside and sublimating its needs? Naturally, there is no answer to this; we can only construct hypotheses (as always in psychoanalysis). But if we were dealing with an analysis, the analytic work could allow the analysand to find his path—in other words, through this and other seductions, overcome the se-ductions after having identified them as such. This is possible precisely because the analyst, as Freud (1915a, p. 166) says, follows a course for which there is no model in real life. What Freud explains in the same article concerning the behaviour the analyst must exhibit could also be expressed in these terms: do not play the patient ("He must take care not to steer away from the transference-love or to repulse it and so make it distasteful to the patient") nor be played by her ("but he must just as resolutely withhold any response to it"), but, rather, to play with her, thus showing here that it is only play ("He must keep firm hold of the transference-love but treat it as something unreal"—Freud 1915a,

p. 166). By considering it a serious thing, the patient precludes access both to the play and also to something real.

We have already discussed and examined some examples of the complementary nature of the playful/serious aspects. It is well known that Freud, with reference to the (dynamically considered) pairs of opposites, proposed pairing play with the real rather than with the serious. His statement quoted above might therefore also be read as treat the transference-love as something playful. Otherwise there is the risk that what happened to Ferenczi will come about, of which Freud (1933c, p. 229) says: "The need to cure and to help had become paramount in him" [*Das Bedürfnis zu heilen und zu hilfen war in ihm übermächtig geworden*]—*übermächtig*, overpowering, irresistible, so as to induce (se-duce) him to the practice and theorization of "active technique", and so on.

In addition to the ironic aspects we have already seen in clinical psychoanalysis and psychoanalytic theorization, we might dwell for a moment on the ironic side that is intrinsic to psychoanalytic practice. We could say that it is necessary for the analyst to let himself be se-duced (in the original meaning of the term) so as to reach the objective indicated so memorably by Freud (1933a, p. 80): "Where id was, there ego shall be" [*Wo Es war soll Ich werden*]—where *Ich* is not only conscious. The methodology the analyst uses, his disposition (free-floating attention), and his exposition to the patient's free association—in other words, his showing everything even, or precisely because, it is known there will in any case be gaps—is tantamount to continually allowing himself to be se-duced, with the aim, however, of helping the patient to find what has been repressed and his possibilities of *reculer pour avancer* along a different line from that followed in the past, helping him flee from his demon, i.e. from repetitiveness. It is, we might also say, letting himself be se-duced so as to seduce the patient.

But what kind of se-duction is this? It is a seduction that follows the opposite course to the one Baudrillard claims deviates the subject from truth, and therefore from genitality. It is a seduction that can be compared to stable irony and not to infinite unstable irony. And in analytic theorization? Here, too, it is necessary for the analyst to allow himself to be seduced. By whom? By what? By the Witch Metapsychology, Freud tells us, without which we cannot move forwards—or, rather, we cannot play with a fantasy, which is in addition feminine, or, rather, bisexual, and which naturally concerns magic—regressing, therefore, but then to return, moving forward in the clinical work and, on the other hand, staying firmly "still" in the "doctrine".

> Granting with liberality every theoretical effort, he [Freud] was intractable about doctrinal discarding. Or more, to say this in another way, theory and doctrine may establish an antagonist relationship. [Granoff, 1975, p. 205]

Here it would seem natural to compare this with the primal scenes that Freud supposes are a kind of phylogenetically inherited prehistoric truth, used by the child in particular to fill the gaps of an individual truth by creating phantasms or primal fantasies [*Urphantasien*], which are often, at a level of memory, elaborations and maskings. Thus, returning to the history of psychoanalysis, according to Granoff (1975),

> the doctrine is the framework of the myth that states the difficulty of fate. Theory will be the effort to resolve it. But also to flatten it, to erode it, to utilize it. It tends to a growing neutralization and a numeric increase of the elements: to their desexualization. . . . Within, the doctrine always remains a focal point for the difference between the sexes. . . . The instinctive duality is in Freud a point of doctrine. . . . And lastly, if nowadays we consider the trajectory of the analytical movement as a whole . . ., can we not see that the question posed about the future of its cause, *die Sache*, as Freud called it, is much closer to a doctrinal extinction than a theoretical dessication? [pp. 205–206]

This is as if it were saying that in psychoanalysis theoretical proliferations, just like "infantile theories", may be necessary fantastic constructions for the thought that tends to a representation and a solution of the greatest enigmas. And the risk is not that these theories will cease to be produced, but that their proliferation, rather than elaborating enigmas in the sense of a truthful solution, tends to mask—or at least to inflate—through an increasing number of increasingly less primal phantasies (including those that claim to go back to the very first ontogenetic origins), the "difficulties of fate", those contained in the myth. This risk felt by Freud (who insisted on the typicality and the limited numbers of the *Urszenen* that have their roots in the onto- and phylogenetic substratum)—and still felt today by a sizeable number of analysts—lies at the basis of Freud's intractability about doctrine, which, according to Granoff's expression, is "the framework of the myth that states the difficulty of fate", of something that is, in the original meaning of the term, ineluctable. The themes found in primal fantasies (primal scene, castration, seduction) have—as Laplanche and Pontalis (1967, p. 432) note—a common nature: they all refer to the origins. In the primal scene—which seems like a sadistic act—there is represented and/or concealed the reality of the parental coitus, i.e. of the origin of the subject. The fantasies of seduction—which appear to be operated by the parental figure—reveal (or re-veil) the origin, the source of sexuality in the subject (and of his desire to seduce). The fantasies of castration—which show the feminine as castrated—reveal (or re-veil) the origin of the difference between the sexes and, we might add, of the disjunction between the fate of the species (potentially immortal) and that of the individual (mortal). Moreover, we know that, at the conscious level, the image of castration is equivalent to that of death. On the whole, we are dealing with enigmatic and ineluctable events. This ineluctable nature works in such a way that the "solution" the primal fantasies claim to bring to those enigmas may lead more towards reality (i.e. of the acceptance of the ineluctability) or towards desire or defence (i.e. possibly of the disavowal of ineluctability).

Of the three events revealed (re-veiled) in the primal fantasies, parental coitus and the difference between the sexes cannot in the adult be disavowed in the psychoanalytic meaning of the term except at psychotic levels or in fetishistic perversions. Disavowal is, however, possible at the neurotic level, as far as the onset of sexuality in the subject is concerned. Hence the possibility that the relative fantasies, those of seduction experienced, persist at the service of disavowal through the transformation into the opposite—*Verkehrung ins Gegenteil*—of the libidinal-emotional reality. [The change, of course, that has characterized the relations between myth and fantasy has been explored by Valabrega (1967)—see chapters two and three; see also Sacerdoti (1971).]

It is for this reason that Freud interpreted what the hysterical patients revealed (re-veiled) in his first analyses as revelatory. Freud's greatest se-duction in his theoretical and clinical progress (towards truth) was perhaps possible because it was precisely a fantasy of seduction which, reactivated in the transference situation, had had a certain countertransferential effect on Freud, albeit unlike the effect it had on Breuer and any other predecessors. This, then, allowed Freud to grasp precisely what was the object of revelation, and more besides.

Perhaps despite (or thanks to) all the recent sophistications, on the countertransference plane, the theme of seduction in analysis has not yet been fully explored and examined from the different modern points of view.

The mechanism through which the fantasies of seduction repress or disavow the inner reality of the onset of sexuality is that of the defence from fantasy through another fantasy raised to the rank of reality, the content of which is reversed (seduction experienced). This whole sequence tends to be repeated in analysis in order to avoid the return of the repressed. Moreover, the "solution" offered by the fantasy of seduction as regards the onset of sexuality functions (in the defensive sense) relatively better than both the fantasy of the primal scene and the fantasy of castration as "solutions" to the enigmas of one's own origin and of the origin of the difference between the sexes, respectively. That one's own origin is seen to be linked to an aggressive act, of hate rather than love, and that the origin of the difference between the sexes is seen to be connected to a mutilation rather than a differentiation may indeed create more problems than it solves. And here we have only traced a few elements that could account for how the seduction has remained—as regards the other two primal fantasies—more "included" (and not "forecluded", as Baudrillard claims) in the history of psychoanalysis, and in the history of every psychoanalysis, with "complications" of various types. These complications are more subtle, perhaps more potentially fruitful, or perhaps only less exploited, both clinically and theoretically. The subtlety results, amongst other things, from the fact that, if the defensive mechanism activated by the fantasy of seduction before the traumatic nature of the onset of sexuality of the child also tends, like both the other primal fantasies, to recover the control of the situation by magically disavowing reality (which is essentially inner reality in this case) with a reversal, this becomes the starting point for play, which, begun as playing oneself and then the other, may move to a playing with the other. This evolution, which is not without its risks, may paradoxically (the irony of seduction) facilitate access to the supremacy of the real, the true, the genital—a supremacy that does not imply the definitive renunciation of the magic of play. Here, in short, lies the potential fruitfulness of seduction and perhaps also its relatively scarce exploitation because of fears linked to an excessive vigilance towards ambiguity and the risks to which it may lead. This is especially true in modern psychoanalysis, which, besides abysmal discourse concerning countertransference and projective identification, is on average unequivocally more serious and less disposed to risk than that of the heroic age.

Se-duction from what?

Baudrillard (1979) tells an Oriental story that might illustrate the possibilities and the risks (including the mental ones) of seductive play, especially with regard to the confusion or the distinction between realistic and magic thought, between freedom and determinism, between autoplasticity and alloplasticity: A soldier meets Death at a market and thinks he sees him making a threatening gesture towards him. He rushes to the King's palace and begs him for his fastest horse, so as to flee from Death during the night, riding to far-off Samarkand. Then the King calls Death before him at the palace so as to reprimand him for having frightened one of his best servants. But Death, with great surprise, replies: "I didn't intend to frighten him. I was only amazed at seeing the soldier here, because I have an appointment with him tomorrow at Samarkand."

In Baudrillard's opinion, the truth of the appointment at Samarkand is that the signs follow unconscious paths, and *acts manqués* (parapraxes) are the most successful, but this does not explain the seduction of the story that is certainly not an apology of truth. To the fortuitousness of the meeting is added the fortuitousness of Death's *ingenuous* gesture, which against his will acts as a gesture of seduction. There is no way the event could not have taken place, and yet it maintains the lightness of chance, of the furtive gesture, of the accidental meeting, of the illegible sign. This is how seduction works. On the other hand, the soldier goes to meet Death because he attributed to a sign a meaning it did not have and that did not concern him; he took for his something that was not directed towards him. Here lies the maxim of seduction: not to have any. The seduced man is caught up against his will in the network of signs that lose themselves. And this story is seducing precisely because the sign is deviated from its meaning, because it "seduces". Indeed, signs become seducing only when they are seduced. If death itself is only an innocent element, and this is the secret irony of the story, the manifest irony of Baudrillard's comment is that, on the one hand, he makes the statements quoted here and, on the other, he categorically states that there is neither the unconscious, nor metaphor, nor psychology in all this.

I shall limit myself here to touching on two points that are pertinent to our discussion. Taking Baudrillard's phrase quoted above ("signs become seducing only when they are seduced") in the light of the fact that the soldier "took for his own something that was not directed towards him", we might refer it (with no offence to semiologists) to the theme of "who seduces whom", concerning what takes place between the soldier–child–patient and death–mother–analyst. The former may, or must (insight or return of the repressed), if possible, leave space for his instincts (sexual and/or of death), therefore for the perception of his desire to be seductive, only through the protection of the fantasy of being seduced. If it is more the return of the repressed or insight that may be worked through, it will also depend on how the repressor—the fantasy of being seduced (threatened) and the behaviour aimed at confirming it (the horse ride)—is treated by the death–mother–analyst. The behaviour of death is comparable, except perhaps for an excess of narcissism, to that recommended by Freud in the treatment of transference-love, and the appointment will take place with a benevolently neutral death, which at the right moment will perhaps be able to give the soldier the ability to distinguish reality from fantasy and to accept the death of some parts of the fantasy, accepting, instead, the presence of other parts. [This is quite different from the behaviour of the mother of Patient F, who used to say to her daughter: "If you get pregnant, I'll hang myself from a pole", who fantasized killing herself for "love", which is what the patient will later do (or will fantasize having done) in reality in a direct form (murder) instead of the inverted form (suicide). It is well known that the primitive image of death is that of a murder.]

Another example of how seductive play may take place on the two registers of the *libido* and the *destrudo* and how courage (in the sense of libido), or, rather, fear (in the sense of *destrudo*), amongst other things, may be a decisive element in tipping the scales, is a clinical fragment I have quoted elsewhere (Sacerdoti, 1977b). A patient uses the following provocative–provoking phrase in a conversation with her husband: "Hey, do you know how often I would love to stick a knife into someone's back!" At this point, her husband throws a knife on the table and turns his back to her. She bursts into tears, and the scene ends there.

The patient had refused for some time to have sexual relations with her husband, whom she considered "irretrievable" and completely without interest for her. Any comment I made that questioned this immediately provoked a reaction of resistance. A similar effect was produced when I tried to show her how the scene contained the aggressive masking of her sexual provocation, an invitation to her husband to take his role and to place her in her own, thus moving together from the dramatization of hate to that of love. Since in reality the thing came to nothing, the patient tried again with better results, in a dream (brought to the following session): "I was on a bridge over a railway line, and the train was going under it. Smoke was coming up through the grating of the bridge. I was with my husband. When we got to the other side, there was a precipice (much deeper than in reality). My husband went ahead and forced me to move back. I hung on to something that at a certain point gave way. . . . Later I was in a valley, and near me lay the crushed body of someone wearing my trousers." About the smoke, she says that she knows it annoys me when she smokes during the session (I often open the window) but that, on the other hand, she learnt it from me in the past. Making the connection with the episode quoted above, I interpret that when she had threatened her husband and he had come forward, thus putting her in the position to be able to brandish the knife, he had somehow forced her to move back. In other words, this had allowed her to realize that it was not the possession of the knife that she wanted. Her crying could have also been the expression of her not feeling that she was completely understood. At this point she wanted her husband to come further forward and to be the one who used the "knife" by "killing" the male part in her, taking away any handhold so as not to take the plunge, so as not to "leap", as happens, instead, in the dream. Probably during the session her cigarettes are an invitation for me to get out my cigar, as in the early sessions, and she is continually frustrated because I open the window instead. Only in the third year did the patient recover her capacity to play in analysis, and in the story mentioned above she had moved this capacity to the relationship with her husband, challenging him (play is often also a challenge). He had only gone along with her until the stakes seemed to be aggressiveness, and in any case his wife's phallicism, withdrawing as soon as with her crying she had revealed her wish to lose the stakes, to leave them to her husband so as to move on to play, which, beginning as such, could then move to the serious, as happens when two partners each accept the reality of their own sex and therefore also that of the other.

This leads directly to another point I believe we can extract from "death in Samarkand". If we do not fear—as Baudrillard does—breaking the spell, the magic, the play, which is for a moment necessary, if we do not expect it to remain an end in itself (all good play should be short), then, precisely because of the fact of distinguishing the story, as Baudrillard would have it, "from a moralistic apology or from a banal story of death instinct", I believe it could be used to make progress with the problem of the realistic and fantastic elements in auto- and alloplastic behaviours.

Are investment and "playing stakes" irreducible?

We may agree with Baudrillard when he states that play, playing stakes, and challenge are the figures of passion and seduction and that, more generally, every materiality—of money, language, sex, affection—completely changes meaning according to whether it is mobilized in investment or "reversibilized" in playing stakes. We cannot, however, agree when he claims that "the two figures are irreducible" (Baudrillard, 1979). The image of irreducibility, therefore of antithesis and isolation, evokes obsessive behaviour, which may perhaps be strengthened by social conditions. Morgenthaler (1977, p. 3) notes that in our production-based society, a deep gulf usually appears between play and seriousness. He stresses the educative element that tends to test the seriousness of life within working processes so that we cannot wonder at the fact that the playful aspect of a holiday is only a morbid, compensatory type of agreement. The everyday becomes monotonous, sexuality is missing. We may compare the relationship between the dominating society and the perverse to that between the analyst and the boy–cow–bull. [Morgenthaler (1977) had been asked by a child analyst who was fortyish, unmarried, with no children, to give a consultation. She was agitated about what was happening with a young boy of eight who had been in analysis for two years. He was maladjusted but had recently shown no odd behaviour; he was intelligent, precocious, and imaginative. He had recently come to the session asking the analyst to explain what happens when a bull mounts a cow from behind. The analyst tried to give the boy the sexual explanation she was able to. At the end of the session, the boy observed: "If you don't want to tell me what happens when a bull mounts a cow, I'll go and ask people in the street." At the next session, he repeated the same thing. The analyst was becoming increasingly disorientated, the boy increasingly obstinate, almost tangibly aggressive. The supervision with Morgenthaler clarified for the analyst that the boy wanted to know if she had already had sexual relations, if she had a man to make love with. In the following session, the boy was calm and asked no more questions. Morgenthaler concludes it was as if the boy had been present at the conversation. This was the unconscious (pp. 2–3).] The inability to face and understand what is play seriously and what is serious jokingly leads to a falsity that hides a profound uncertainty. Society feels threatened by manifest perversions because they consider its microstructures, which are perverse, as the boy considered his analyst's sexual sphere. In society the consequences are misunderstanding, hostility, and negative evaluation in the judgement of perversions.

Paradoxically, it is precisely when we must assume roles, when institutions and formalizations become determinant, when, that is—as Morgenthaler (1977) notes—brains are one-directional, that the perverse characteristic is excited and becomes perversion. Rigidity keeps pace with the adaptation required by society or even partly substitutes for it. The assumption of roles and institutionalizations, formalizations, and manipulations conditioned by society contain the perverse microstructure of the form of "normal" relationships. There is an intensified reaction on both sides: the pervert strengthens his perversion; society intensifies its attitude and ritualizes its forms of relationship as regards the pervert (pp. 6–7).

I believe that this analogy, with all the limitations inherent in an analogy between the individual and society, is indicative, and that to what Morgenthaler notes we might add a hypothesis that would further associate the two protagonists of the discussion—the individual and society—and which could hold, *mutatis mutandis*, also for the protagonists of the story quoted in the previous section—the soldier and death. In both cases, both actors, each in his own time (as regards death, in the story of Samarkand, we may note that the soldier is young, healthy, and loved by the King!), did not want to accept the ineluctability with which the great themes, the fates linked to the biological root, are carried out—those represented on the one hand in collective myths, on the other, in primal fantasies, which are, unlike the former, ambiguously revelatory. Correspondingly (and this may perhaps seem a paradox, but is probably only a shift and a kind of defensive coherence) the other themes—and in particular the social ones—are faced without that behaviour and even without that alloplastic expectation with which we may legitimately regard things that are not supported by *anánkē*, almost as if this had been shifted from its natural site to others to which it does not belong, leaving no space for play (including ironic play) nor, through this, for all the unexpected events that may result. [As Freud (1924e) says: "We call behaviour 'normal' or 'healthy' if it combines certain features of both reactions [neurotic and psychotic]—if it disavows the reality as little as does a neurosis, but if it then exerts itself, as does a psychosis, to effect an alteration of that reality. Of course, this expedient, normal behaviour leads to work being carried out on the external world; it does not stop, as in psychosis, at effecting internal changes. It is no longer *autoplastic* but *alloplastic* (p. 185).]

We might ask ourselves about the "nature" of a certain philosophy which, considering—as does Gans quoted in Blumenberg—that man must come to the idea of considering himself above nature, laughs at Thales because, absorbed in his thought, he does not end up on the state but in the water, the origin of all things (Blumenberg, 1983). Blumenberg comments that the observer, following Hegel, has acquired familiarity with the reasons of history; he has a formula to define the founder of the philosophy of nature absorbed in contemplation of the sky, a formula that provides a tardy articulation to the servant-girl's smile: the first philosopher was beyond all reality. To our question we might therefore reply, following Freud, that a similar philosophy is by nature defensive: the "superior gods" are part of man's (inner) reality as much as the "lower gods", and in both, in order to know them, we must be prepared to end up inside them.

"Unicuique suum": the renunciation of the "alibi" and the reappearance of the space of irony

The perspective opened up by this long detour allows us to return to the question of the lack of a "fissure in the rock of what is" (Adorno, 1951) and to consider the perception of this lack (or, in other words, the lack of perception of the fissure) as a defensively co-determined distortion, operated through disavowal and shifting. Certainly the interlocking, by collusion, in the relationship between the individual and society (which reaches its peak in the case of the so-called perversions) may give the impression that the underlying bedrock is there, in the "social", effectively as a fate, without fissures. This is, paradoxically, all the more so the greater the incongruities, which best lend themselves to shifting the primal conflicts, even when they are not the expression of them. In fact, the underlying bedrock, the lack of the fissure (and the fissure itself), the *anánkē*, are elsewhere. But how can we find the courage to renounce the *alibi*, exposing ourselves at the same time to those real risks that are run when we refuse a socially-shared appearance and therefore indicate it as such? And yet, despite the real risks of the latter, it is from this (from the surface) that we must begin, thinking also that we will never finish, and therefore that we must always keep the appearance in sight in order to be able to put it in its place and do the same thing with reality.

A kind of circularity may thus be set in motion. The double vision of (stable) irony and also that of self-directed irony may almost paradigmatically help to exit from the impasse. In particular, self-directed irony "at its best" (Schlesinger, 1979) may make up the first stage (the most difficult one), which permits the creation of a space at the level of inner reality; hence it may be relatively easier to perceive a fissure also "in the rock of what is" (following the preconstituted paths, since we are referring here to realities characterized by incongruities)—not, therefore, the faith that moves mountains, but irony which, unlike what Adorno indicates, may still find the fissure in the rock.

Clinical psychoanalysis teaches us that the capacity for insight concerning ironic aspects (of the "unstable" type), and therefore the capacity to grasp a certain kind of (provocatory) message, may confer the possibility both to play and not to play the game—or, in other words, to play it within certain limits (which in analysis are obviously those of the setting). In this way, we may at times manage to begin an evolution that leads either to the fall of the "unstable" ironic attitude or to its evolution in the direction of "stable" irony. "Stable" irony basically corresponds to reaching the postambivalent genital position and may indeed be a certain guarantee for its maintenance in (the most varied) situations in which it is particularly difficult and therefore necessary to maintain both the disenchantment and a good objectal investment. In other words, we want to be consciously, or realistically, utopistic.

Certainly, when—to use Adorno's (1951) words—"behind the one who is falling echoes the mocking laughter of the perfidious object that has made him impotent", it may also happen to great spirits that they feel themselves irrevocably without handholds, especially if he who had been masked as a champion of utopia (equivalent to the good primal object) reveals himself to be perfidious. This happened to Walter Benjamin (1940) when the pact between Stalin and Hitler was drawn up. It was in recovering from this shock—as Scholem (1972) tells us—that Benjamin, in his "Geschichtsphilosophische Thesen", described and interpreted the painting by Klee entitled *Angelus Novus*, to which he gave enormous symbolic and/or allegoric significance.

> There is an angel that seems to be about to move away from something it is gazing fixedly at. Its eyes are staring, its mouth open, its wings outstretched. The angel of history must look like this. It has its face turned to the past. Where we can see a chain of events, he sees a single catastrophe that incessantly accumulates ruins and throws them down at his feet. He would dearly love to remain, to raise the dead and recompose the destruction, but a storm blowing from heaven has been caught up in his wings, and it is so strong that he can no longer close them. The storm blows him

> irresistibly towards the future, to which he has his back turned, whilst the accumulation of ruins rises before him into the sky. The storm is what we call progress.

Scholem comments that here we have Benjamin's personal angel, which stands between the past and the future and induces him "to return from whence he came", in a new interpretation of Klee's painting in which he has become the angel of history. But if before it was the *patience* of the waiting lover, now it is the *storm* from heaven that propels him towards the future, even without his having to turn his face. Paradise is at the same time both man's origin and his remote past, as well as the utopic image of his future of redemption—in a conception of the historic process that is more cyclic than dialectic. Here, too, "the origin is the end".

But if the end is the origin (tomb–womb), there is no space for an object that is different from the primal one, except in appearance. In this case, there is no discarding between appearance and reality, nor therefore really a handhold for irony.

In addition to the elements mentioned here, the ironic formulation is probably the one that best lends itself to reassume, we might say, the movement from a pregenital position to a genital position, which favours both inner and outer reality in the most global sense. The supremacy of reality, after all, presupposes that the appearance is also contemporaneously present. Moreover, the highlighting of how reality disentangles itself from appearance and com-prehends it may also be a way of recalling a step and therefore of rendering less operative or inoperative the regressive tendency to return to it, to stay there, to repeat patterns in a sterile fashion. It is well known that this takes place especially at moments of difficulty and it is probably for this reason that irony flourishes most (and may be most necessary to avoid definitive, perhaps masked retreats by bringing about tactical retreats) precisely when because of circumstances or choice there are difficulties to be faced.

We may now better understand Schlesinger (1979) when he states that

> the anxiety consequent to the inhering incongruities of the Jewish life . . . stimulated the creative capacities of the

> gifted to create verbal and conceptual resolutions in this setting. The stories and humor thus invented gained currency and were retold by people sharply aware of the incongruent aspects of their existence and also highly responsive to the relief in the form of laughter that such a conceptual resolution brought them. [p. 318]

A certain, widespread judgement of this kind of humour, of irony and self-directed irony, which stresses its (sado)masochistic, or cynical, or nihilistic aspects, therefore seems to operate a distortion (which scotomizes, amongst other things, the context) to the detriment of the "genital" aspect evident in what has been observed above (see Booth's "stable" irony). Given that the conditions characterized by incongruities and antitheses (pairs of opposite states of mind—*geistige Gegensatzpaare*), which are in a certain way analogous and relative dilemmas, could—as we have already said—today be considered almost ubiquitous (Schlesinger, 1979), the exploration (which permits the recall to clinical and theoretical psychoanalytic material) of dynamics operating in irony, especially "stable" irony, therefore appears very topical, as is also a more precise characterization of the best Jewish humour.

In the best of Jewish humour, as mentioned above, the distinction between victim and spectators is minimized, and their identification may be more or less complete. We may observe that the roots of this lie in previous ages and in much more serious texts (thus confirming the serious aspect of these jokes). In the Passover *Haggadà* [the popular story of the Jewish Passover that is read at the family table on the first two evenings of the festivity], for example, it is imagined that psychologically different young people ask for explanations about the injustices undergone by the Jews in Egypt at the hands of the Egyptians. One of these young men (who is classified as wicked) poses a question formulated in the third person. He is the only one for whom the *Haggadà* prescribes condemnation, because he rejects not only tradition, but also identification with society. The reference in the first person to those events that are past, also concerning aspects of suffering, is not for reasons of masochism—especially as Passover is the celebration of the liberation from slavery—but as the expression of a capacity to participate (in the primal sense) in sorrows (as well as in joys)—in other words, to live again, identifying oneself, for better and for worse, with a great historical event of one's own people. This comes close to another of the characteristics of many ironic Jewish stories: that of possessing a certain magnitude and dignity. According to Freud (1927d), this characteristic is peculiar to humour. We have already seen elsewhere how most of the best Jewish humour is realized through irony. It is often thanks to irony that it manages to unite sophisticated and intellectual aspects with its wide communicative, community value. As the *jüdische Witz* could count on a high level of values and shared emotional experiences, it has been a folkloristic manifestation, even though it also shows characteristics that are usually prerogatives of élite manifestations. We have here another pair (popular/élite) concerning which modern means of communication of mass culture, by a kind of irony of fate, have operated not in the direction of reconciliation but in that of the highlighting of contraposition.

Summary of main points

To conclude: starting from the question of why Freud's work on *Witz* has remained practically isolated from his later work, we have sought an answer mainly through a survey of certain elements that could be connected with the theme "Freud as ironist" in works other than that on *Witz*. What emerges from this survey is the presence of a political component, in addition to the personal and professional components, in the ironic aspects of Freud's expressions.

We have therefore tried, in a historical perspective, to frame these aspects also in the characteristics and the dynamics of the *jüdische Witz*, which flourished before Freud's time but was still cultivated in his day, even by Freud himself. In those Jewish minorities, the socio-political situation (as well as the cultural and religious tradition) greatly encouraged the development of a sense of humour, of irony, and of self-directed irony, of which the masochistic, cynical, or nihilistic elements corresponding to "unstable" irony have been distortedly stressed, to the detriment of the "genital" aspect, corresponding to "stable" irony. This is characterized by the tendency to compose, as constructively as possible—privileging inner reality without scotomizing outer reality—a series of incongruities and antitheses that, starting from the "objective" situation, were formed into pairs of states of mind [*geistige Gegensatzpaare*]. Analogous conditions and relative dilemmas (Schlesinger, 1979) have today become ubiquitous and universal. The exploration (which the recall to clinical psychoanalytic material permits) of the ironic viewpoint, especially in the direction of "stable" irony, and the broadening to the preconscious and unconscious spheres, therefore appears to be very topical.

Some claim that in today's society the medium of irony has disappeared (Adorno, 1951), because ideology has resigned itself to the confirmation of reality through a pure and simple duplication. Nothing, therefore, is left but "bloody seriousness, including truth". But perhaps it may be possible to attempt to recover a space for ironic play through an operation that allows the use of a wider horizon. Thus a detour or a leap into clinical psychoanalysis and the theoretical and doctrinal developments that derive from it may draw on elements that allow us to return to consider the historical and social reality in a perspective from which the possible "fissures in the rock of what is" on which the "talons of irony" may take hold are visible. The consideration of the equivalences of "truth" at an unconscious level, which clinical psychoanalysis allows to be unequivocally grasped, makes an exploration of the theme of se-duction in comparison with social reality vitally important.

The framing of a certain seduction as a form of unstable irony leads us, in the wake of earlier studies, to examine once more seduction in psychoanalysis and, obviously, the psychoanalysis of seduction. Briefly we might say that seduction, as well as the two other primal fantasies, has remained more "included"—and not at all excluded or "foreclosed" as Baudrillard (1979) claims—in the history of psychoanalysis and also in the history of every psychoanalysis. These psychoanalyses also differ from those of two generations ago because modern society intensifies more subtly and pervasively the tendency to silence needs and desires with surrogates that are well known to analysts, which are directed, in repetition, into the neurosis of transference. However, from the analysis of this—which is also an artificially encouraged surrogate—needs and desires, rather than being silenced, are made to speak. Se-duction may therefore produce different results. We might say that in the second case it follows the line of stable irony, even becoming an ingredient of it, whilst in the first case irony cannot, and indeed does not, develop. This does not happen, however, through the adherence of ideology to reality, but through collage (by means of seduction) of the surrogate over the more regressive needs, with the obliteration of the evolutive potentials and of the access to non-anachronistic but actual needs, that is to reality.

When we speak of seduction it is therefore necessary to have a longitudinal vision that clarifies its evolutive line or its tendency (towards what?), which is equivalent to precisely describing at the same time its primal significance: se-duction away from what? The viewpoint in which seduction has a direction is the opposite of that maintained for example, by Baudrillard (1979), according to whom seduction and operations of direction (playing the stakes and investment) are irreducible and therefore deadly enemies (hence Freud's alleged disavowal of seduction).

Maintaining this irreducibility appears to be in line with what is usually manifested in our production-based society (Morgenthaler, 1977) in which there is a deep furrow between play and seriousness. On the other hand, recourse to clinical psychoanalysis may be very instructive and clarifying. It teaches us, amongst other things, that the defensive aspects of the fantasy of seduction before the onset of sexuality tend to disavow magically, to mask this reality through a reversal in order to maintain control; this often becomes the starting point for play that, begun as playing first oneself and then the other, may become a playing *with* the other. Paradoxically through this evolution, which is not without risks, there may be facilitation (irony of seduction!) of the access to the supremacy of the real, the true, the "genital", a supremacy that does not imply renunciation but rather the com-prehension of the apparent, of the deceptive, of the magic of play. Comprehension therefore does not necessarily signify renunciation: certainly, it signifies the possibility of distinguishing, of knowing therefore also which things are truly ineluctable and which are not. Amongst the former are the great themes (fates) linked to the biological root: those represented on the one hand in collective myths, and on the other in the primal fantasies (which are ambiguously revealing/re-veiling). The less ineluctability is accepted, the other themes (the non-ineluctable ones) are faced without that behaviour and alloplastic expectation with which we may legitimately re-examine the things that are not supported by *anánkē*. And the social often tends to be presented (especially) by the holders of power, with characteristics of ineluctability. We may therefore easily establish a collusion between maskings with the semblance of omnipotence on the one hand (society, its rulers) and with those of impotence on the other (the individual).

Renouncing this alibi, besides renouncing the defence operated thereby, by shifting, as regards the true ineluctability of human fate, may certainly entail exposing oneself at the same time also to those real risks that are run when we refuse a socially shared appearance and therefore recognize it as being merely an appearance. But, once we have regained the space to begin this operation at the level of inner reality (and self-directed irony at its best may be a great help in contrasting narcissistic indulgences), it is relatively easier to continue it at the level of outer reality where, for example, in the incongruities between words and actions, the talon of irony may find its space once more. The *jüdische Witz* may be paradigmatic of the success of this operation, a success that presupposes, besides the investment in the great enigmas of life, the use of the pathos of the distance as regards a large part of socio-political reality and especially its every idolization.

We might expect that the lack of ironic and self-directed ironic vision and of the capacity for insight concerning preconscious and unconscious ironic dynamics contributes to the formation of all the more tragic vicious circles, which in certain ways recall those that may be established between acting and counteracting in analysis. To avoid this ending tragically, it is essential that the analyst possess the capacity for ironic double vision. This ironic vision must then concern himself (self-directed irony), both as a person and as an analyst, and therefore also the conceptual bases of his work. Flournoy (1986, p. 87), for example, finds it seductive to reverse the thesis according to which the Oedipus complex preexists the treatment, for which we may thus (better) imagine a possible end, in so far as Oedipus exists "thanks to the analyst who introduces seduction into the experience of the treatment".

In other words, the (non-tragic) end of the analysis will be possible because Oedipus (Rex) is not *then* a tragedy: that is, (reading the negation) it *is* a tragedy, a dramatization, a fiction [*eirōneia*] rather than a *historia morbi*. But this will surface at the end, thanks to the double vision, characteristic of irony, that is always present in the analyst's perception.

BIBLIOGRAPHY

Abadi, M. (1978). Meditazione su (l')Edipo. *Rivista di Psicoanalisi 24*, 390–424.

Adorno, Th. W. (1951). *Minima moralia. Reflexionen aus dem beschäftigten Leben.* Frankfurt am Main: Suhrkamp Verlag.

____. (1967). *Ohne Leitbild. Parva Aesthetica.* Frankfurt am Main: Suhrkamp Verlag.

Alexander, J. (1969). De l'ironie. *Revue Française de Psychanalyse, 33*, 441–450.

Alexander, J., & Friedman, J. (1980). The nature of psychic defence. *International Journal of Psycho-Analysis, 7*, 490–509.

Alexander, J., & Isaaks, J. (1963). Seriousness and preconscious affective attitudes. *International Journal of Psycho-Analysis, 44*, 23–30.

Bahia, A. B. (1977). New theories: their influence and effect on psychoanalytic technique. *International Journal of Psycho-Analysis, 58*, 345–363.

Baudrillard, J. (1976). *L'échange symbolique et la mort.* Paris: Editions Gallimard.

____. (1979). *De la seduction.* Paris: Galilée.

Benassy, M. (1973). A la recherche d'une définition de l'humour. *Revue Française de Psychanalyse, 37*, 517–522.

Benjamin, W. (1940). Geschichtsphilosophische Thesen. *Schriften*. Frankfurt am Main: Suhrkamp Verlag, 1955.

Beres, D. (1980). Certainty: a failed quest? *Psychoanalytic Quarterly, 49*, 1–26.

Besançon, A. (1975). *Histoire et experience du moi*. Paris: Librairie Ernest Flammarion.

Bettelheim, B. (1982). *Freud and Man's Soul*. New York: Alfred A. Knopf.

Bibring, G. L., Dweyer, F, Huntington, D. S., & Valenstein, A. F. (1961). A study of the psychological processes in pregnancy and of the earliest mother-child relationship. *The Psychoanalytic Study of the Child, 16*, 9–72. New York: International Universities Press.

Bion, W. R. (1962). *Learning from Experience*. London: Heinemann Medical Books. [Reprinted London: Karnac Books, 1984.]

____. (1970). *Attention and Interpretation. A Scientific Approach to Insight in Psycho-Analysis and Groups*. London: Tavistock Publications. [Reprinted London: Karnac Books, 1984.]

Bloom, H. (1975). *Kabbalah and Criticism*. New York: The Seabury Press.

Blumenberg, H. (1976). Der Sturz des Protophilosophen zur Komik der reinen Theorie, anhand einer Rezeptionsgeschichte der Tales-Anekdote. *Poetik und Hermeneutik, 7*, 11–64.

Booth, W. C. (1974). *A Rhetoric of Irony*. Chicago, IL, & London: University of Chicago Press.

Brenner, C. (1980). Metapsychology and psychoanalytic theory. *Psychoanalytic Quarterly, 49*, 189–214.

Butler, S. (1970). *Erewhon*. Harmondsworth, Middlesex: Penguin.

Chasseguet-Smirgel, J. (1984). The femininity of the analyst in professional practice. *International Journal of Psycho-Analysis, 65*, 169–178.

Cremerius, J. (1981). Über die Schwierigkeiten, Natur und Funktion von Phantasie und Abwehrmechanismen psychoanalytisch zu erforschen und zu definieren. *Quarta conferenza della Federazione europea di Psicoanalisi*, Rome.

Derrida, J. (1971). La mythologie blanche (le métaphore dans le texte philosophique). *Poétique, 5*, 1–52.

Deutsch, H. (1933). Psychologie der manisch-depressiven Zustände, insbesondere der chronischen Hypomanie. *Internationale Zeitschrift der Psychoanalyse, 19*, 358–371.

Devoto, G. (1966). *Avviamento alla etimologia italiana*. Florence: Le Monnier.

Erikson, E. H. (1968). *Identity, Youth and Crisis*. London: Faber and Faber.

____. (1977). *Toys and Reasons*. London: Marion Boyars.

Favez, G. (1971). L'illusion et la désillusion dans la cure psychanalytique. *Nouvelle Revue de Psychanalyse, 4*, 43–54.

Ferenczi, S. (1921). Weitere Ausbau der 'aktiven Technik' in der Psychoanalyse. *Internationale Zeitschrift für Psychoanalyse, 7*, 233–251.

Flournoy, O. (1986). La séduction réhabilitée ou La passion de l'enfant oedipien. *Etudes Freudiennes, 27*, 63–87.

Freud, A. (1986). *The Ego and the Mechanisms of Defence*. London: Hogarth.

____. (1965). *Normality and Pathology in Childhood*. London: Hogarth. [Reprinted London: Karnac Books, 1989.]

Freud, S. (1887–1904). *The Complete Letters of Sigmund Freud to Wilhelm Fliess*. Cambridge, MA: Belknap.

____. (1900a). *The Interpretation of Dreams*. *S.E., 4–5*.

____. (1901b). *The Psychopathology of Everyday Life*. *S.E., 6*.

____. (1905a [1904]). On psychotherapy. *S.E., 7*.

____. (1905c). *Jokes and their Relation to the Unconscious*. *S.E., 8*.

____. (1905d). *Three Essays on the Theory of Sexuality*. *S.E., 7*.

____. (1905e [1901]). Fragment of an analysis of a case of hysteria. *S.E., 7*.

____. (1906c). Psycho-analysis and the establishment of the facts in legal proceedings. *S.E., 9*.

____. (1907a). *Delusions and Dreams in Jensen's "Gradiva"*. *S.E., 9*.

____. (1908c). On the sexual theories of children. *S.E., 9*.

____. (1908e [1907]). Creative writers and day-dreaming. *S.E., 9*.

____. (1911b). Formulations on the two principles of mental functioning. *S.E., 12*.

____. (1912–13). *Totem and Taboo*. *S.E., 13*.

____. (1913i). The disposition to obsessional neurosis. *S.E., 12*.

____. (1914c). On narcissism: an introduction. *S.E., 14*.

____. (1914d). On the history of the psycho-analytic movement. *S.E., 14*.

____. (1914g). Remembering, repeating and working-through. *S.E., 12*.

____. (1915a). Observations on transference-love. *S.E., 12.*

____. (1915c). Instincts and their vicissitudes. *S.E., 14.*

____. (1916–17). *Introductory Lectures on Psycho-Analysis. S.E., 15–16.*

____. (1917c). On transformations of instinct as exemplified in anal erotism. *S.E., 17.*

____. (1918b [1914]). From the history of an infantile neurosis. *S.E., 17.*

____. (1919a [1918]). Lines of advance in psycho-analytic therapy. *S.E., 17.*

____. (1921c). *Group Psychology and the Analysis of the Ego. S.E., 18*

____. (1923b). *The Ego and the Id. S.E., 19.*

____. (1924b [1923]). Neurosis and psychosis. *S.E., 19.*

____. (1924e). The loss of reality in neurosis and psychosis. *S.E., 19.*

____. (1925d [1924]). *An Autobiographical Study. S.E., 20.*

____. (1926d [1925]). *Inhibitions, Symptoms and Anxiety. S.E., 20.*

____. (1927c). *The Future of an Illusion. S.E., 21.*

____. (1927d). Humour. *S.E., 21.*

____. (1930a). *Civilization and its Discontents. S.E., 21.*

____. (1933a). *New Introductory Lectures on Psycho-Analysis. S.E., 22.*

____. (1933b [1932]). *Why War? S.E., 22.*

____. (1933c). Sándor Ferenczi. *S.E., 22.*

____. (1939a [1937–39]). *Moses and Monotheism. S.E., 23.*

____. (1937c). Analysis terminable and interminable. *S.E., 23.*

____. (1937d). Constructions in analysis. *S.E., 23.*

____. (1941e [1926]). Address to the members of the *B'nai B'rith. S.E., 20.*

____. (1950a [1887–1902]) A project for a scientific psychology. *S.E., 1.*

Fromm, E. (1926). *You Shall Be as Gods. A Radical Interpretation of the Old Testament and Its Tradition.* New York: Holt, Reinhart and Winston.

Frye, N. (1981). *The Great Code. The Bible and Literature.* New York: Harcourt, Brace, Jovanovich.

Gaddini, E. (1981). Note sul problema mente-corpo. *Rivista di Psicoanalisi, 27,* 3–29.

Gaddini de Benedetti, R. (1976). Formazione del sé e prima realtà interna. *Rivista di Psicoanalisi, 22,* 206–225.

Geelerd, E. R. (1965). Two kinds of denial. Neurotic denial and denial in the service of the need to survive. In: N. Schur (Ed.), *Drives, Affect and Behaviour, Vol. 2.* New York: International Universities Press.

Gendrot, J. A. (1968). Introduction au colloque sur analyse terminée et interminable. *Revue Française de Psychanalyse, 32,* 215–225.

Gibson, R. O., & Isaac, D. J. (1978). Truth tables as a formal device in the analysis of human actions. In: E. Jaques (Ed.), *Levels of Abstraction in Logic and Human Action.* London: Heinemann.

Gill, M. M. (1976). Metapsychology is not psychology. In: M. M. Gill & P. S. Holzman, Psychology versus metapsychology. *Psychological Issues, 9* (4), 71–105.

Gillibert, J. (1973). L'acteur, median sexuel. *Nouvelle Revue de Psychanalyse, 7,* 71–77.

Good, E. M. (1965). *Irony in the Old Testament.* London: S. P. C. K.

Granoff, W. (1975). *Filiations.* Paris: Les Editions de Minuit.

____. (1976). *La pensée et le féminin.* Paris: Les Editions de Minuit.

Greenson, R. R. (1967). *The Technique and Practice of Psychoanalysis, Vol. I.* London: Hogarth.

Groupe μ (1976). Ironique et iconique. *Poétique, 36,* 427–442.

Hart, H. H. (1961). A review of psychoanalytic literature on activity and passivity. *Psychiatric Quarterly, 35,* 331–352.

Hartmann, H. (1950). Comments on the psychoanalytic theory of the Ego. *The Psychoanalytic Study of the Child, 5,* 74–96. New York: International Universities Press.

____. (1969). Introductory comments on "Menschenkenntnis". *International Journal of Psycho-Analysis, 50,* 529–531.

Hendrick, J. (1942). Work and the Pleasure Principle. *Psychoanalytic Quarterly, 11,* 311–329, 1943.

____. (1943). The discussion of the "Instinct to master". *Psychoanalytic Quarterly, 12,* 563–565.

Horkheimer, M., & Adorno, Th. W. (1947). *Dialektik der Aufklärung, philosophische Fragmente.* Amsterdam: Querido Verlag.

Hutcheon, L. (1978). Ironie et parodie: stratégie et structures. *Poétique, 36,* 467–477.

Isay, R. A. (1977). Ambiguity in speech. *Journal of the American Psychoanalytic Association, 25,* 427–452.

Jabès, E. (1980). *Du désert au livre.* Paris: Belfond.

Jacobson, E. (1946). The child's slaughter. *The Psychoanalytic Study of the Child, 2,* 39–60. New York: International Universities Press.

____. (1965). *The Self and the Object World.* London: Hogarth.

Jones, E. (1953). *S. Freud: Life and Work* (3 volumes). London: Hogarth.

Keats, J. (1935). *The Letters of John Keats,* edited by Forman. New York: Oxford University Press.

Kerbrat-Orecchioni, C. (1976). Problèmes de l'ironie. In: *Linguistique et Sémiologie. Travaux du Centre de recherches linguistiques et sémiologiques de Lyon, 2,* 9–45.

____. (1977). *La connotation.* Lyon: Presses Universitaires de Lyon.

Kierkegaard, S. (1834–1842). The journals. In: R. Bretall (Ed.), *A Kierkegaard Anthology.* Princeton, NJ: Princeton University Press (1951).

____. (1841). *The Concept of Irony with Constant Reference to Socrates.* Bloomington, IN: Indiana University Press (1968).

____. (1843). *Le ripresa. Tentativo di psicologia sperimentale di Constantin Constantius.* Italian translation. Milan: Edizioni di Comunità (1954).

Klein, G. S. (1967). Peremptory ideation: structure and force in motivated ideas. In: *Motives and Thought: Essays in Honor of David Rapaport.* New York: International Universities Press.

____. (1970). Two theories or one. *Bulletin of the Menninger Clinic, 37,* 99–132, 1973.

Knox, N. D. (1972). On the classification of ironies. *Modern Phylology, 70,* 53–62.

____. (1973). Irony. In: P. P. Wiener (Ed.), *Dictionary of the History of Ideas, Vol. II.* New York: Scribners.

Koestler, A. (1976). *The Thirteenth Tribe.* New York: Random House.

Kohut, H. (1971). *The Analysis of the Self.* London: Hogarth Press.

Kris, E., & Kaplan, A. (1952). Aesthetic ambiguity. In: E. Kris (Ed.), *Psychoanalytic Explorations in Art.* New York: International Universities Press.

Kubie, L. (1951). The distortion of the symbolic process in neurosis and psychosis. *Journal of the American Psychoanalytic Association, 1*, 59–86.

Lacan, J. (1964). *Le séminaire de Jacques Lacan. Livre XI. Les quatre concepts fondamentaux de la psychanalyse*. Paris: Éditions du Seuil, 1973.

____. (1988). Truth emerges from the mistake. *Seminar I*. Cambridge: Cambridge University Press.

Lagache, D. (1964). Fantasie, realité et verité. *Revue Française de Psychanalyse, 29*, 515–538.

____. (1965a). La psicoanalisi come sublimazione. *Psiche, 2*, 2–3.

____. (1965b). Le modèle psychanalytique de la personalité. In: *Les modèles de la personalité en psychologie*. Paris: Presses Universitaires de France.

Landmann, S. (1960). *Der jüdische Witz*. Olten und Freiberg im Breisgau: Walter Verlag.

Laplanche, J., & Pontalis, J. B. (1967). *The Language of Psychoanalysis*. London: Hogarth, 1973. [Reprinted London: Karnac Books, 1988.]

Lavagetto, M. (1985). *Freud, la letteratura e altro*. Turin: Einaudi.

Lewin, B. D. (1950). *The Psychoanalysis of Elation*. New York: Norton.

Lopez, D. (1970). *Analisi del carattere ed emancipazione. Marx, Freud, Reich*. Milan: Jaca.

Madsen, K. B. (1969). Theories of motivation. In: B. B. Wolman (Ed.), *Handbook of Psychology*. New York: Prentice Hall.

Meltzer, D. (1973). *Sexual States of Mind*. Perthshire: Clunie Press.

Morgenthaler, F. (1977). Forme di rapporto della perversione e perversione delle forme di rapporto. *Psicoterapia e scienze umane, 2* (New series), 1–14 (1979).

____. (1978). *Technik zur Dialektik der psychoanalytischen Praxis*. Frankfurt am Main: Syndakat Verlag.

Morier, H. (1975). *Dictionnaire de Poétique et de Réthorique* (second edition). Paris: Presses Universitaires de France.

Muecke, D. C. (1969). *The Compass of Irony*. London: Methuen.

____. (1970). *Irony*. London: Methuen.

____. (1978). Analyse de l'ironie. *Poétique, 36*, 478–494.

Musatti, C. L. (1957). *Trattato di psicoanalisi*. Torino: Edizioni Scientifiche Einaudi.

____. (1972). Introduction. In: S. Freud, *Opere, Vol. 5,* pp. 3–6. Turin: Boringhieri.

____. (1982). *Mia sorella gemella la psicoanalisi.* Rome: Editori Riuniti.

Nunberg, R. (1926). The will to recovery. *International Journal of Psycho-Analysis, 7,* 64–78.

Ornston, D. (1982). Strachey's influence: a preliminary report. *International Journal of Psycho-Analysis, 63,* 409–426.

Pasche, F. (1969). *A partir de Freud.* Paris: Payot.

Pessoa, F. (1931). Autopsicografia. In *Obras Completas de Fernando Pessoa.* Lisbon: Ática, 1942–74.

Peller, L. E. (1954). Libidinal phases, ego development and play. *The Psychoanalytic Study of the Child, 9,* 178–197. New York: International Universities Press.

Racker, H. (1968). *Transference and Countertransference.* London: Hogarth Press. [Reprinted London: Karnac Books, 1985.]

Rapaport, D. (1944). The scientific methodology of psychoanalysis. In: M. M. Gill (Ed.), *The Collected Papers of David Rapaport.* New York: Basic Books, 1967.

____. (1953). Some metapsychological considerations concerning activity and passivity. In: M. M. Gill (Ed.), *The Collected Papers of David Rapaport.* New York: Basic Books, 1967.

____. (1957). A theoretical analysis of the superego concept. In: M. M. Gill (Ed.), *The Collected Papers of David Rapaport.* New York: Basic Books, 1967.

____. (1960). The structure of psychoanalytic theory. *Psychological Issues, II,* 2.

Rapaport, D., & Gill. M. M. (1959). The points of view and assumptions of metapsychology. In: M. M. Gill (Ed.), *The Collected Papers of David Rapaport.* New York: Basic Books, 1967.

Reich, A. (1950). The structure of the grotesque-comic sublimation. *Yearbook of Psychoanalysis, 6,* 194–207.

Reik, T. (1929). *Künstlerisches Schaffen und Witzarbeit, Lieb und Lied in dem Witz.* Vienna: Internationaler Psychoanalytischer Verlag.

Ricoeur, P. (1974). Hermeneutics and psychoanalysis. In: P. Ricoeur, *The Conflict of Interpretation.* Evanston, IL: Northwestern University Press.

Ripellino, A. M. (1973). *Praga magica.* Turin: Einaudi.

Robert, M. (1974). *D'Oedipe à Moïse.* Paris: Calmann-Levy.

Rogers, R. (1978). *Metaphor. A Psychoanalytic View*. Berkeley, Los Angeles, CA, & London: University of California Press.

Rosen, V. H. (1977). Obsessions as comic caricatures. In: *Style, Character and Language*. New York: Jason Aronson.

Sacerdoti, G. (1971). Fantasmi, miti e difese nell'assistenza psichiatrica. *Rivista di Psicoanalisi, 17,* 84–110.

____. (1974). Il concetto psicoanalitico di istinto di fronte all'etologia. In: A. Balestrieri, D. De Martis, & O. Siciliani (Eds.), *Etologia e psichiatria*. Bari: Laterza.

____. (1976). Metafore spaziali e temporali: raffigurazioni del mondo interno. *Rivista di Psicoanalisi, 22,* 333–345.

____. (1977a). Transfert, preconscio e clichés culturali. *Rivista di Psicoanalisi, 22,* 215–229.

____. (1977b). Spunti clinico-metapsicologici in tema di (dis)continuità con particolare riguardo al sogno. *Rivista di Psicoanalisi, 23,* 372–390.

____. (1979). Le "contre-acting" et ses rapports avec l'"insight" dans les problèmes psychotiques. *Revue Française de Psychanalyse, 43,* 335–342.

____. (1986a). Riflessioni sulle bipolarità inerenti al processo psicoanalitico con particolare riguardo alla continuità-discontinuità. *Rivista di Psicoanalisi, 32,* 195–208.

____. (1986b). Luci e ombre dell''insight' teorico. *Gli argonauti, 28,* 17–32.

____. (1986c). Ebraismo e psicoanalisi davanti all'assimilazione. In: D. Meghnagi (Ed.), *L'altra scena della psicoanalisi*. Rome: Carucci.

Sacerdoti, G., & Spačal, S. (1985). Insight. *Rivista di Psicoanalisi, 31,* 59–74.

Schafer, R. (1968). On the theoretical and technical conceptualization of activity and passivity. *Psychoanalytic Quarterly, 37,* 173–198.

____. (1976). The psychoanalytic vision of reality. In: *A New Language for Psychoanalysis*. New Haven, CT, & London: Yale University Press.

Schilder, P. (1935). *The Image and Appearance of the Human Body. Studies in the Constructive Energies of the Psyche*. London: Kegan Paul.

Schlesinger, K. (1979). Jewish humour and Jewish identity. *International Revue of Psycho-Analysis, 6,* 317–330.

Schmid, C. (1960). Preface. In: S. Landmann, *Der jüdische Witz*. Olten und Freiburg im Breisgau: Walter Verlag.

Scholem, G. (1972). *Walter Benjamin und sein Engel*. Frankfurt: Suhrkamp Verlag.

Schorske, C. E. (1973). Politique et parricide dans "L'interpretation des rêves" de Freud. *Annales, 28*, 309–328.

Sereny, G. (1974). *Into that Darkness*. New York: Random House.

Singer, E. (1977). The fiction of analytic anonymity. In: K. A. Frank (Ed.), *The Human Dimension in Psychoanalytic Practice*. New York: Grune & Stratton.

Slochower, H. (1970). The Hebrew memory of a chosen God. The book of Job. In: *Mythopoyesis. Mythic Patterns in the Literary Classics*. Detroit MI: Wayne State University Press.

Sperling, O. E. (1963). Exaggeration as a defense. *Psychoanalytic Quarterly, 32*, 533–548.

Stone, L. (1961). *The Psychoanalytic Situation*. New York: International Universities Press.

Valabrega, J. P. (1967). Le problème anthropologique du phantasme. In: *Le désir et la perversion*. Paris: Editions du Seuil.

Vossius, G. J. (1643). Réthorique de l'ironie (Document), *Poétique, 36*, 495–508 (1978).

Wangh, M. (1979). Some psychoanalytic observations on boredom. *International Journal of Psycho-Analysis, 60*, 515–527.

Webster, S. (1970). *Seventh New Collegiate Dictionary*. Springfield, MA: Bell; London: Merriam.

Weiss, E. (1970). *Sigmund Freud as a Consultant*. Intercontinental Medical Book Publishing.

Winnicott, D. W. (1935). The manic defense. In: *Collected Papers: Through Pediatrics to Psychoanalysis* (pp. 129–144). London: Tavistock (1958). [Reprinted London: Karnac Books, 1991.]

____. (1951). Transitional Objects and Transitional Phenomena. In: *Collected Papers: Through Pediatrics to Psychoanalysis* (pp. 229–242). London: Tavistock (1958). [Reprinted London: Karnac Books, 1991.]

____. (1960). Ego distortion in terms of true and false self. In: *The Maturational Processes and the Facilitating Environment*. London: Hogarth (1965). [Reprinted London: Karnac Books, 1990.]

____. (1971). *Playing and Reality*. London: Tavistock.

Winterstein, D. W. (1932). Contribution to the problem of humour. *Psychoanalytic Quarterly, 3*, 303–316, 1934.

Zaltzmann, N. (1976). Du sexe opposé. *Nouvelle Revue de Psychanalyse, 14*, 183–206.

Zapparoli, G. C. (1967). *La psicoanalisi del delirio*. Milan: Bompiani.

INDEX